Leadville

Edward Platt was born in 1968 and lives in London. He is a regular contributor to various magazines and newspapers. *Leadville* is his first book.

- - -

'Weird and wonderful'
Selina Hastings, *Sunday Telegraph*

'A small, gritty, monoxide-scented epic'
Peter Conrad, *Observer*

'[Platt] breathes flesh and blood into surely the most depressing four miles of tarmac in England . . . He invests it with the human drama of a Cairo or a Bombay. He is a reporter of fearless imagination'
Simon Jenkins, *The Times*

'An important and highly readable addition to the literature of London'
Nicholas Royle, *Time Out*

'An original talent and an excellent book'
Norman Lewis

LEADVILLE

A biography of the A40

EDWARD PLATT

Photographs by Catherine Platt and Gigi Sudbury

PICADOR

First published 2000 by Picador

This edition published 2001 by Picador
an imprint of Pan Macmillan Ltd
Pan Macmillan, 20 New Wharf Road, London N1 9RR
Basingstoke and Oxford
Associated companies throughout the world
www.panmacmillan.com

ISBN 0 330 39263 8

3 5 7 9 8 6 4

A CIP catalogue record for this book is available from
the British Library.

Typeset by SetSystems Ltd, Saffron Walden, Essex
Printed and bound in Great Britain by
Mackays of Chatham plc, Chatham, Kent

Acknowledgements

The names of most of the people in the book have been changed.

I am grateful to everyone on Western Avenue who agreed to talk to me, and I would also like to thank the following people for their advice and support: John Carey, Petra Cramsie, Caroline Dawnay, Ursula Doyle, Natasha Galloway, Simon Grant, Annabel Hardman, Cassian Harrison, Caroline Taylor, and my parents.

The following books have been particularly useful: *The Intellectual and the Masses*, by John Carey; *Cities of Tomorrow*, by Peter Hall; *Dunroamin*, by Paul Oliver, Ian Davis and Ian Bentley, and *The Hundred Mile City*, by Deyan Sudjic.

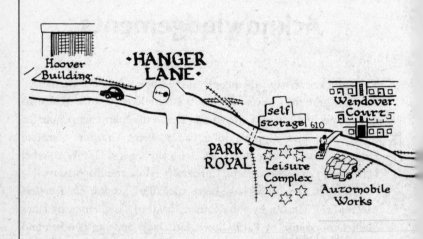

Hoover
Building

•HANGER
LANE•

self
storage | 610

Wendover.
Court

PARK
ROYAL

Leisure
Complex

Automobile
Works

N

← OXFORD & THE WEST →

Map artwork by Gigi Sudbury

LEADVILLE

A40

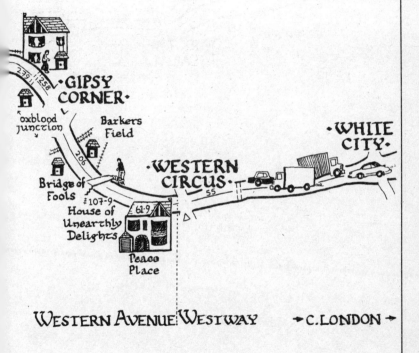

GIPSY CORNER·

·WESTERN CIRCUS·

·WHITE CITY·

oxblood junction

Barkers Field

Bridge of Fools

House of Unearthly Delights

Peace Place

WESTERN AVENUE WESTWAY   ·C.LONDON·

Contents

Introduction

I did not live in London until I was twenty-three, but I visited the city often when I was a child. In my mind, London is mapped through the roads that connect it to the parts of England where I have lived: the A11 to Essex, where I was born; the A1 to the north, where I grew up; the A3 to Hampshire, where I finished school; the A4 to Bristol, where I went to university. The fact that I now live in west London, close to Western Avenue – the A40 – completes my map of the city's roads.

Whenever I was driven into London, I watched the houses which lined the road: as the car travelled towards the centre of the city, the houses marched in the opposite direction; dirty and anonymous, pinched and choked by an endless, ragged chain of cars and lorries, they looked uninhabitable, yet the blackened cars parked on the pavements suggested otherwise. It seemed incredible that there were people living within ten yards of the car in which I was sitting.

One afternoon in January 1995, as I drove along Western Avenue, I did what I had never done before: I parked the car in a side-street, and walked on to the road. I found myself standing at the bottom of a valley, beside a set of traffic lights. The air tasted sugary, and the rhythm of the passing cars was hypnotic: each one drew me after it, seduced by the soft, cushioned violence of its motion, and it was only when it had gone that I realized how fast it was travelling; then it was too late – another took its place, then another, each one becoming a blur of trailing colour, like a melted sweet, as it fell through the slotted mouth between the rows of terraced housing which lined the road. Dirty brown and oddly insubstantial, the houses seemed to have been moulded from damp cardboard, rather than brick and glass; some were derelict, others seemed to have been abandoned. There was no one in sight.

I began to read about the arterial roads. I discovered that most of them were constructed between the wars, during a building boom which transformed the landscape of Britain. Four million homes were built between 1921 and 1936, as the city centre slums were demolished, and their inhabitants relocated to the outskirts of town. The population of central London fell by 400,000, but more than a million people moved into the new houses on its periphery. In 'the vast new wildernesses of glass and brick' on the edge of town, the entrenched patterns of English life were thought to be changing. 'Everything and everybody is being rushed down and swept into one dusty arterial road of cheap mass production and standardised living,' wrote J.B. Priestley, in *English Journey*, an account of his travels around England in 1933. He believed a 'cleaner, tidier, healthier, saner world' than we had known before was being systematically assembled on the edge of England's cities – and so did George Orwell: 'The place to look for the germs of the future England is in light-industry areas and along the arterial roads,' he wrote in 1941. 'In Slough, Dagenham, Barnet, Letchworth, Hayes – everywhere, indeed, on the outskirts of the great towns – the old pattern is gradually changing into something new.'

In 1995, I was working as a freelance journalist. I have never had a full-time job, and I had never wanted one; I preferred to work from my home in Shepherd's Bush, which meant Western Avenue lay within easy reach. The houses I had seen beside the road had begun to preoccupy me; I wanted to know if Orwell had chosen the right place to look for England's future. I decided to go back to Western Avenue.

If I have learnt anything as a journalist, it is that I can usually persuade people to talk to me. I did not know what I would find on Western Avenue, but I came to a decision: I would visit each of the houses beside the road, I would talk to the people who live in them, and I would collect their stories.

Western Avenue begins at a junction called Western Circus. Within a hundred yards, the houses begin their steady march: suburban villas line each side of the road as it travels west, climbing steadily for half a mile before it crosses a railway bridge. Here, advertising hoardings flank the road; as it banks through a gentle turn, the cars pass between giant advertisements for other cars – faster, glossier cars than those stalled in the queues of traffic. The road passes more houses on the left and a modern block of flats on the right, crosses another bridge, passes a garage and begins to descend to a junction called Gipsy Corner. There are houses on the left, and factories and workshops on the right; the road widens to six lanes, and the traffic picks up speed, until it rips through Gipsy Corner at sixty or seventy miles an hour.

This is the point where I had first walked on Western Avenue. Two weeks after my first visit, I returned to Gipsy Corner and began calling at the houses beside the road.

PART ONE: 1995

And above all, it is *your* civilisation, it is *you*. However much you hate it or laugh at it, you will never be happy away from it for any length of time ... Good or evil, it is yours, you belong to it, and this side the grave you will never get away from the marks that it has given you.

George Orwell, *The Lion and the Unicorn*

Up till 1900 no-one had any idea, even the faintest notion, of the phenomenon about to burst on the world. First came the motor-car; then the air-plane ... And all the time the universal use of machinery continues to produce its consequences.

Le Corbusier, *The City of Tomorrow*

1. Enchanted Land

The worst times are the summer afternoons, when the flood of traffic on Western Avenue thickens and congeals into a fetid stew of metal which clogs the road and gums up the air. Sometimes, Trevor Dodd wants to rush out and smash the cars with a hammer. 'Everyone's beeping, everyone's bad-tempered, it's hot, it's hard to breathe, it's stinking with all the exhausts . . . it's just a wind-up.' He rests his hands on the window-ledge overlooking Western Avenue and then runs a finger along the glass; it comes away smeared with dirt. 'Look how filthy the window gets,' he adds, disdainfully.

The glass vibrates gently, in tune with the traffic on the road beneath us; it is Saturday afternoon, and the cars flow freely through Gipsy Corner. As Trevor begins to introduce me to the horrors of life beside an urban motorway, there is a kind of pride in his voice. 'It's dirty, it's dusty in the summer, and if it's raining, the whole place goes brown – it's like this misty cloud all over the road. Walk up to the shops and you get covered in dirty spray; stand out there by the traffic lights and you get blown around – the lorries come screaming through the junction at seventy miles an hour, and you actually get moved off your feet.'

Enthused by the ugliness of his neighbourhood, he is, already, unrecognizable from the hostile, suspicious man who had answered the door five minutes ago. He'd had reason to be suspicious – I had come to call at his house unannounced and uninvited; he had no idea why I was there, and I was not sure I could explain it properly myself.

227 Western Avenue was the third house I visited. I had begun, randomly, at 213 Western Avenue – a house which stands to the west of Gipsy Corner, in the shadow of the car supermarket which straddles the junction. A dirty sheet hung in the window beside the front door, and the garden was sown with thick, pale grass. It was almost a relief when there was no answer to my knock. For some reason, approaching the houses beside the road made me nervous.

I soon discovered it was not just me who was nervous: at 217 Western Avenue, an elderly woman edged the front door open, and slammed it shut again before I could explain why I was there. It is hard to blame her. I was beginning to think I might be wasting my time, and 227 Western Avenue did not give me much encouragement: an upturned arm-chair lay in its overgrown front garden, its paintwork was chipped and cracked, and its brickwork had been flayed bare by the passing cars. I rang the bell anyway.

After a moment, the door shuddered, sticking against its frame before it opened. I was confronted by a stocky man in his early thirties: his face was rounded, but the flesh was laid on in sparse flat planes, and a cap of closely cropped hair topped his powerful figure. A thickening belly pressed against the waistband of his jeans. I'm writing a book about Western Avenue, I said, and I'd like to talk to you; I felt ridiculous. He looked at me dumbly, his heavy, unshaven face closed like a fist. 'Are you winding me up?' he said, scornfully.

An Ulster accent thickened his words. For a moment, I thought he might hit me. He kept one hand pressed against the door – if necessary, he could throw his weight against it, and shut me out. I took a step backwards; I would try elsewhere. Then, for some reason, he relented. 'All right,' he said, suddenly, 'you'd better come in.' With surprising graciousness, he opened the door wider, and I stepped into the cramped, gloomy hallway of his house. I followed him up the stairs, climbing over the boxes and bin-bags which litter his flat, and emerged into his shabby sitting-room.

With a proprietary gesture, he showed me to the window, with its panoramic view of Western Avenue. Beyond the ugly knot of the junction, the warehouses and factories of the Park Royal Industrial Estate gathered on the horizon. It was only two o'clock in the afternoon, but there was little light left in the day – the landscape was drained of colour, and its perspectives peculiarly flattened, as if the houses were pressing themselves backwards, away from the noise and dirt of the road. We stood in silence for a moment and watched the traffic.

'The noise fucks you up,' he says, conversationally. 'I think that's one of the things which will come out in the next ten years – you'll get people running out there with machine guns.' He makes tea in the dirty kitchen, which overlooks the road, and then settles on a gilt-embossed chair in his sitting-room. The room is littered with junk: I notice a decrepit stereo, and a bin-bag stuffed with clothes; beside my feet is a scrap of paper with a telephone number for 'film and TV extras', and a candle in a bottle rests on a set of cardboard bookshelves under the window. In the bedroom, a half-finished copy of a Van Gogh painting stands against the wall. Trevor used to be a painter, but he says he is too lethargic to bother anymore. It makes sense: living beside a motorway would drain the life from more dynamic people than Trevor Dodd. It would certainly drain the life from me – if I lived here, I imagine I would never get out of bed. Trevor makes a sporadic living as a French polisher, and when things are quiet, as they are now, he fills in with painting and decorating.

He tells me he left Belfast thirteen years ago, when he was eighteen, and hitch-hiked to London to look for work.

'Everywhere in Britain, people are drawn to London – if I'd known it was like this' – he gestures vaguely towards the window – 'I wouldn't have bothered. But once you've come, you can't really go back again.' As he begins to talk more fluently, he seals each of his sentences with a precise downward movement of his lips: it is a curiously feminine gesture, at odds with his bullish physical presence, and it lends his speech a rhythm which makes everything he says seem more considered and thoughtful than it might first appear. His instinctive hospitality has conquered his suspicion, and the intimidating façade he presented at the door has dissolved. Yet he remains guarded: he is persuasive and entertaining, but he tells me little about himself.

He was living in a squat in Willesden when the Housing Association offered him a flat on Western Avenue. He had little choice but to take it. For almost two years, he lived in a house 400 yards to the west of Gipsy Corner. Four months ago, he moved to number 227 – his second home on the road. He has hardly even bothered to unpack. 'What's the point? I'm being kicked out soon.'

I ask him why, and he looks at me in surprise. 'Did you not know?'

'What?'

'I thought that was why you were here. They're knocking the houses down.'

'They're doing what?'

He laughs at my astonishment. 'They're rebuilding the road – they're building a flyover here.' He walks to the window. 'Most of this is owned by the Department of Transport.'

The sweep of his arm covers the houses on both sides of the road. Many of them, he says, have been marked for demolition, and work will soon begin on the flyover which is designed to carry the traffic above Gipsy Corner. Soon, the tenants will be evicted, the houses will be destroyed, and the construction crews will occupy the road. It is a shock: I had no idea the road was being rebuilt. It is not why I came to Western Avenue, yet had I waited six months, it would have been too late; the life of the road would have been destroyed.

Trevor does not particularly care that he is being evicted. He has no attachment to the area: there is nothing to do here – no good places to go, no interesting people to see; he cannot drink, because he used to have a drinking problem, but when he does go out, he visits friends in Kilburn. He takes a thick sheaf of letters, detailing the terms of his impending eviction, from the writing desk which stands haphazardly in the middle of his sitting-room, and spreads them out on the floor. He is bemused by the intricacies of the process, but he does not resent it. 'I'm not sorry to be leaving Acton – not at all – but I'm sorry I'll be losing my own wee flat.'

He pauses to point out the view from his bedroom window. In the back garden of the house next door, a willow tree blooms luxuriantly, its branches spilling into the gardens of the neighbouring houses. 'That's a beautiful view, if you live on Western Avenue.' It is the first positive comment he has made. 'Have you found anyone else to talk to?'

I say I haven't really tried.

'Well, you won't find anyone who is sorry to leave. Most people are happy to go – they just want somewhere to go to.'

He's right, I think, as I walk out on to the road again. When the lights turn red, and the cars gather in the valley, the fumes are so thick it is as though a warm, wet hand has been clamped over my face. Surely everyone will welcome the chance to leave this behind them. Leaning into

the wind which funnels down the hill, I walk back towards
my car.

— — —

At night, the arterial roads are an illuminated necklace
wrapped around the city's throat – an adornment which
threatens to choke it to death. By day, they are an escape
route, though in the humiliating inevitability of rush-hour
traffic jams, they are also a trap. The city's streets were first
described as 'arteries' and 'veins' in the eighteenth century,
when planners began to model traffic systems on the blood
system of the body. According to the urbanist Richard
Sennett, they believed that if motion through the city
became blocked, then the 'collective body suffers a crisis of
circulation like that an individual body suffers during a
stroke'.

— — —

I park in the shadow of the car supermarket, and walk on
to the road for the second time. It is Tuesday morning.
Yesterday, I rang the Department of Transport, and I was
told that more than 200 houses have been marked for
demolition on Western Avenue.

There is a removals van parked in a side-road, and in
the distance I notice a man walking along the pavement
with a duvet tucked under his arm. Suddenly, the signs of a
random and widespread departure from the road are obvious. I do not know yet which houses will be demolished,
and it is with a new urgency that I begin my house-calls.
I start on the hill above Western Circus, on the side of
the road which carries traffic east, towards the centre of
London.

At 152 Western Avenue, the black man who answers
the door dismisses me with an abrupt wave. He has lived

here for only a year, and he has nothing to say. Next door
lives Mr Clopet, who fixes one staring eye on the wall
beside my head while the other contemplates the sky behind
me, and whispers that his mother is inside the house. He
invites me to return another day. An old woman from
Whitstable talks to me through a crack in the wooden fence
which seals her back garden – she will not come outside, or
open the gate to allow me into her garden. She insists she
has nothing to say. Her face is as dry and roughened as
bark, and she works her jaw fiercely as she talks, as though
she is chewing a wad of tobacco. 'I like it round here –
there's good and bad in every race,' she says, defiantly.

I reach the flat summit of the hill above Gipsy Corner,
where the traffic masses between the railway bridges before
it begins its thunderous descent to the junction. There is a
stretch of a hundred yards where all of the houses beside
the east-bound carriageway have been abandoned – except
for one. 186 Western Avenue is the last occupied house in
its block. The doors and windows of the neighbouring
house are sealed with metal plates, painted a thick, dirty
red, and weeds lace together the fractured tarmac scalp of
its driveway. Yet the woman who answers the door at 186
seems oblivious to her surroundings: Oh yes, she says,
brightly, I like it here. She hardly notices the traffic. Her
name is Mrs Johnson. Her husband appears from inside the
house, clutching a pair of glasses – a crisp, Mediterranean
accent shaves his speech. With scrupulous courtesy, he
writes down my phone-number, his crimped, greying hair
poised above a scrap of paper cushioned on the palm of his
hand. They promise they will call me, but I do not believe
them – they are just being polite. As I turn away, I bang my
head sharply on the hanging basket suspended from a hook
above the porch; it hurts, but I pretend it doesn't, and we
all laugh, nervously.

It is a bitterly cold morning; by lunchtime, my fingers can hardly hold a pen. It begins to rain, and I give up and go home.

— — —

In 227 Western Avenue, Trevor Dodd is bothered by a nuisance caller: 'Leave a message,' says his answer-machine irritably, 'and whoever it is that keeps ringing me up and playing music down the phone, will you please stop doing it?' I hang up, guiltily, though I have no reason to feel guilty.

— — —

The suburbs began life as a rural isolation ward: from the thirteenth century onwards, fear of plague prompted a periodic exodus from the city, and the modern suburb was born when epidemic cholera persuaded the prosperous middle classes to abandon the confines of Victorian London. Yet the suburbs built in the 1840s were restricted to those who could afford to travel to and from the city, and London remained notoriously congested. In 1884, a Royal Commission on the 'Housing of the Working Classes' discovered that eight people to a room was commonplace in the 'pestilential human rookeries' of London's slums and tenement buildings.

— — —

I have noticed 219 Western Avenue before: with its low wooden fence and its tidy front garden, it is a model of suburban propriety – neat, self-contained, and sheltered from the road by a disciplined bank of trees. A security-conscious sticker beside the front door warns visitors they will be required to identify themselves: it is obvious that elderly people live here, and most of the old people I have met have been neurotically reluctant to talk to me; many will not even open their doors. It is Saturday, 11 February. I push the gate open, and walk up the neat path to the front door. I knock, and stand back. The thrill of anticipation as I wait to see who will answer is always the same – a peculiar mixture of fear and voyeuristic curiosity.

The door is opened without hesitation, and I find myself facing an elderly woman. Animated by the need to impress her, I begin what is, by now, a familiar introduction. She listens politely, and then, without hesitating, she says, 'Well, you'd better come and talk to my husband.' She opens the door wider, and ushers me through a wood-panelled hall into the sitting-room at the back of the house. It takes a moment for my eyes to adjust to the gloomy interior.

There is an old man sitting in an armchair inside the door; he half stands, twisting his neck awkwardly to see who I am, and then subsides into his chair again. He is no more surprised to see me than his wife had been. He nods enthusiastically while she explains why I am here, gripping my hand as if he wants me to pull him to his feet. 'I'll tell you some stories about the Transport Board,' he says, fervently. I have not mentioned the 'Transport Board' – in fact, I have hardly had a chance to introduce myself, yet Mr and Mrs Green have responded to my presence so eagerly that I am left with the strange suspicion they had been expecting me to call.

The Greens have lived on Western Avenue for thirty-five years. Now, the 'Transport Board' is buying their house by compulsory purchase, for it is one of the many marked for demolition. They do not want to leave their house – what's more, they do not want to leave the road, and Mr Green is furious that the money they are being given as compensation is not enough to buy another house on Western Avenue. 'We've never had any complaints,' he says, belligerently. 'Why should they reduce the price of the house because of the noise? There's no noise. Listen! Can you hear anything?'

Mr Green, a balding old man in a tweed jacket, holds up his hand, like an elderly schoolteacher stilling a noisy assembly. I wait politely while he contemplates the familiar atmosphere of his home; for a moment, there is a beatific look on his face. The distant rumble of traffic is plainly audible, yet Mr Green does not notice it – age, or familiarity, or both, has seduced his senses, and he does not hear what I am hearing. He lowers his pipe and appeals for vindication: 'They're talking through their hats – there's no noise, and there's no pollution either.' In fact, Mr Green counts proximity to the main road as one of the major advantages of life on Western Avenue. 'Where else can you get a house where you can step out of your front door and get a bus to Greenford? Go around the corner and you can catch a bus to Shepherd's Bush, or Hammersmith – or Harlesden!' he says, with wide-eyed enthusiasm.

It is the Department of Transport, with its scheme for rebuilding the road, which attracts his scorn. The men who came to value the property sat on their sofa for five minutes, and then strolled around the house. Its first owner was the head of a furniture firm in Kensington, and its fittings are good quality – better than they could have afforded, Mr Green admits – yet all they cared about was the amount of land the house occupies. 'My daughter wants that fireplace for her sitting-room, and we'll take it, whatever they say. Look!' With the stem of his pipe, he stabs at the gold leaf which edges the panelling on the wall. His indignation is so intense that he cannot imagine other people do not share it; had it not been me, he seems to think, then surely someone, sooner or later, would have come to hear his grievances.

Photographs of children and grandchildren cluster on

the mantelpiece. From the security of his buttressed arm-chair, Mr Green overlooks the back garden, which has been bedded down for the winter: the lawn is neatly cropped, and plants climb a trellis set against the fence. The gardens were a source of pride to the home-owners who arrived on Western Avenue in the 1930s, but most of them are disappearing under a sprawling, uninterrupted tangle of weeds; only one or two householders still maintain the neat demarcations of suburban life.

Though the demolition crews have begun to mark out their territory, nature has not yet deserted the road – Mr Green says their garden is like a bird sanctuary. 'We've got two blackbirds who've been with us all these years. We'd sit out in the garden with our two deckchairs and these two birds, the mother and father, would come, and we'd put out food for them. In the morning when we get up they all seem to fly into our garden because they know there'll be something for them to eat. We had a squirrel in the garden, as well – was it after Christmas, or before? Well, I don't know what those two blackbirds are going to think when we're gone.'

Briefly, they tell me their history: they met at a police ball in 1935, and married in 1937 – she is from County Cork, he is from County Durham, and their accents have not lost their distinctive edge, though they have softened and grown more alike over the years. 'He's English, but I'm Irish, and I always will be,' says Mary Green, firmly. They have three children, the youngest of whom, Robin, still lives with them; he is forty-seven years old, and a town planner.

The Greens arrived on Western Avenue in 1959. The road was already colonized by houses and factories, yet the Greens remember it as a quiet residential district – London's 'Queen of Suburbs', as an advertisement in the *Acton Gazette* described neighbouring Ealing, in 1931. 'For

pedestrians who delight in rambles, the region might be
called Enchanted Land,' said a brochure published in 1930,
describing Ideal Homes in another nearby suburb.

Recently, Mrs Green has noticed that many of the
houses around them have been converted into 'flats for the
homeless people', but they never see their new neighbours,
and they often wonder whether the houses are really occupied. The Greens' reclusive neighbours are less real to them
than the people who lived there thirty years ago. 'You
should see the front gardens! They're only here temporarily,
and they don't even bother to pick up the rubbish. It's a
real tip now, Western Avenue,' says Mrs Green. 'We're
ashamed to have people come over to see us.'

She does not open the door at night anymore. In their
back garden, the gate into the lane is secured with five
bolts, and they say the house is like a prison, with locks
and bolts on every door. 'We've had to make this house
very secure, because we've been burgled twice . . . I don't
know why they pick on us. You know, we had our car
stolen from the back, and then a fortnight ago, haven't we
had our car stolen again?' Mrs Green settles at a table
against the wall, instinctively ceding the floor to her
husband.

'Yes, I had a Ford Cortina and I parked it at the back
one evening and when we got up the next morning, it was
gone. We've never seen it from that day to this. Then we
got another Escort and Robin parked it on the other side of
Western Avenue – he'd only left it two hours and that was
gone.' Mrs Green thinks it's because people are unemployed, and 'trying to get something for themselves', but
her husband, who served in the Metropolitan Police for
thirty years, blames his old colleagues: since the day the
bobby went off the streets, he says, they've lost all touch
with the public. Yet the image of an elderly couple barri-

caded into their house is undermined by their unquestioning hospitality. They never ask why I am here, or what I want from them. At one point, Mrs Green disappears into the kitchen, and a moment later, she places a plate of ham sandwiches on the low table in front of me.

'You know, if I'd been younger, I would have loved to have written a book – what I've done and what I've seen would have gone well in a book,' says Mr Green, suddenly. My tape-recorder turns noisily, capturing Mr Green's breathing, as well as his pipe-roughened old man's voice, as he begins to tell me about the places in the neighbourhood that have acquired mythical significance for him: the shops, the bank, the hospital, all of which have disappeared; the house in Horn Lane, where Lord Nelson used to live with his 'girlfriend', Lady Hamilton; the tall house where a 'famous cricketer' called Fry used to live; and the car showroom, which used to be owned by two brothers. 'Those two brothers!' he says, with an indulgent chuckle, as if he was recounting the antics of two naughty schoolboys. 'One had all the business over on the other side of the Thames, and the other brother this side of the Thames, supplying all the greengrocers with vegetables. They were going to start a market here, but the two brothers . . . they never got it off the ground. They went out of business and this place was left empty for quite a long time. Then the showroom came instead, and altered the place a lot.'

He once escorted King George V to the Ideal Homes Exhibition, in Olympia, and after the war, when the Russians and the British were struggling for control of Berlin, he guarded a Russian hostage in Hammersmith police station – a diplomat whom the British had kidnapped in Berlin and brought back to Britain. 'Who was he? I can't remember now. Some important man,' he says, irritably. The question upsets him.

'He's forgotten,' says Mrs Green fondly. 'Will you tell him about Ruth Ellis?' she prompts gently, repairing the damage.

'Oh yes . . .' Mr Green sighs with satisfaction. 'Well, being a sergeant, I was fortunate enough to have two periods at the Old Bailey – that's for the summer, when the Old Bailey was in session. Well, I happened to be inside the court when the case of Ruth Ellis, the last woman to be hanged in England, was up. I was present inside the court when the judge asked her – I'm not quite sure now if it was two or three times – to reconsider her plea of Guilty. He wanted her to go down to the cells, and think it over, because whenever he asked how she pleaded, she said Guilty. And he kept asking her to change her mind. He sent her downstairs to the cells two or three times to reconsider her plea, and each time she came up she said the same thing – Guilty. So of course, he'd given her that opportunity to reconsider her plea, and he had no alternative – he picked up the black hat which was at the side, you know, he puts that on his head, and he told her what was going to happen . . . I look upon that as something very unusual – to think I was there when Ruth Ellis, the last woman to be hanged in England, was sentenced! I mean, you could meet hundreds of people and they wouldn't be able to tell you all these things. And what I'm telling you is the truth! You could talk to hundreds of policemen in the Met, and they'd never once have had a period offered to them at the Old Bailey. No, I never regretted being in the police – I had a wonderful time, and I had some wonderful experiences. I got a Commissioner's Recommendation for catching four Post Office workers, during the time of the blackout once . . .'

My tape-recorder clicks to an abrupt halt: the noise it makes startles me, but Mr Green does not notice – he has begun to tell me about the time he was involved in a car-chase, pursuing two house-breakers through the suburbs of Kew and Richmond.

There is silence for a moment when he reaches the end of the story, and then they both speak at once: 'We'll be glad to get out of the area now,' says Mrs Green, unexpectedly.

'The old lady next door . . .' begins Mr Green.

'She's been here longer than us.'

'Yes, just longer than us,' says Mr Green, vaguely. I had met the old lady next door: she did not want to talk to me – she would not even open her door to me – but I will hear about her anyway.

'She came in this morning, Mrs Broadbridge, and she's very upset about leaving. She's a nice woman. She used to be an accountant at Harrods. She said this morning, I feel really ill. Ever since I heard I had a date to leave, I've been feeling sick. And she's on her own – we're fortunate we've got our son to help us. Well, we feel dreadful about it, of course, but what's the point? We hate it, but what can we do?' Her memory is sharper than her husband's, but it is Mr Green who takes care of their shared past: while he endlessly recomposes the story of his life, she is more concerned with the immediate practicalities of their day-to-day existence. It is a pattern I am familiar with – my grandparents have perfected it.

'Do you do the lottery?' says Mrs Green, in a conspiratorial whisper, when she shows me to the door ten minutes later. 'We do – we haven't collected yet, but we'd put the Transport Board in a mess if we did.' She opens the door and the liquid rush of the traffic floods the hall. 'I'd tell them they'd have to put up with us until they came up with the right offer – they'd have to get the bailiffs in.'

The Green's gate swings shut behind me. I walk west, away from Gipsy Corner. 229 Western Avenue – the house next door to Trevor's – has been abandoned; oxblood plates are nailed to its façade. A thin wind blows down the road – a following breeze, hurrying the traffic along, through the suburb of East Acton. Rubbish collects in the gutters and spills on to the pavement.

At 239 Western Avenue, the front door is ajar. Tentatively, I push it open, and step inside the house. The air is damp. Curled like an upside-down question mark, a wire trails from the overhead light socket, and the long, brown tendrils of a dying plant hang limply in the stairwell. The sitting-room door has been ripped off its hinges; inside, a handful of green pills have melted into livid, spreading spots on the damp carpet. In the back garden, for no apparent reason, the components of two dismembered lawn-mowers are scattered across the grass. The L-shaped garden shed contains the assorted props of someone's life – a pair of skis, a filing cabinet, a fishing rod, a clutch of ties, a typewriter instruction manual, and a shelf of jars full of pink and blue paint.

I climb the stairs. Holes have been driven through the floorboards in each of the bedrooms, and the toilet has exploded; all that remains is the jagged stem, which cups a fetid pool of water. In the bath next door, there is a human shit, and in the bedroom above the road, a carpet lies over the hole which has been driven through the floorboards; I step carefully around it. Underneath the window, I find several letters from the DSS, and amongst them, handwritten on a piece of dirty white tissue paper, a poem:

> I WOZ 'ERE, but now
> I've gone, I've left
> My name to CARRY ON,
> Those who know me, know me well,
> And those who don't, can
> GO TO HELL.

It is signed 'SMUDGER'. I read it out loud and my voice echoes alarmingly in the empty house. The capitals have been gouged crudely into the paper. It looks as though it was written by a grotesquely overgrown child.

Flies circulate noiselessly around my head, and dust catches in my throat. I should not be here: the house does not feel deserted – the gleeful violence with which the bailiffs have set about it is sickening, and the stench of an ill-timed and reluctant departure thickens the air. The vibration of the heavy lorries on Western Avenue makes the floor creak beneath my feet – a warning of the sustained violence which is to follow when the demolition of the houses begins, and the traffic invades the space once coloured by human presence. I leave the house quickly, letting the door slam shut behind me. Outside, on Western Avenue, the air seems fresh in comparison.

There is a fox which lives near Gipsy Corner. It crosses the road using the subway which emerges close to Trevor's front door. No one ever sees a fox killed on the road.

The symbol of the nineteenth century, said H.G. Wells, was a 'steam train running upon a railway', and it was the railways which prised open the bunched fist of the Victorian city. At a conference on workmen's trains in 1893, the general manager of one railway company complained that the prospective route of a new line ran across a vast expanse of open fields, where 'houses were scarcely to be seen'. 'They will soon come,' he was told. 'Run the trains and they will come.' At first, suburbia was a 'railway state' – a world defined by the configuration of railway station, local shops, and open fields.

— — —

Mr Green once knew a man who owned seven greengrocer shops, and lost them all betting on the dogs at Park Royal. He last saw him in Hammersmith, selling tins of tomatoes from a stall. Mr Green still has a bet every day, but he makes sure that he 'never goes over the limit'.

— — —

I have brought with me the neatly drawn plans which arrived this morning from the Department of Transport. It is 13 February. I spread them out on the floor of Trevor's sitting-room, and we study them, united in contemplation of the destruction of his neighbourhood. Of the 210 houses which will be demolished, most lie on the westbound side of the carriageway between Gipsy Corner and Western Circus; many are grouped around Gipsy Corner.

Trevor walks to the window: 'I think those are the worst houses over there – on the other side of the road. Are they leaving those houses there? You're kidding! They're terrible – they've got traffic on both sides . . . Let's have a look at the plan . . . You're right . . . those houses are still there.' He shakes his head in disbelief: the rebuilt road will pass in front of the downstairs windows of the houses opposite. It is hard to believe the proposal is serious – life for the people who remain beside Gipsy Corner will be laughably difficult. 'They've never solved a traffic problem by building a road – quite the opposite, in fact. But I don't know – I don't drive, so I've never been stuck in a jam. You'd have to measure how many people get fucked by the road, measure how many get fucked by the traffic jams, subtract and see who wins.'

Trevor does not know whether the Housing Association will offer him another flat when he is evicted from 227 Western Avenue – at the moment, it is saying there are no more homes, but he does not believe it. 'I have never, ever heard of a Housing Association turning round and saying, "We've no more property – fuck off!"' There is a tenants' meeting on 16 February, when the question will be finally settled, and he invites me to come along.

Raids on the abandoned houses have begun. Most people blame the squatters who are beginning to colonize Western Avenue, but Trevor says its the kids from the White City estate. 'People go in and take out the pipes and the boiler and the floorboards. You just don't give a fuck – the bailiffs move in and smash the toilets, then people come in one by one and nick everything in the house.'

He was raided by the police in his first flat on Western Avenue. 'I was sleeping in the front room on a mattress, and there was a bang on the door – it must have been about half-five in the morning. I heard all these boots on the floorboards, so I got up, and the door was punched in; this noose – a long stick with a noose – came round the corner. I thought, Jeez, what a way to wake up! I didn't know then it was the police. I had this Stanley knife – I was putting veneer in so I had a knife there – and I'd got to the door with the knife when I saw the guy with a number on his shoulder. If I hadn't seen that, I'd have taken his head off. What goes through your mind is just terrifying. The noose was for the dog – they obviously thought there was a dog in there, in case we were drug dealers or something. They had a warrant for Class B drugs – dope, like, soft drugs – and they searched the place. They kept my mate upstairs, and they kept me downstairs, and they went though the whole house. I had a drill, an electric drill, and I didn't have a receipt for it. Well, you don't keep receipts, do you?

But once they'd done the door, they weren't just going to
go away. We were brought down to Acton nick, and that
was it – we were released. Did they charge us? Did they
fuck! I've never been raided before. It was frightening – a
couple of thousand policemen standing on your mattress
first thing in the morning going – ' he shapes his hands into
a megaphone, and mimics the booming voice of a policeman – ' "DON'T MOVE". It was Operation Bumblebee –
they raided every fucker in the whole world.'

– – –

In the nineteenth century, the built-up area of London
increased five times over. Suburbia, complained *The Times*
in 1904, was 'a district of appalling monotony, ugliness
and dullness . . . Now London stretches to Croydon. It is
no longer possible to escape from the dull suburb into un-
spoiled country.' Yet, despite the thickening belt of housing
which surrounded London, the city remained almost as
congested as it had been twenty years earlier, and the
Fabian Society announced that it would 'rather face a civil
war than such another century of suffering as this one has
been'.

– – –

15 February. The back lane which runs behind the Greens'
house is overgrown with forsythia. It is peaceful here, for
the condemned houses muffle the noise of the traffic. Birdsong chimes with the distant ring of metal on metal; someone is working beneath the bonnet of their car on Park
View, one of the side-roads abutting Western Avenue. A
froth of domestic detritus has spilled on to the back lawn
of one of the abandoned houses, and in the garage lies a
clutch of washers, screws and metal pipes – the knuckles
and joints which held the house together. I pick through

the wreckage like a bargain-hunter at a car-boot sale, not knowing what I am looking for.

— — —

'Have you ever had an eviction notice pinned to your door?' The angry middle-aged Irish woman gets to her feet and points accusingly at the three women who sit, side by side, at the far end of the room. 'I haven't been able to sleep for the last month. Even if it's only a bedsit, will you find me somewhere to put my stuff – or is it going to end up on the streets?'

The rain taps lightly against the uncurtained windows, and a thin veil of disinfectant rises from the scuffed lino. Children's drawings on the wall depict 'The Contents of the World', and racks of plastic chairs fence in the tenants, who sit in a rough semi-circle, facing the representatives of their Housing Association.

Lulled by Trevor's nonchalant attitude towards his eviction, I had expected the other tenants to react the same way; I was wrong. When the meeting began, in a church hall 500 yards behind Western Avenue, it seemed as if they were only waiting to be told where and when they would be rehoused. Their faith in the Housing Association was touchingly complete; it was also misplaced. 'If there were more homes, we would give them to you . . .' begins Sinitta, the Asian woman who is acting as the main spokesperson for the Housing Association.

In front of us sits the man who shares Trevor's house – an Irishman with heavy eyes and a startlingly large head. Trevor told me he goes to sleep at night and leaves his television on at full volume, and had introduced me to him one afternoon last week. While the television played inside his flat, Donal leant heavily against his half-open door and stared fixedly at my forehead. 'There's nothing to say about

the road – there's nothing to say about it. It's just a place
to live,' he said, repeatedly. Tonight, Donal has been staring
at the floor with the intensity of a mystic; now, he swings
his heavy head up – it gathers pace, slowly, like a wrecking
ball – until he is staring at Sinitta. 'BOLLACKS!' he shouts.
'BOLLACKS!'

The noise is so loud it makes me flinch, and the hall
echoes to Donal's ugly bark. For a moment, there is an
uncomfortable silence; then someone finds the courage to
speak, and the tempo of the tenants' complaints picks up
again. As an outsider, it seems obvious to me that their
demands will not be met: the Housing Association does not
have homes to give them. Yet the tenants do not want to
accept what they are being told: terrified by the prospect of
being made homeless, and united by the conviction that
they are being denied what is rightfully theirs, their inter-
ruptions drown out Sinitta's measured replies. The neat
agenda laid out for the evening is soon forgotten. 'Could
we at least have a definite decision not to evict anyone until
we have another meeting? Everyone's together here, but
people will get thrown out on the streets one by one,' says
a jockey-sized Irishman with a halo of crazed blond hair.

During the last two weeks, I have visited most of the
condemned houses around Gipsy Corner, but I have met
very few of these people. Perhaps they are scared to answer
the door, since the only visitors they expect are the bailiffs.
Yet as I look around the room, I realize that I recognize
more people here than anyone else does. Most of them have
never met each other; why should they have? I have lived
in the same house in Shepherd's Bush for four years, and I
have only just begun to meet my neighbours. It is strange
to think that I already know more people in the condemned
houses than the people who have invested years of their
lives here.

It is only now that they find they have friends on the road. One by one, the tenants strike up informal alliances with their neighbours in the hall. They have a common cause: the Housing Association has betrayed them. Some are vehement in their anger; others are more docile – they are used to waiting while other people decide where and how they will lead their lives, and they watch placidly while the recriminations spill out around them; others applaud those with the courage to vent the frustrations shared by everyone in the hall.

As the heat generated by sixty bodies begins to dry our damp clothes, an unmistakable atmosphere seeps into the room: it is redolent of underfunded, institutionalized charity – dowdy, well-intentioned and inadequate. Before I met the Greens, I did not understand how anyone could enjoy living on Western Avenue; tonight I am confronted with a much simpler and much sharper emotion – fear. The tenants do not love Western Avenue – they do not want to leave, simply because they have nowhere else to go.

'We're trying to come to an agreement with the DoT to agree the last date on which they want the properties back,' says Sinitta.

'I don't see why you're so keen to evict people when you're so unwilling to help people make alternative arrangements,' says a man with pale cropped hair seated in the front row. An open briefcase rests on his knee.

'We have legally binding contracts, and we won't get any more DoT properties unless we comply,' replies Sinitta.

'BOLLACKS!'

'Do you want any more, if this is the way people are treated?'

'It's not ideal, I know, but it's better than nothing.'

'Well, "nothing" is all some people are going to get.'

'BOLLACKS!'

No one pays any attention to Donal's outbursts any-more.

The man with the briefcase suggests, menacingly, that the 'popular press' might be interested to hear how the Housing Association is treating its tenants, and no one points out the obvious truth: the 'popular press' does not care about the tenants of Western Avenue.

The tenants begin to change their approach: if they will not be rehoused, why can't they stay where they are for the time being? Not only has 'fucking West Hampstead fucked up' and run out of homes, but it is also initiating proceed-ings to evict its tenants. They believe the houses will not be demolished for some time – instead, they will be boarded up and left empty, stained with the blood-red paint that marks the abandoned houses beside Gipsy Corner.

In her neat black business suit, Sinitta is the best-dressed person in the room, and the tenants think she is cheating them. They do not believe there are no more houses, and they are right: there are empty houses all over London. But if the tenants think the Housing Association can be bullied into action on their behalf, then they are wrong; it is no longer a radical organization; it is now part of the estab-lished chain of government, trying to balance its obligation to the Department of Transport with its obligation to the tenants. It is an awkward position to be in. According to the man with the briefcase, the head of the Housing Asso-ciation is on a paid sabbatical in America – the money which should be spent on housing its tenants is funding paid holidays for its employees instead.

'I want to make some points,' says a black woman in a leather jacket, as she gets to her feet. 'You told me to go to the council. Well, councils don't rehouse single people, period. I'm told they don't have to rehouse me. They told me I should have a child – then they'd have to house me.'

There is general applause. 'It doesn't matter which way I turn, I get the door slammed in my face. You say we shouldn't rely on you, but why not, since you put us here?'

The prospect of becoming homeless is bad enough, yet to be snubbed by the organization which said it would provide for them is worse: the bewildered anger of the tenants makes a pitiful spectacle, for it is a measure of their powerlessness. It is a painful occasion, and a peculiarly intimate one. No one knows what I am doing here, and if they did, they would probably ask me to leave, for I am a witness to the evening's inexplicable humiliations.

At 8.30, the meeting begins to break up. In the crowd, I catch up with Trevor Dodd. He has come off worse than most: none of the tenants will be rehoused, but many will be compensated for leaving Western Avenue; he will get nothing, since he has lived in his house for less than a year. Surprisingly, he does not care: 'If I am being shafted, I don't feel like I am. The Housing Association have always been very helpful and very courteous,' he says.

The other tenants, still hoping for a reprieve, gather in disconsolate clumps by the door. Outside, it is raining hard, and the slick, black streets are quiet.

— — —

At 217 Western Avenue, an estate agent's board hangs above the gate. Mrs Broadbridge, the Greens' neighbour, is 'digging into her savings' to buy another house in the area. She likes to think she can still smell her dead husband's cigarette smoke in their home, and she wants to stay close to the place where they lived together.

— — —

Trevor squints through the cracked glass in his sitting-room window towards the house next door.

'Do you think . . .?' I begin.

'Do I think what? Do I think Planet Hollywood is a good restaurant?'

His unexpected sarcasm is a shock. I had begun to take his good-natured tolerance for granted, but several days have passed since the Housing Association meeting, and his patience is running out. Two days ago, he was offered a room in The Approach – a side-road on the other side of Western Avenue – but he turned it down. 'You know – "Do you want to live in hell, or do you want to live in a hard place, Mr Dodd?"' He apes the well-meaning tones in which the Housing Association conducts its business.

The gas has been disconnected in his flat. He has 'done his back in' and can't work – his doctor has told him he should lose weight. Confined to his condemned house, he sits in the gilt armchair in his sitting-room, and fires stones through the window with a fat steel catapult; cracks spiral outwards from several neat, round holes in the glass.

I leave 227 Western Avenue for the last time; within two weeks, both Trevor and the Greens are due to move away. In Park View, where I parked my car, rows of suburban villas face each other across a wide, peaceful street; it is a secure and irreproachable world – a reminder of what Western Avenue must have been like when the broad, concrete road was free of traffic, and the arterial roads were a blank screen on to which people projected contrasting visions of the future. I nudge into the stream of traffic on Western Avenue: the cars make way for me, and then ease together again. We are barely moving – I could turn off my engine and let myself be borne along by the mass of cars travelling towards the heart of London.

– – –

In 1909, the newly established London Traffic Branch
invited a man called Colonel Hellard to prepare a study of
the city's arterial roads. His report recommended the construction of four new roads, including the Western Avenue,
and its counterpart on the other side of the city, the Great
Eastern Avenue. 'The open ground to the south of Wormwood Scrubs presents an opportunity of forming a good
Western outlet which should on no account be lost,' it said.
In 1913, at the Greater London Arterial Roads Conference,
plans were approved for 255 miles of new roads around
London.

2. Leadville

Chalked on the oxblood panel is a map of London's roads: 'YOU ARE HERE', says the legend beside an arrow pointing to Western Avenue. The house has been labelled to avoid further confusion: 'NUMBER 251, WESTERN AVENUE, ACTON, NORTH LONDON, nr HANGER LANE AND NORTH CIRCULAR ROAD.'

— — —

It was the futurists who first claimed the car as the symbol of the new century: 'We affirm that the world's magnificence has been enriched by a new beauty ... a beauty of speed,' said the Italian poet Marinetti in 1909 – the same year that mass-production of the Model T Ford began in America, marking the birth of the 'automobile age' – 'A roaring motor car that seems to run on shrapnel is more beautiful than the Winged Victory of Samothrace.' Others claimed that the invention of the car had revolutionized our lives: 'The norm of our existence has been completely demolished and reversed,' wrote Le Corbusier, a leading figure in the architectural avant-garde of the post-war years.

— — —

William Conlin runs his hand over the wooden doorframe at 237 Western Avenue. 'You know what? You can choose your neighbourhood – but you can't choose your neighbours.'

It is strange to hear William echo the refrain of the home-owning residents of Western Avenue – many of whom would regard an unemployed Irishman in a Housing Association property as an undesirable addition to the road. Yet William has reason to be wary of his neighbours. His fingers trace the pale scars which pock the wood of his doorframe: they mark the hinges from which his front door used to hang. One day, the woman who lived in the flat above him knocked the door down with a hammer. 'You can't win with people like her. It was every which way but lose.' There is no bitterness in his voice. It is difficult to imagine what might provoke him to anger. William is a solidly built man yet there is a diffidence about him which makes his physical presence unthreatening, even in the confines of his tiny hallway.

I follow him into the darkened sitting-room of his flat. The room has green walls, green-stained floors and shuttered windows. It feels like a sunken garden – faintly damp, and sheltered from the sun. In the middle of the room stands a long table littered with black-and-white photographs. William gestures towards the open door of his bedroom, at the front of the house: a mannequin's head topped by a bowler hat stands on the window-ledge facing the road, but the blind is lowered, and the room is dark – William has turned his house back to front to escape the traffic on Western Avenue. 'I never even pull the curtain. It's such an ugly looking scene out there.'

William – an unshaven Irishman with a straggling ponytail of dirty-blond hair – has lived on Western Avenue for six years, but time has not dulled his appreciation of the road: when he answered the door, and I told him I was writing a book about Western Avenue, he responded enthusiastically. 'I call it Leadville,' he said, as we stood on his doorstep. 'You can put that in your book . . . Me and my mate did a survey – we reckon eighty million cars pass

this house every year. Jesus!' he added, absent-mindedly.
'You should see the trees round here!'

His troublesome neighbour was called Alison, and
William used to avoid talking to her. 'She was capable
of anything – she was a complete nut. First of all, I said,
"Look, you live upstairs – I live downstairs; if you want to
see me, phone me." Later I said, "Look, I don't want to see
you or talk to you at all." I didn't want anything to do
with her. It was getting really out of hand – she was calling
me up at all hours of the day and the night, going on at me,
accusing me of taking pornographic pictures – she was a bit
of a berserko feminist, you know, but for all the wrong
reasons. She used to lean out of the window and shout at
me as I was going down the road, "You're a coward –
you're not a man!" I had a van out there, and she used to
vandalize it – you know, she'd scratch the paint off, and all
this . . . She used to go on about men being violent, but
when she knocked my door in and I didn't kick the crap
out of her, I was a coward. She used to say all men were
child molesters, and then she went off to Australia and
came back to London six months pregnant.'

He picks a hand-rolled, half-smoked cigarette from an
ashtray, and relights it. He has probably told the same story
many times before, yet the way he talks makes it seem
unrehearsed – almost as if he were hearing it for the first
time, he seems fascinated by the possibilities it presents.
Perhaps I have been seduced by the Irish accent which
glosses his words, yet it seems to me that William is a
natural storyteller. Behind me, a heavy, gilt-edged mirror
hangs on the wall above my head; pinned inside its frame is
a spray of black-and-white photographs of a semi-naked
woman. Her head is shaved, and her face concealed in
shadows, yet it is plain the pictures were taken in this room.

William stands up and walks to his kitchen, which is set against the sitting-room wall; he flicks on the kettle. One afternoon, Alison had a visitor from Australia. William met her in the hall, and they started talking. 'I asked her in for a cup of coffee, and she was down here all afternoon – just chatting about this and that. She came in at about one, and stayed until six. We were getting on really well, and all this time we could hear Alison banging around upstairs . . .' He raises an eyebrow towards the ceiling with a weary look, suggestive of the trouble Alison had put him to over the years. 'Eventually, her friend said, "I'd better go back, hadn't I?" So she went upstairs, and Alison came clattering down the stairs one minute later – she was out there in the hall, banging on the door and giving me all kinds of abuse about this and that, shouting, "You were stopping me from feeding my fucking baby." ' William picks a shred of tobacco from his lips. 'Then she went berserk – she smashed the door down with a hammer.'

He is interrupted by a dull, muffled thud; it sounds as though a pocket of gas has ignited somewhere in the flat, but William is unconcerned. 'My electricity is a bit dodgy – watch.' He switches the kettle on again, and steps away from it. A moment later, the plug spits from the socket, and dives over the edge of the sideboard, trailing its skittering flex behind it. 'It's a sign I should get out of this house,' says William impassively. More to the point, it is a sign he should not be boiling water, but he nonchalantly waves away a puff of steam and plugs the kettle in again; it erupts once more before it boils. Finally, he presents me with a bowl of tea. 'A very West Hampsteady cup of tea – remember that! It's exactly like the Housing Association.' He laughs, and the sound is startlingly loud – a clattering, raucous cheer.

Alison moved out a year ago, in the middle of the night,

when her son was six months old. The Housing Association had offered her a flat for a single parent in Southall, which was left empty – and since no one knew she was leaving, her flat at 237 Western Avenue was empty as well. 'People like that don't understand cause and effect – she doesn't know how much damage she does,' says William, earnestly. He knows only too well that the Housing Association has few properties to spare, yet there is another element to his disapproval: he feels kinship with the boy who will grow up without knowing his father, for his own father died before he was born. 'He was a gorgeous little boy, and I couldn't even say hello to him – you know, where does he stand by now? He must be lost in space.'

I ask him whether it made a difference to him not knowing his father, and he repeats the question wonderingly: 'Did it make a difference? Jesus! Heaps! It's a big hole in your life – it's only when you get older that you realize what a difference it makes.' He says he has no balance in his head when it comes to relationships, and few other reference points – he'd never seen a man and a woman having an argument, for instance, and it took him a long time to figure out he could say no to a woman, just like a woman could say no to him. 'I grew up on social welfare and when you do that you never say no, you always say "yes", and "please"; it takes a long time to learn you can say no . . .'

William has four older brothers and sisters, all of whom knew their father: they are all married and live in Ireland. It is William – the youngest son, the boy whose father died while his mother was pregnant with him – who has become the wanderer. Yet he insists his childhood had positive aspects, as well: the reason he mainly photographs women is because he has a feminine perspective; he is used to seeing the world through his mother's eyes. 'Maybe that's why I

can take decent photographs – because I'm sensitive,' he
suggests.

He is pleased when I ask if I can see more of his
photographs. I follow him into his bedroom, where he
opens a chest of drawers which stands under the window;
it is filled with prints and contact sheets. Wreathed in the
killing-bottle scent of chemicals, we crouch over the thick,
glossy stack of paper and flick through the images. Some
of William's photographs are portraits: in one, a blonde
woman stares into the camera, her conventionally pretty
face composed and unrevealing. William holds the picture
up to look at it better; the light filtering through the blind
bleaches its edges. 'Isn't she beautiful?' If she were famous,
he adds, people would be falling over themselves to publish
the photograph. William's pictures have been rejected by
magazines and agencies, but he does not care: he suspects
that the media is simply a glorified network of friends –
and he is, at least, partly right.

'The first time I photograph a person, I say to them,
look, just come along, dress how you want, and don't do
anything you're not comfortable doing. So we have a cup
of tea, and a chat – one girl came along at ten in the
morning, and we were still chatting at four in the evening,
and we hadn't taken one photograph. Do you know what I
mean?' Whether he is a good photographer or not, there is
one thing at which William excels: making friends. 'I tell
you something, Edward, generally my head will be blank
before I start.' The way he uses my name so confidently is
an aspect of his easy, relaxed charm. 'But I always get
something exclusive to the person, you know what I mean?
And I find, you know, sometimes that I can draw people
out of themselves.'

Many of William's pictures are candidly pornographic.

One contact sheet contains a set of images of a naked woman kneeling on William's bed: her hands are clenched on the brass bedstead, the white counterpane is pooled around her knees, and a black leather whip curls between her buttocks; the whip, it seems, is William's favourite prop. Yet his appreciation of nudity is not purely voyeuristic: he shows me a series of self-portraits, in which he sits on a window seat in a French château, gazing soulfully towards the camera, which is positioned in the garden beneath him; his knees are drawn up to his chest, and he is naked.

He has been taking photographs regularly for three years. Before he moved to London, he had lived in various European countries, 'just travelling around and making the most of it'. He had begun to ask himself what he was going to do with his life, when he woke up one morning and decided he would like to become a photographer. His plan was to take people's portraits and sell them back to them – it sounds simple, but he hasn't worked out how to go about it yet.

William returns the contact sheets to their place, and straightens up. 'What appeals to me in London is that I can retain my anonymity, which is really interesting. All the things you can dig up ... Plus as well, all the interesting people. When you go to Dublin, you know, it's very, very rare that you'll see a black face or a Chinese face, or anything ... I really notice in London that you can walk around the streets, and see the faces. Anyway, I don't think I could take photographs like that in Dublin.'

He is probably right: his mother might have inspired his interest in photographing naked women, but it is hard to believe 'an ordinary Catholic woman' would approve of the results. Alison once sent William a postcard from Australia,

with a simple message: 'I'm pregnant – ha ha!' When
William told his mother about the card, she responded by
saying she was going to church to say a prayer for Alison.

Four days have passed since the tenants' meeting, and
William has accepted that he will have to leave his home.
He would stay longer if he could, for the place 'suits him
down to the ground' – he uses the garden as a studio and
he has turned his bathroom into a darkroom. 'When I move
into my new place, I won't have that, which means I can't
experiment. It could ruin my career before it even takes off!
The Department of Transport are philistines – will you put
that in your book? They don't understand what they're
doing to us.' His barking laugh takes me by surprise again.
'But maybe, you know, maybe, I think to myself, if I get
kicked out of here, it will make me get my finger out a bit
more, because I'm in a comfortable little rut here; I've got a
nice little lifestyle, it's nice and easy . . .' Most people would
regard life on the dole on Western Avenue as painfully
austere, but William said that he grew up learning to be
grateful for what he was given.

Besides, he knows it is not fair to blame the Housing
Association. 'We did sign contracts saying we would go
if they wanted to kick us out, so we haven't really got
a leg to stand on. It's not their fault – they're just badly
organized, do you know what I mean? They have all this
positive discrimination stuff, and they can't even make a
decision – when they need to do anything, they've got to
have a meeting, you know, and they've got to have, like,
refreshments – and holiday snaps!' He laughs raucously.
At the tenants' meeting, I remember William contributing
to the chorus of abuse, but little upsets him for long; he has
forgiven Sinitta already.

His only concern is that they will be evicted sooner than
necessary: if he moves out in a month, he does not want to

drive past in two years' time and find the house still
standing. The work could take years to complete. 'They're
going to do an underpass out there, and they're building
bridges and widening roads all around here. It's not just a
question of sorting out the A40 – it's a mega-job, and they
work at a snail's pace, so I don't see what the panic is; it's
not like the M11, where we're all barricading ourselves in
and threatening to stay here for ever. We just want a bit
more understanding, but they're a bit, you know . . . hard-
line about it.'

He gestures towards the road outside. 'That whole corner is going to be like the Bullring – it's going to dehuman-
ize it even more. I mean, who's going to walk from one side
of the road to the other now? The only way you're going
to get across that road is by going through a subway. It's
going to be like Elephant and Castle. Do you know what I
mean? I got lost in Elephant and Castle once, and it's really
hard to find your way out. When you go underground,
you're disorientated – you don't know where you are, and
they're giving you all this north, east and south side, and
all that . . . Oh God, it's difficult! It's just crazy . . . It's
going to become an ugly, sprawling, disgusting mess . . .
They put the car first – they put the speed of the car first,
and the convenience of the car, and if you haven't got a
car, the whole system seems to be against you. It's a shame
really, as it could be such a nice place . . . Would you like
some more tea?'

I refuse hurriedly, not wanting to sit through William's
pantomime with the kettle again. He makes me promise I
will come back. Without leaving the sanctuary of his hallway, William leans forward and knocks on the front door
of the neighbouring flat. 'Loads of women have told me
she was in love with me,' he says, casually, 'But I don't
know . . .' It is his last reference to Alison – and perhaps

the most significant. The flat is now empty: after Alison left, four illegal immigrants from Brazil moved in, and then a man called Dennis arrived; he stayed for five months. 'He was sound – kept himself to himself,' says William, approvingly. 'Suited me down to the ground.'

— — —

There is another city called Leadville: Leadville, Colorado, was the largest mining town in the Rocky Mountains. The hills around the 'Magic City' were a rich source of gold and silver.

— — —

The day after the Armistice, in 1918, Lloyd George promised to provide 'habitations fit for the heroes who have won the war'. As the government began to address Britain's housing shortage, 'Homes for Heroes' became an election slogan. Lloyd George, who believed the housing problem had become 'a threat to the stability of the state', regarded the money spent on houses as an insurance against 'Bolshevism and Revolution'. The new houses – 'each with its own garden, surrounded by trees and hedges, and equipped internally with the amenities of a middle-class home' – were to provide 'visible proof of the irrelevance of revolution'. A programme of 'public works' began, consisting, primarily, of the construction of roads and houses, and designed to drive Britain's post-war revival.

— — —

In search of Robin Green, the town planner who lives with his parents, I return to 219 Western Avenue.

I had met Robin briefly on my first visit, when he passed through the sitting-room. He was dressed casually, in cords and a nondescript sweater, yet his clothes seemed curiously

formal on his neat figure, and he moved with a delicacy
that matched his appearance; his presence barely disturbed
the atmosphere in the room. For some reason, the subject
of concentration camps had come up, and Mrs Green told
me that Robin has been to visit Belsen. She raised her voice
to call to her son in the adjoining room: 'I said – you've
been to Belsen, haven't you?'

'Yes,' replied Robin.

Five minutes later, I saw him stoking a bonfire in the
frost-bound garden; a thin plume of grey smoke rose from
the damped-down pile. I wanted to meet him again.

It is Mrs Green who answers the door, and invites me
inside, as she did last time. Mr Green is settled in his
armchair inside the door. As I lower myself into their sofa,
Mr Green raises his hand. 'You know, we've had a lot of
trouble with this affair – I'm not happy, not happy at all.'
His hand drops to his side, falling sluggishly, as through it
were travelling through a thicker medium than air. The
movement heralds the beginning of another account of the
crimes committed by the Transport Board. The fact that a
month has passed between my visits does not make much
difference to what I am hearing – I have simply re-entered
the room at a different point in an endless loop of conversation.

As politely as I can, I interrupt him, and explain I have
come to talk to Robin; unfortunately, he is out.

'Would you like me to show you round the house?' says
Mrs Green, suddenly.

Mr Green bites on his pipe, in a wordless protest, but
gets to his feet to follow us. He pauses by the wooden chair
in the hall. 'That's over a hundred years old, you know.'
A black-and-white photograph of the Catholic members
of the Metropolitan Police who served during the Second
World War hangs beside an illuminated view of a town in

the south of France. Upstairs, there are two pictures hanging beside their bed: one is a Catholic icon, the other a
pencil portrait of a young man; it is Mr Green's cousin,
who died of meningitis when he was nineteen years old –
or was it consumption? Mr and Mrs Green cannot agree.
They argue amicably for a moment, before Mr Green
pronounces a verdict: it was consumption – his sister died
of it, as well. They seem perfectly content to find me
standing in their bedroom, and their openness is so natural
that it no longer surprises me.

Mrs Green pushes open the door of the spare bedroom,
which is cluttered with books and files and boxes; it is
Robin's office. The room is not large enough to contain all
the boxes, and they overflow on to the landing of the
Green's house.

'I'll make sure he calls you,' says Mrs Green, as she
shows me to the door.

'He's gone into the history of Acton a lot,' adds Mr
Green, proudly. 'And he's got three degrees, you know!'

– – –

In the back garden of 237 Western Avenue, two young
women stand, topless, in front of William's bathroom
window; the image is composed so that the frilled leaves of
two marijuana plants emerge between their bare shoulders.

– – –

In 1919, the Ministry of Transport was formed, and road-
building began in earnest. Two years later, Middlesex
County Council approved the construction of the first
portion of Western Avenue. The road was to cross the open
land that lay to the north of East Acton, which meant that
the work would be free 'from those dilatory and costly
obstacles which haunt all clearance schemes'; only Barker's

Field – an old athletics ground which had been converted into allotments – lay across the road's projected route. On the night when intimation of the approval of the scheme was received, notice was given to the allotment holders on Barker's Field.

– – –

I receive a handwritten letter from Robin P. Green – B.A. Dip.T.P., M.R.T.P.I., Chartered Town Planner. 'Sorry I wasn't able to see you when you called,' it begins. 'I don't think that your research would in any way adversely prejudice our situation, and, therefore, I raise no objections. Indeed I would welcome your interest in recording the life and times of this area.'

– – –

Koforola spends her days in bed with the radiator turned up to insulate her against the English winter. She rarely leaves her house in the evenings, either. Most of the time, she just sits in her room at 233 Western Avenue. Koforola hates the English weather, and she hates Western Avenue.

Like most of the people in the condemned houses beside Gipsy Corner, Koforola is preparing to leave her home; the little furniture that remains in the sitting-room is hidden beneath stacks of cardboard boxes. It is dusk, but the room is poorly lit, and it is almost as dark inside the house as outside. Koforola sits on the far end of the sofa, her hands folded demurely on her knees. She is in her early twenties – a slim woman with an almond-shaped face and shoulder-length dreadlocks – and she holds herself with an elegance which is faintly severe. Thinking that I am practised at conducting this kind of meeting, I ask what seems to me a simple question: what did she think of England when she first arrived? There is silence for a moment. 'What did I think of England?' she says, wonderingly. After a moment, she repeats the question again: 'What did I think of England?'

Finally she says, 'I went to school, which was OK. I got used to the system – and the cold, for one thing.' It is a politely uninformative answer.

I first met Koforola a week ago. When I rang the doorbell at 272 Western Avenue, it was answered by an athletic-looking man dressed in shorts and a sweatshirt. Keeping the door half-closed, he told me his name was Tony, though the way he said it suggested he was not telling the truth. Koforola appeared behind his shoulder. Squeezed inside the half-open door, perfectly at ease in one another's presence, they looked, to me, like lovers. I explained again why I was there, and Koforola reacted with far more enthusiasm than 'Tony' had done. She said she would like to talk to me, and she told me her address: 233 Western Avenue. It was a moment before I appreciated its significance: 233 stands on the opposite side of the road to 272 Western Avenue. William says the road is like the Berlin Wall – he does not even recognize the people who live on its far side – yet 'Tony' and Koforola have breached the barrier of traffic. I had discovered my first cross-carriageway romance, or so I thought.

I ask her about Tony, and she frowns, blankly: she does not know who I mean.

The man who lives on the other side of the road, I say, and her face dissolves into a smile. He is not called Tony, and he is not her boyfriend, either – just the brother of a friend, who happens to live on Western Avenue. 'I used to go round there a lot,' she recalls. She would cross the road by the traffic lights at Gipsy Corner – although their houses were no more than fifty yards apart, it would take her five minutes to walk from one to the other.

She falls silent again, so I ask another question, and she answers it with no more enthusiasm than before, yet, gradually, her story emerges. Koforola is from Sierra Leone. She was born in England, but her parents moved back to Africa when she was very young. She lived there until her father died, in 1987, and she returned to England with her mother. Her father used to manage a firm called PZ Industrial – the detail emerges unprompted, though her memories of her childhood in Africa seem as vague as her impressions of England.

I do not blame Koforola for her reticence. Since I started visiting Western Avenue, I have been surprised by the readiness with which people talk about themselves; in their place, I would be less willing to share my life with a stranger, and I would understand if Koforola were reluctant to talk to me. Yet she is not – or she does not seem to be: instead, she seems puzzled by my questions; if only she could see their purpose, she would willingly answer them. She looks at me quizzically, almost accusingly, as though she held me responsible for her peculiar inarticulacy. It is not my fault I cannot answer your questions, she seems to say – it is your fault: you are asking the wrong questions.

Although she looks English, Koforola is, in fact, African, and perhaps the instinct to remake the past is a cultural reflex which she does not share. It does not interest Koforola – she feels no obligation to order its confusions into a comprehensible pattern; she has no ready-made answers for me, because she has never considered the questions I am asking.

For the time being, she lives on Western Avenue, and she does not like it. 'When it's hot, during the summer, I think I prefer it, even though I can't open my windows because of the noise. I prefer it when it's warm,' she adds, in a rare moment of enthusiasm.

Now, her friends are leaving 272 Western Avenue, and she knows none of her other neighbours. Perhaps one of the reasons she was willing to talk to me was that she knows few other people in the area – few people in London, for that matter. Soon after she arrived on Western Avenue in 1993, she was forced to give up her part-time job as a shop assistant because she began to suffer pains in her stomach, and she had an operation a month ago to discover what was causing them. 'It's a severe problem. I've had nothing like it before. It's something to do with my period as well, because it comes two weeks after it.' She is matter-of-fact about her illness, but there is one subject which rouses her to anger – the way the Housing Association has treated her. 'I'm not happy with them,' she says, repeatedly. 'I'm not happy with them at all.' At the tenants' meeting, it was Koforola who stood up to announce that the council had told her to become pregnant if she wanted to be housed.

In the last twenty minutes, as the light in the sitting-room has strengthened in comparison to the deepening gloom outside, the uncurtained window behind me has darkened slowly. Koforola's illness might explain what appears to be a languid indifference to life; it certainly explains her passionate condemnation of the Housing Association.

I ask her what she will do next, and she shrugs: there is nothing for her in Sierra Leone, but there is little to keep her in London, either; if she could afford it, she would consider joining her mother in America. 'If I had the money, I could go anywhere I wanted to,' she says, with a kind of weak defiance.

I stand up: the window behind me is black; I cannot see through it, though the traffic spills flickering beads of light across its oily surface. The fact that Koforola cannot imag-

ine her future may explain why she cannot make sense of
her past: if you do not know where you want to go, it is
hard to understand where you have been. Feeling oddly
inadequate, I follow Koforola to the front door. She opens
it without meeting my eye, and as I step out of the house, it
closes quietly behind me; I do not even have a chance to
say goodbye.

— — —

On the day that work began on Western Avenue, one man
was injured in 'the crush amongst applicants for relief at
the council offices'; the *Acton Gazette* blamed falling levels
of employment on a 'trade depression resulting largely from
the financial condition of Europe', but others attributed 'the
epidemic of unemployment' to government neglect. 'During
five years of Armageddon,' said a local councillor, 'the
country was spending at the rate of eight millions a week,
and it now has to find money for the men who fought its
battles.' The Western Avenue workmen were to be recruited
from the local labour exchanges; 'good men – not unem-
ployables' – should be taken on alternately to give as many
as possible a chance.'

— — —

On the day William moved into 237 Western Avenue, he
found himself stuck in a traffic jam on the wrong side of
the road – he could see his flat, but he could not reach it
for over an hour. Sometimes, when the traffic is 'bumper to
bumper', he parks on the other side of the road, and walks
the last 500 yards to his house.

— — —

'It was a constant theme throughout a memorable child-life
– from the age of seven up to pre-adolescence, I was always

collecting model cars. It was one of the principal expenditures of pocket money.'

Seated on opposite sides of a low table in his parent's sitting-room, Robin and I are discussing childhood games in a manner which I find disconcertingly formal. When Robin told me, a moment ago, that playing with dinky toys and sections of road layout was the primary influence on his career, I thought at first he must be joking, yet there is nothing in his expression to suggest that he is anything less than serious: he sits upright, his hands arranged in his lap, his hair neatly parted to one side, and his handsome features composed and unrevealing. We have been talking for five minutes, yet his face has betrayed no emotion, and his voice has not broken stride or changed pitch; it is almost robotic in its regularity. He seems so placid and emotionless that it is difficult to know how to approach him.

For many years, Robin worked in the Town Planning Department of the London Borough of Hounslow. I ask him what it is that appeals to him about town planning, and he looks at me steadily for a moment. It is impossible to know what he is thinking – it is not inconceivable that the question has upset him, and it is a relief when he begins to reply in his usual, measured tones. 'I enjoy the exercise of logic and reason – basically common sense – which it entails; I also enjoy engaging my past familiarity with maps and plans and the 3-D relationship of buildings and facilities with each other – as per my days of playing with dinky toys and building model towns.'

There are family photographs ranged on the window-sill behind me, and the sofas are veiled in white linen antimacassars. The net curtains bleach the sunlight passing through the window, and diffuse shadows pass across Robin's face. Like everyone else who lives on Western Avenue, Robin was not born there. He was born in Shep-

herd's Bush, and moved to Western Avenue with his parents
when he was eleven. He remembers looking at pictures in
the school library of the archetypal suburban man – a
Surbiton commuter with rolled umbrella and bowler hat –
and he was aghast when he learnt that his family was to
move from the centre of the city to its fringes.

'I wasn't used to the suburban landscape,' he says,
mildly. 'I was much more used to what you'd call an inner-
city environment, with the houses close to the roads and
close to one another.' Yet, when he arrived on Western
Avenue, he discovered that the road offered certain attrac-
tions. Above all, he was struck by its access to transport
facilities: every weekend, Robin had a Red Rover travel
ticket, discounted for children – the detail is recalled with
characteristic clarity – and he was able to get 'out and
about' on the buses and trains. Ironically, it is what Robin
calls 'the transport theme' which has proved the undoing of
the house, yet his adventures on public transport were an
important element in his education, for they fed his bur-
geoning fascination with the landscape of the city.

Robin Green's childhood obsessions have remained
remarkably real to him. The preoccupations which structured the child's view of the world have been absorbed,
intact, into the professional reflexes of the adult; he dis-
cusses the subject of his pocket money with the same seriousness as he considers the financial strategy of a borough
council.

He has not worked since 1986 – he never tells me why,
and I do not ask. For some time he called himself a freelance
consultant and worked from home, but his life has changed
recently. He tells me he is in London only to help his
parents negotiate their departure from the road; in 1994 he
began dividing his time between Western Avenue and his
parents' house in Ireland where he grows vegetables and

searches the forest for wood, in an attempt to be self-
sufficient. 'Self-sufficiency is the theme of the 1980s and the
1990s, it must be if we are to try and accommodate future
generations on the planet,' he says. Since town planning
aims to promote careful husbandry of scarce resources,
he detects a reassuring continuity between the aims of the
town planner and the conservationist.

It is difficult to be self-sufficient while he is in London,
but he attempts to live by the same principles which govern
his life in Ireland: at night, he scavenges on the Park Royal
Industrial estate, where he picks up wood, electrical goods
or 'other things which "the industrialist" discards'. He
stresses the title; I imagine Robin's industrialist as a sinister
figure in top hat and fur coat, a predator despoiling the
planet. Of course, Robin is too sensible to be carried away
by such far-fetched ideas – he would point out that Britain's
wealth was generated by industrialists – yet there is something about his manner, at once so inscrutable and yet so
insistently rational, which prompts me to imagine strange
ideas circulating behind his calm façade.

Characteristically, his interest in conservation does not
stretch to apocalyptic fantasies; instead, he is interested in
prudent economies. 'The minimum cost for a packet of
screws at Texas is fifty pence, but I can walk around the
industrial estate and pick them up for free. Self-sufficiency
has always been central to some people, but we're now
trying to convert the middle classes – those people with the
greatest disposable incomes.'

It is a modest rallying-call – given Robin's downbeat
delivery it could hardly be anything else – yet it is a radical
one as well. Oddly, perhaps, Robin presents a greater
challenge to the conventions of middle-class life than many
of his less respectable neighbours do: in some ways, his
frugal self-sufficiency is more subversive than William's

flamboyant bohemianism. I ask Robin whether the recent arrivals on the road have affected him, and his answer is a model of pragmatic diplomacy: he is as scrupulous in his criticism of others as he is in his assessment of his own character. 'The newcomers tended to be . . . I don't know what the politically correct term is – itinerants . . . Which, in a sense, was the ministry caring for the history of the area – which is called Gipsy Corner.'

I realize it is Robin's joke, the first he has attempted. He smiles shyly, and his still features are transformed. Initially, I had looked for a distancing irony in his deadpan manner, but I soon learnt that everything he says must be taken at face value. When he wants to make a joke, he will signal the change of register. His habitual seriousness reasserts itself immediately. 'It would be scurrilous to say it has given rise to an increase in crime or petty theft – I don't think it has done, but it has affected the value of the property. It sounds very materialistic, but we are interested in the money we can get for this property.' More than once he apologises for the state of the house and its garden: 219 Western Avenue looks perfectly respectable to me, yet Robin explains there are many improvements they would have implemented, were it not for their impending eviction.

Robin's childhood holidays in Ireland were another stage in his education as a town planner, for they alerted him to the contrast between urban and rural environments – a theme which has informed much of the debate about the merits of suburbia. The Greens' predecessors saw the suburbs as a means of escaping the polluted city. 'We all crave the sun, light and air,' wrote one contemporary social historian; or, as W.H. Auden put it, 'The sun is one of our emotive nouns.' Until the Green Belt Act of 1938 dampened the city's expansion, the suburbs were consuming 70,000 acres of farmland a year, yet many people believed that the

exercise was a self-defeating one: the person who goes to
the suburbs 'seeking the edge of the countryside', only
succeeds in 'pushing the countryside further away from
somebody else' said the town planner, Thomas Sharp, in
1940. 'The more they strive to embrace the object of their
desire, the more it escapes them; the more they try to make
the best of both worlds, the more they make the worst.'
The new arrivals, hoping to escape the city, brought the
city with them.

'There are atmospheric problems apart from the obvious
ones of noise and dust pollution,' says Robin. 'This is a
hollow in the ground, and the basic effect, hemmed in by
buildings, is to create an adverse microclimate of pollut-
ants.' Other people might say the air is foul, but Robin
resists such melodramatic formulations. Still, he has no
desire to leave the road: in fact, he has dedicated a great
deal of energy to preserving it in its present condition. In
1989, when the Public Inquiry was held to consider arguments for and against the proposed reconstruction of Western Avenue, Robin deployed his professional expertise to
argue that the scheme was misconceived, and the houses
should be left intact.

He tells that he discovered 'significant discrepancies' in
the Department of Transport's proposal, and he promises
he will send me a copy of his Proof of Evidence. He says he
is not unduly disappointed that his protest has failed, for
he has assessed the task of diverting the Department of
Transport, and concluded it was beyond his powers; since
the Department had planned to rebuild Western Avenue
since the 1960s, it would have required a 'sea-change in
national policy' to persuade it to abandon the scheme.
'Recently, the politicians appear to have caught up with
professionals on the matter of road planning. They're saying we can't accommodate the projected increase in road

traffic, and that new roads generate new traffic. Well, the man in the street knows that to be true.' The change has come too late to save Western Avenue.

I ask him how he feels about the impending eviction, and he does not reply for a moment. Again, I think I might have upset him: since his engagement with the landscape of Western Avenue animated his childhood and inspired his career, perhaps he is dreading the day when they will leave the road. Yet when he speaks, his manner is as calm and measured as always: he was merely considering an appropriate response. 'I don't particularly enjoy living next to a busy main road, so there is that advantage in moving, but I'll regret it because we've invested so much of our lives here . . . I suppose I have different reactions, depending upon which hat I'm wearing. As a planning professional, I have to accept decisions which are made in the proper way, but when I'm viewing the proposal as a resident, I acknowledge some disquiet at the prospect of being decanted from the area.'

It is such a beautifully modulated expression of regret that it is difficult to believe it has not been prepared in advance. Robin seems utterly detached from the events he is describing, as though it were someone else's life we are discussing. Eager to prompt a more emotional reaction, I ask him whether he will miss the house he has lived in since he was eleven. Robin rebuffs the question with ease. 'Certainly one develops a fondness for what one is familiar with . . .' He does not sound convinced. He begins again: 'If I have a fondness for this house, it's because it has performed its functions satisfactorily: it's structurally sound, it's weather-tight and it has good access to central London – I can even walk in. It has accommodated us as a family satisfactorily.'

For some reason, it is a very moving answer. There is

something heroic about Robin Green and his insistent, dogged rationality; there is also something beguilingly strange about him, for the dry plantations of his mind are watered by a flood of childhood dreams and images – an underground stream which renews itself constantly and which stains his thoughts a strange shade; stranger, per-haps, than he might like to acknowledge. I do not want to ask him anything more. I can hardly do justice to the depth of his knowledge of the area, but I promise I will read the documents he sends me.

'We're leaving in a week,' he reminds me, as he shows me to the door.

– – –

On 3 March, a sign appears in the window of 233 Western Avenue, Koforola's house. 'TO THE BAILIFFS,' it says. 'THREE PEOPLE LIVE HERE AND ARE AT PRESENT AWAITING ACCOMMODATION WITH THE WEST HAMPSTEAD HOUSING ASSOCIATION. WE ARE LEGAL TENANTS, STILL PAYING RENT. THANK YOU.' Although I call several times at 233, there is no answer; I never see Koforola again.

– – –

'Beyond the Great Western Railway, the avenue will pass the Isolation Hospital, cut across the old Alliance Flying Ground, and make for the Hanger Hill district', reported the *Acton Gazette* in April 1922. 'A critical year' lay ahead for the North Acton plotters: in July, Councillor Wade, the champion of the allotment holders' interests, urged the council to postpone the construction of Western Avenue; he said it was an 'awkward time for allotment holders to be deprived of their plots', but the Highways Committee was unsympathetic. It could not postpone a 'useful public work which was providing relief for the unemployed'. Besides, the provision of 'a fast exit from the city' had become an urgent priority – already, 'enormous tidal waves' of commuters were engulfing London morning and evening.

– – –

In 1907, there were 32,000 cars on Britain's roads. By 1995, there were more than 23 million – each of which, according to William's calculation, drove past his house three times a year.

3. Gipsy Corner

'Kane! Get off! Off!'

Mrs Shaw lowers the teapot and wafts her hands at the giant Alsatian whose head rests in my lap. Kane lifts his ears and raises his head fractionally. A thin web of drool trails between the fat, purple flesh of his lip and my knee; it breaks suddenly, and recoils into his mouth.

'Oh, Kane!'

Mrs Shaw is horrified, but Kane settles his head on my leg, fixes his eyes on the plate held in my right hand, and sighs contentedly. Kane is on cake-watch, while his companion – an ancient labrador called Cindy – tracks back and forth in front of the sofa, buffeting my knees and murmuring quietly to herself. Once, visitors to the Shaws' household were prey for Cindy; now she must wait in line behind Kane. Miming exaggerated embarrassment at her dogs' behaviour, Joan Shaw passes me a cup of tea, and retreats to an armchair on the far side of the room. Fortunately, I like dogs, and I say so, and Mrs Shaw resumes the story she began before Kane distracted us.

Fifteen years ago, when the traffic on Western Avenue became unbearable, the Shaws turned their house back to front – they built a garage and a back entrance on to the road which runs behind their house, and for many years, they did not use their front door at all. Then the council began to let its houses on Western Avenue: two years ago, the Shaws found that their neighbours had changed. 'I work at the hospital, and I'm at work at six o'clock in the morning,' begins Mrs Shaw – a stocky woman dressed in trousers and a sweatshirt; she has short sandy hair and tinted oval glasses which cast a pale shadow on the upper half of her face.

'I used to go out in the morning, and there'd be a big van – a big lorry, parked right in front of the gates, so I couldn't get the car out. People didn't park in front of the house until we got people next door . . .' She hesitates. 'Well, they're gipsies, actually.' The confession comes in a rush – she does not want to appear prejudiced, yet she is relieved to identify the people who have disrupted her life. 'Well, there have been absolute murders over it, I can tell you!'

She settles more comfortably in her armchair; she tells the story with practised relish. 'Well, I got really fed up with this. You know, you put up with it for five times, and then all of a sudden, I blew . . . I went along, and I said, "Look, this has got to stop – you know there's a car in there, why do you park in front of the drive?" And I just got a load of abuse – the woman said, "Within six months, we'll have you all out," she said, "And we'll have some more friends in there . . ." Which I was horrified at . . . I've heard of these sort of stories before, but I never thought . . .' Suddenly, she laughs, and her manner softens: 'She did come back and apologize – she said she was very sorry, she didn't really mean it . . . She's got her mother living down the road, and her mother said to her – "Well, that wasn't a very good thing to say, was it?"'

My view of Mrs Shaw is obscured by Cindy's wagging tail, which passes back and forth in front of my face with metronomic regularity. If I were to lean sideways, I would see her better, but my movements are hampered by Kane's head, which balances on my knee – as warm and heavy as a loaded teatray. In the circumstances, it is difficult to be sure of anything, yet it seems to me that the appalled fascination with which Joan Shaw details her neighbours' misdemeanours contains an element of self-mockery; she is not bitter – in fact, she seems genuinely amused by the predicament in which she found herself.

In the end, she chose to compromise – rather than putting her car in the garage, she began to leave it in the road, where it could not be hemmed in by her neighbours' lorries. 'I just picked the easy way out, because at this stage I don't want hassle with the car – at the end of the day, it's only a car. Our attitude is just let it go, because if you get involved . . .'

Joan Shaw has reason to be wary – seven years ago, one of their dogs was poisoned by a piece of meat which someone had thrown over the back fence. Since she cannot understand why anyone would want to kill their dog, she has chosen to regard the incident as a mistake. She can think of only one possible explanation: the couple living next door had a dog who raised a litter of puppies in an old car at the back of the house; the puppies used to bark all night, and the Shaws wondered if somebody thought it was their dog that was barking. We agree that it hardly seems an adequate reason for poisoning a dog, but they could not take the matter any further. 'You know, if you started to wonder . . . do they have a grudge against us?'

She does not know who their enemy might be, for the simple reason that she does not know many of her neighbours. 'This is going to sound awful, but when we had a family it was enough to keep us going – we didn't have a lot of time for much on the outside.' Both her daughters have now left home. Yet her love of privacy is coupled with an enthusiastic appreciation of the world around her. She has none of the gossip's mean-spiritedness, and none of the gossip's intrusive curiosity, but she shares the gossip's delight in the dramas of daily life – a quality which equips her well for life in suburban England. Yet Joan Shaw is not English – like Mrs Green, she came from rural Ireland to live on Western Avenue.

She arrived in England in 1958 and met her husband, John, when she was working for a builder's merchant in Shepherd's Bush. His trade is a specialized one: he matches bricks according to their colour and texture. The Shaws have now been married for thirty-five years, which means Joan Shaw has lived in England longer than she lived in Ireland. 'I like it here because I like a bit of life,' she says, simply.

I feed Kane a morsel of biscuit, and his jaws grind together lazily. I brush crumbs from my hands, and show him they are empty, and his interest in me begins to fade; he slumps to the floor by my feet. His presence must explain – in part at least – why Joan Shaw is so relaxed with a stranger in her house, for he is one of the largest dogs I have ever seen.

When the Shaws moved to Western Avenue thirty years ago, they could pull up to the front of the house in their car, and Mrs Shaw used to walk across the road with her youngest child in her arms. Now, the pollution rots their curtains and fabrics, and stains the carpets. In the summer they can never open their front windows, and when the lorries go past, they feel the house vibrate. Four years ago, the noise became so loud they could not hear the television, and they took out another mortgage to double-glaze the front windows – it was the best thing they ever did: 'It kept us sane, to be honest with you,' she says, lowering her voice as though she was entrusting me with a great secret.

They knew there were plans to widen the road when they arrived on Western Avenue, but they did not know what form the development would take. Six years ago, when they were finally told they would lose five feet from their front garden, they asked the Department of Transport to buy their house: it refused – a rebuff aggravated by the fact that it had begun to lease out its properties to 'problem families'. Mrs Shaw's house is one of the better-kept houses on the road – climbing plants frame its wooden porch, and it is neatly tended – yet they would 'jump at' a chance to sell it.

If the Shaws were to swap places with Mr and Mrs Green, then perhaps they would all be satisfied, yet the Shaws cannot afford to leave Western Avenue for the time being. 'The last three and a half years have dragged us right down – everything has gone wrong for us, really,' says Joan Shaw, matter-of-factly. Three years ago, Mr Shaw was made redundant by the firm which had employed him for twenty-six years; he lost his pension, as well. Inspired, perhaps, by the 'enterprise culture' in the 1980s – a copy of Margaret Thatcher's autobiography rests in a miniature bookshelf beside the fireplace – Mr Shaw attempted to set up in business on his own; the venture failed. Now, he is working for his old firm again. Mrs Shaw has had to keep working for longer than she anticipated, but she does not waste time feeling sorry for herself. 'The plan now is to work till we're both sixty-five, and then get out – if we survive that long; we're just going to keep the place going – and nothing more.'

She dreads the prospect of the roadworks, yet the sooner the work is begun, the sooner it will be complete – and then, she tells herself, things will improve. In the narrow hall, her dogs barrel past her, and almost knock her over; she brushes them away, ineffectually. She does not want me to leave with the wrong impression, and as she opens the door, she adds, stoutly, 'We're going along steady, and we're going to keep it up; people are more important than bricks and mortar.'

— — —

On Saturday, 30 July 1922, a mass meeting was called at Barker's Field: the North Acton Plotters were 'up in arms against dispossession'. The plotters had no wish to 'hinder the interest of the unemployed', but the task of bridging the railway lines which bracketed Barker's Field had yet to begin and they calculated that there was at least a year's work to be done before the allotments need be touched at all. One plotter claimed that 'the authorities should not be permitted to ignore the human element like they did'. A disturbing precedent had been set: the men working on the road had dug up Councillor Wade's crop of potatoes and left them to rot – an example of 'how things should not be done'.

— — —

Of the 23.8 million cars in Britain, one belongs to me: a C-reg, three-door, four-gear Peugeot, with a busted radio and a seat that spews handfuls of dirty yellow foam between the driver's legs; once maroon – now mottled brown; once a family car in which my three sisters and I learnt to drive – now used more or less exclusively for travelling back and forth along Western Avenue.

— — —

A heavy envelope arrives at my house, postmarked London W3. It contains the Proof of Evidence of Robin P. Green, of 219 Western Avenue, presented at the Public Inquiry into the Department of Transport's Proposals for Gipsy Corner and Western Circus, held between July and August 1989. 'My name is Robin Patrick Green,' it begins. 'I am a chartered Town Planner, and a member of the Royal Institute of Town Planning . . .'

– – –

'NOT WANTED!' says a sticker on a lamp-post beside the road. 'Richie Rich – the Westway's very own wanker and top hand-pump. Avoid this senile tosser like the plague! £23,000 reward for foreskin'.

– – –

The Saturday morning traffic scythes through Gipsy Corner. It is 6 March, and spring is coming to Western Avenue. In William's sitting-room, he flips on his exploding kettle and lights a cigarette. The date has not been set yet for his eviction, but he is looking forward to it. 'I'll enjoy it. I'm going to stand up and make a bit of a speech in court.' He laughs raucously. 'I've every intention of giving them a bit of my philosophy . . . I've checked out most things – I've read loads of books, done this and that, checked out my horoscope . . . I'm Leo – I used to be into it heaps, but the problem is you lose touch with the day-to-day grind of your life and when you get back to nine to five, you can't cope. You've got to keep a balance. I've been signing on, but I want to start earning some money now – it's time I made an impression.'

William's philosophy is spacious enough to accommodate an opinion on most aspects of modern life – the changing landscapes of British cities, as well as rape, adoption, imperialism, subways, taxi-drivers, contraception, consumerism, aesthetic terrorism and organized religion. 'It's a crazy world we live in,' he says, more than once. 'All the great empires are falling . . . Thatcher's gone, Maxwell's gone, the communist regimes in Eastern Europe have all gone – these people thought they'd be here for ever, and it's all collapsing round their ears. Even what we call democracy is collapsing, and people are making their own arrangements – there are people living in squats who work in the City, or people who used to be brain surgeons living in tepees in Wales – it's all collapsing, and it's a good thing too.'

It is easy listening to William – he is stoned, as he often is, but he is not stupid or dogmatic, and he is never boring. His attitude to life is gently anarchic, but his subversive instincts are not fuelled by anger – he does not want to change the world, but he appreciates its complexity and takes pleasure in its absurdities.

He picks up a framed photograph of two women, and props it up on the table for us to look at. 'They're mother and daughter,' he says. 'They got kicked out of their house because they couldn't pay the mortgage and they went to the council and they were told they'd made themselves intentionally homeless. It's Catch-22, isn't it? I mean, it's sick . . . Anyway, they put them into South Acton Housing Estate, and they couldn't handle it there. The mother is an artist, and she painted half a picture in the whole year they spent there.' He points to the older woman who stands at the back of the composition, arms draped around her daughter's neck: William used to do life drawing classes and she was his teacher. A copy of *Ulysses* – the emblem of the literate Irish exile and the only book in William's room – stands on the bookshelf as evidence of his artistic ambitions.

I leave 237 Western Avenue at one o'clock, and walk west. 245 Western Avenue has been abandoned, but the task of sealing it is incomplete; the unsecured metal plates which hang on its façade flap in the strong wind. I stand on the pavement and listen to the ugly, percussive rattle of the boards as they bang against the house. The gritty wind which blows across my face scours my skin, while the traffic behind me threatens to pull me backwards, into the road.

A selection of vintage sports cars – their sculpted, polished snouts turned into the oncoming flood of traffic – are ranged on the pavement in front of a block of buildings which once housed an off-licence and a corner shop. The MG showroom – *Former Glory* – is the last shop beside Gipsy Corner to remain open. Sunk within the polished surface of a blue MGB is a distorted image of 265 Western Avenue – the first derelict house in the block abutting the garage.

There is an attendant leaning against the garage's grooved double doors. He buffs his hands on a chamois leather.

'Nice cars,' I say, casually.

Not surprisingly, he seems to agree.

'When are you moving?'

'Not in the foreseeable future.'

'But what about the roadworks?' I ask.

'Oh, that's all up in the air,' he says, vaguely.

Is he referring to the flyover? Or is he suggesting that nothing has been decided? The phone rings inside his garage, and he goes to answer it.

– – –

Pasted to a pillbox is a plan for the redevelopment of Western Avenue: it is signed 'D.D. Munro, Grade 7 Officer, Department of the Environment', dated 31 May 1989, and tattooed with a silver penis.

– – –

'There's nothing for the children, which is a shame,' says Sandra Parker. 'For us, it's not so serious, because we can always go out if we want to, but you can't let them wander around on their own; they do complain about it, I suppose – oh yes, I'm a very wicked mother!' Mr Parker used to be a semi-professional footballer; Mrs Parker works for the NHS. They have three children, two boys aged sixteen and eleven, and a girl aged ten – the first children we have met on Western Avenue. 'Someone only has to stop on the hard shoulder and pick up your kid, and they're gone – you'd never see them again,' she says.

– – –

'The problem of the house is the problem of the epoch,' declared Le Corbusier. Lloyd George was not alone in seeing the post-war housing shortage as a threat to the stability of society: surveying the conditions in France, Le Corbusier declared society to be faced with a simple choice: 'Architecture or Revolution'. But the kind of houses Le Corbusier wished to build had nothing in common with Lloyd George's 'Homes for Heroes'. He believed that the advent of the machine had transformed every aspect of our existence, except for one: the houses in which we lived. The house was a machine like any other – 'a machine for living in' – and the suburban semi was a poorly designed machine: nostalgic, sentimental, and ill-equipped to meet the demands of the age.

– – –

The evidence is as fresh in his mind as it was in 1989: flicking through the pages of his Proof of Evidence, Robin explains his arguments with a certainty and fluency which compels attention.

I have spent the last week attempting to unravel the document. The substance of his objections to the planned reconstruction of Western Avenue was clear enough: the scheme was 'inordinately disruptive' and ultimately futile, for the volume of traffic on Western Avenue would soon exceed the projected capacity of the rebuilt road. So far, so good, but when Robin abandoned general principles in order to begin attacking the Department of Transport's plan on 'points of detail', I found his arguments impossible to follow. I have come back to 219 Western Avenue to ask him to explain them to me.

It seems that he discovered a loophole in planning law which meant the Department of Transport had no 'absolute right' to some of the land it was planning to acquire on Western Avenue. The land in question had been set aside for developments designed to 'mitigate the environmental impact' of the rebuilt road. 'Strictly speaking,' he says, his features as impassive as ever, 'had the owners chosen to exercise their rights, then the Department of Transport would have been required to cede the rear gardens to them.' In other words, the displaced residents of Western Avenue could have conspired to sabotage improvements designed to make life more bearable for the people left behind – yet had they done so, they would have been forced to sacrifice much of their compensation, in a piece of legislative vandalism of no conceivable benefit to anyone.

'Yes, well, as it was, not many people . . . well, in fact, I doubt if anybody knew about it – and anyway they didn't wish to exercise the right to receive back half their land; they wanted the totality of their money in order to get housing elsewhere,' he says, candidly acknowledging the absurdity of the idea. 'Besides, who would want bits of garden land beside a motorway, anyway? They couldn't have done anything with it.'

Robin had tunnelled so deeply into the recesses of planning law that he emerged into a world far removed from the practicalities which govern most people's lives –

including his own. He had discovered a flaw in the government's case, but it was one nobody would ever think to
exploit. Still, there had been 'a lapse in the public consultation process', and Robin could not resist pointing it out.
His desire to see the correct procedures observed overwhelmed all other considerations.

It is no wonder I was confused: the argument makes
little sense – but then, nor did many of the proposals he was
contesting. Robin points out, with relish, that the Department of Transport's calculation that the 'noise climate'
of the area would be improved by the scheme was based on
the absurd premiss that once the houses were destroyed,
fewer people would be affected by the noise. By the same
logic, he points out, destroying west London in its entirety
would reduce the 'noise pollution' emanating from Heathrow Airport.

'I don't know whether the Proof of Evidence said much,
but it kept everyone occupied for a day,' he says, mod-
estly. And it is unfair of me to belittle his work: responding
to his Proof of Evidence, the inspector thanked Robin for
his 'considerable contribution' to the inquiry. 'You have
an extremely well-set-out case and obviously you are both
professionally competent to comment and of course person-
ally very closely affected.'

The inquiry was a fitting conclusion to Robin's years
on Western Avenue – a stage on which he displayed both
his love of the landscape of the area, and his knowledge
of planning legislation. In the official theatre of a public
inquiry, Robin enacted the twin obsessions which have
structured his life. Six years later, the bureaucratic procedures with which he is so intimately acquainted have run
their course. 'We're leaving in a week,' he reminds me. He
is perfectly content: in accordance with the laws ordained

by the gods of planning, the Greens' occupancy of Western Avenue is drawing to its appointed end.

– – –

Joan Shaw knows of three people who have died on Western Avenue. One old lady was killed when she was standing on the edge of the pavement waiting to cross the road beside the car showroom – a lorry caught her and pulled her under its wheels.

– – –

There was 'wide-spread lamentation' at Barker's Field on 10 August 1922. An advance guard of twenty unemployed men had entered the land to peg out the course of the road – preliminaries which involved uprooting the crops in one or two allotments. 'It makes our hearts bleed to see lovely crops and choice rose-bushes being torn up in this way,' said one plot-holder. The produce – potatoes, cabbages, carrots, beetroots, turnips and parsnips – was piled up in heaps beside the dung-track which ran across Barker's Field, marking Western Avenue's future course.

– – –

There is no answer when I ring the bell at 186 Western Avenue. The Johnsons have not rung me and they do not seem to be at home – or not to me at least. The neighbouring houses are derelict, and fire has charred the mock-Tudor façades of 182 and 184 Western Avenue, yet still they refuse to leave.

– – –

'You see, we were a couple whose marriage wouldn't work. When we got married, I was in the army – I was in Rome

with the British army . . . I was in the First Army – I was a
soldier in the British army, and I met her in Rome, you see,
and we got married in Rome . . .'

Katherina Jackson claps her hands, and laughs. 'Yeah!
In '47, wannit?'

Louis Jackson does not answer – despite the stuttering
repetitions which punctuate his speech, he is intent on
completing his anecdote.

'As far as everyone was concerned, they said it wouldn't
work – it wouldn't last, you see. And now we've only got
one more year to make fifty – so we haven't done badly,
have we? For a marriage that wasn't going to last, we
haven't done badly – and it makes you wonder, doesn't it?
It makes you wonder. When you see people today, they get
married, and people say, "How long have you been married?" – "Twenty-five years" – "Twenty-five years!" . . .
You know, they think they've been married a long time –
well, we've lived on the Western Avenue for twenty-five
years! Being married on the Western Avenue for twenty-
five years – imagine what that's like!'

Mrs Jackson claps her hands and laughs raucously – a
gesture which almost lifts her from the chair where she is
sitting. Perched by her side, her husband smiles dryly,
enjoying the response he has provoked. Mr Jackson likes
telling jokes – often, it seems, the same ones – and Mrs
Jackson never fails to laugh.

I first met the Jacksons a week ago, on the pavement
outside their home: the front garden is so narrow that their
front door stands within feet of the road, yet there is a
flowerbed sunk into the concrete, and Mr Jackson was
stooped over it. I stopped and introduced myself. Mr Jackson listened patiently, then, with the mischievous smile of
an overindulged child, he said, 'There's a big road out the
back, as well – I always tell people we live in the middle

lane!' He shifted from one foot to another in a palsied jig
of pleasure; Mrs Jackson, who stood behind her husband
in the porch, smiled contentedly. At first glance, they
seemed a comically mismatched pair: Mr Jackson is a frail
Englishman in his mid-seventies, burdened by a pair of
heavy, black-framed spectacles, while Mrs Jackson is a
picturebook version of a Mediterranean matriarch – extravagantly cheerful and generously proportioned, with her
greying hair pulled back into a neat bun. I left them
standing side by side in their narrow porch – contrasting
icons of domesticity, displayed for the benefit of the passing
cars.

I ask when it was that they arrived on Western Avenue,
and they both speak at once: 'On this road?' begins Mr
Jackson.

'Thirty years!' says Mrs Jackson, with relish.

'On this road? We moved into this road in 1967—'

'Thirty years!'

'—no, 1966.'

'Thirty years!'

Mrs Jackson is looking for someone to share her delight
in the length of their tenure.

'No, we moved here in 1966,' says Mr Jackson firmly.

Twenty-nine years, in other words. Eager to distract
them from their squabble, I ask them where they had lived
before, and the routine begins again: 'We lived across the
road . . .' says Mr Jackson.

'In the fish shop! The fish and chip shop – over there,
yeah!'

'We had the fish and chip shop on the corner.'

'For seven and a half years! Wannit? Over there! Wannit? Seven and a half years! Oh, dear!'

Mrs Jackson fans herself exaggeratedly. In the years she
has spent in England, she has picked up a mixed bag of

English slang, yet her speech has never lost its music-hall Mediterranean lilt. A kitsch day-glo photograph hangs above her head: at first glance, I thought it was a sentimental portrait of the Madonna, but when I looked closer I saw it was another icon of Italian womanhood – Sophia Loren.

The room is littered with ornaments and pictures, including a sleek black-and-white photograph of Mr and Mrs Jackson, and colour photographs of their four grown-up children. The net-curtained gloom, the profusion of glass trinkets and the stillness of long, undisturbed occupancy remind me of the house in Yorkshire where my grandmother lived for thirty years.

'Before the fish and chip shop, we was in Acton before that for a couple of years, as well – we moved out of Acton to Burgess Hill . . .' Mr Jackson tells me.

'Burgess Hill – yeah!'

'. . . to a nice new house in a very quiet road.

'And then we moved back here!'

'That's a story in itself, isn't it?'

'Yeah!'

'No, but we moved because I couldn't get up a train to London every time . . .'

'We moved from Burgess Hill and came over here,' says Mrs Jackson, helpfully reiterating the point.

'But that's not relevant to what you're asking us about, you know,' says Mr Jackson.

He is remonstrating with his wife, but he does not look at her directly: like a child who does not want to acknowledge a younger sister, he addresses his remarks solely to me. Perhaps the years of living together have accentuated their innate differences: Mrs Jackson is unashamedly histrionic, while Mr Jackson – precise, pedantic and sardonic – is a caricatured Englishman: he carries no excess weight, physically or emotionally. Still, the Jacksons agree on one point, at least: they were both perfectly happy living on Western Avenue. 'At that time, we thought, "Well it's not too bad,"' says Mr Jackson. 'Nice neighbours, you know.'

He pushes his glasses up his nose: they are so heavy it is hard to believe they are designed simply to help him see better; they look like some kind of structural support – a plastic girder to weld together the planes of his face. 'There really wasn't much to worry about, but because people moved out and the Ministry of Environment – the Ministry of Transport – bought the houses off them because they were blighted—'

'Oh, we should have went then! Oh! We should have went!' wails Mrs Jackson. She raises her clasped hands to Saint Sophia.

'Well, no, that's . . . That's not . . .'

'Oooh, we should have went away! We should have went!'

'Well, no, well, what we should do or what we shouldn't do isn't relevant to the question.'

Mrs Jackson subsides into her armchair, and folds her hands neatly on her lap. Mr Jackson is eager to limit our conversation to the terms of my original request to talk about Western Avenue. For some reason, he is reluctant to let the discussion move on: perhaps he is concerned that his wife will begin to dominate the conversation if he lets it range freely, or perhaps he simply does not trust me. In any case, once the conversation drifts from his control, he becomes irritable.

'The only reason we should have moved maybe was because of the way the economy balanced itself with property,' he says, peevishly restating his authority. 'When you're talking of buying a house or selling a house you wait till the right time – you can't just put it up for sale when you please, because you've got to move with the market, you know.' I watch his wife carefully: her face is still, but her bunched eyes are bright – she is not in the least abashed by her husband's admonitions.

Mr Jackson does not blame the traffic for the fact that it would be difficult to sell his house now; he blames the 'Ministry of Transport', which bought the neighbouring houses, and let them, via the local council, to short-term tenants – it is their presence, he believes, which has polluted the area.

'We used to have good neighbours,' interjects Mrs Jackson. 'Good neighbours, yeah!' Her right arm flaps once, in a gesture of despair.

'No, no . . . No, you can't complain about the neighbours – you can't complain about people and individual families.'

But if Mr Jackson is not complaining about his neighbours, then what is he complaining about? The answer is prompt – and heartfelt: 'Ealing Council – they're mixing private tenants and council tenants, and you can't expect them to live next door to each other.'

It is not a new complaint – in fact, it is another theme in the great suburban debate. Between 1919 and 1925, local authorities built 600,000 new houses in England, but when the supply of council housing ran out, private enterprise took up the cause instead. During the next fifteen years, more than 600,000 houses were built in Greater London by private firms. The 'speculative builders' responded to their customers' perceived desire for houses which were distinct from their neighbours': some of the houses on Western Avenue have porches, and bay windows, while others do not; some have steeply angled gables, others have flat roofs. The architectural establishment despised the clutter of suburban housing, yet the gables, beams, and porches served a purpose close to Mr Jackson's heart: they distinguished privately owned houses from the uniform rows of neo-Georgian cottages which made up the majority of council houses. There was a particular demand for the kind of house whose 'exterior is so different from the decent exterior of the council house that the casual observer must see at a glance that the owner is not living in a council house'.

Some homeowners went to ludicrous lengths to establish that they were not council tenants. In the north Oxford suburb of Cutteslowe, the developers of a private housing estate built a wall across the boundary separating their properties from the council estate built on adjoining land. The wall was seven feet high, and topped by iron spikes. The Cutteslowe wall remained in place until 1959. As Deyan Sudjic pointed out, in a book called *The Hundred Mile City*, the preservation of the ideal of 'community' 'is a cloak for all kinds of motivations which . . . would be far less acceptable if more openly expressed.'

Since city life is inevitably fragmented and mobile, Sudjic believes our veneration of communal living stems from the enduring power that the countryside exerts upon the Anglo-Saxon mind: 'The model for the "natural" order of urban organization that is the tacit assumption behind the community myth is the farming hamlet and the fishing village, where everybody knows everybody else,' he wrote. Sentimental longing for a rural utopia dies hard. It is ironic that the Jacksons' life has been disrupted by the arrival of a family of gipsies next door – the unwelcome intrusion of a rural way of life into an urban environment.

Yet Mr Jackson believes that sharing the road with council tenants causes practical difficulties: 'If you've got a private tenant next door, and your gutters are overflowing, you can just knock on the chap's door and between you you can get the job done,' he explains. 'If you've got council tenants, they'll say, "Oh, the council's responsible for that,", and it never gets done. I used to do any little bits and pieces like that, but I can't do it anymore – I've got my ladders, but I can't use them anymore; I can't do it.'

'We gotta no privacy now!' yells Mrs Jackson suddenly.

'No, this has got nothing . . . this has got nothing to do with what you've come for—'

It is no good; Mrs Jackson will not be silenced: 'If we wanna sit in the garden, we gotta no privacy!'

Reluctantly, Mr Jackson is forced to concede the point: their new neighbours do not grant them the privacy they feel they deserve.

'Our summers are gone from now on, you see,' he says, sadly. 'So you say – what's it like living on the Western Avenue? Well, the answer now isn't the same as what it would have been two years ago . . . You're not really in the same situation as you was before they let the houses to the Ministry of Transport. And, of course, the people who run the council couldn't care less . . .'

During five years' foreign service in the army, Mr Jackson won five medals, yet he has lost faith in the authorities he once served. Worse – he now believes they have conspired against him. 'What makes it so ironical is that our member of parliament for this area is Mr Young – the housing minister. He's the man who makes all the promises, and he's done exactly the opposite to what he said he'd do – he's mixed the tenants, mixed them all up . . .'

Given that the Jacksons' marriage was born in Rome, in the aftermath of the Second World War, it seems strange that their retirement should be spent agonizing over the distinction between council tenants and homeowners in East Acton. Suddenly, Mr Jackson's breath whistles unexpectedly. It sounds as though there is a kettle boiling in a distant room somewhere in the house. He laughs – sinus

problems, he explains, caused by polyps in the nose; if he
was a Tory councillor, he could have had it fixed. Mr and
Mrs Jackson laugh, and it is nice to be reminded of Mr
Jackson's sense of humour.

From a cupboard set against the wall, Mr Jackson
retrieves one of the many official letters he has received
over the years; his hands vibrate gently as he bends over to
inspect it. 'This thing has been going to be done for years
and years and years – you know, it's been planned, it's been
cancelled, it's been planned . . . When they first put it out
that they was going to build a flyover over this part of the
Western Avenue, these houses were only thirty years old.
And I think to myself, they can anticipate that in thirty
years' time them houses are going to be very handy to the
Ministry of Transport. They've got a hell of a lot of these
houses round here – over the years, they've been collecting
them, you know, one at a time . . . It's a grand plan; they've
been at it a long time – they know what they're doing.'

Confronted by the lumbering machinations of government, Mr Jackson sees conspiracies at work – and perhaps
he is right to do so. Letting properties to tenants with no
interest in the area has had one noticeable effect at least:
there is little prospect of a protest movement gathering
momentum on Western Avenue. None of the recent arrivals
consider the road worth saving, and people like Mr Jackson
will do nothing – he is too old. I find it difficult to share his
enthusiasm for a golden age of owner-occupied housing,
but I recognize that the changes to the area have genuinely
upset him. If he seems bitter, it is because he is powerless,
and the knowledge of his weakness is hard to accept.

I cross the road by the subway. The Greens have left
their home: a forwarding address is pinned to the letter-
box, and fox-holes in the garden mark the plots where
Robin's plants once grew. The sitting-room window at the

front of the house is broken. I reach inside – as someone else did before me – and release the latch. The window opens easily, and I climb inside. The house smells damp. Upstairs, roof-beams lie across the floor of Mr and Mrs Green's bedroom, and on the landing, the attic door is propped open to reveal the vaulted recesses of the roof. The structure of the house has been laid bare, as though Robin were providing me with a final lesson in the history of Western Avenue.

– – –

'DIRTY VEHICLE EXHAUGHTS UNWELCOME IN THIS AREA', says the oxblood panel which seals the downstairs window at 215 Western Avenue. 'EAST ACTON IS A HIGH POLLUTION AREA WHICH DEMANDS CLEANER AIR FOR ITS RESIDENTS'. It is 2 April: the grass in William's front garden is a foot high, and the condemned houses are almost lost behind the blossoming trees; weathered, worn and receding into the resurgent gardens, they seem to be ageing more naturally than before. They look like workmen's cottages in a neglected corner of a country estate.

4. The House of Unearthly Delights

I step on to the wooden box resting against the gate and peer into the rubble-choked passageway which runs down the side of 69 Western Avenue. The house looks abandoned, but I have been given my instructions: I shout – loud enough to be heard in the back garden – and then walk to the front door. The day is hot and still, but it is cool in the shadow of the house.

Five minutes ago, I was standing outside 109 Western Avenue. 'BOLLOX TO YA!' says the slogan scrawled in giant letters across its upstairs windows. 'X amount Arianism = ?' adds the downstairs window, cryptically. Bunting trails from its façade, and a polkadot dress hangs behind the glass in its front door. It is one of several squatted houses on the hill above Western Circus. I rang the bell, but there was no answer; then a battered figure in a dirty T-shirt and olive-green fatigues appeared at the top of the drive.

He paused, swaying slightly, and as I walked towards him he seemed to have trouble focusing on my face. He had baby dreads growing in his thick ginger hair. A lorry paused on the hill behind him, drenching him in shade; its brakes squealed as they held its weight against the slope. Suddenly, he lost his balance and took a step to steady himself; embarrassed by his lack of co-ordination, he frowned. 'I'm a bit messed up,' he said, candidly, in a soft Irish accent.

His eyes were smeared and empty, and his jaw was furred with stubble; he had been up all night. 'We're trying

to get a bit more organized,' he began. 'Knock through the
gardens, get a load of tents and caravans in there . . . Give
them a whole load of shit.' He swallowed; he did not look
capable of causing trouble. 'Go to number 69 – there's
another squat there. They're in the garden – just shout –
they'll hear you . . . I could talk to you now, man, but I'd
just talk a load of shit.' I believed him. He turned to go
inside the house, and I walked down the hill, into the rising
tide of traffic, until I reached 69 Western Avenue.

The man who answers the door does not seem surprised
to see me. Instead of a shirt, he wears a neck-brace of
sunburn, and there are red-raw bracelets on his skinny arms
– the negative of the T-shirt he was wearing yesterday, or
the day before. He leaves the door open, and walks through
the hall, disappearing into the greasy shadows of the house.
The image of his pale flesh dies slowly, and I follow his
fading trail into a kitchen overlooking the garden. On the
wall beside me is a lurid mural – a green-and-red painting
of an alien creature, with horned face and scaled skin. The
door to the back garden is open; tentatively, I step outside,
and emerge into the bleached light of the squatters' garden.

A carpet of baked earth encircles the back of the house,
and spreads towards a low wooden table where three
people are sitting. 'Sit down, man,' says the skinny man
who answered the door, in a thick Glaswegian accent. His
blond hair curls to his shoulders, and the thick lenses of his
glasses distort his eyes. He is perhaps thirty-five. An apple
tree blooms above our heads. Thirty feet beyond the table,
the garden dies in a tangle of plants and grasses. The house
next door is sealed; and the next; and the next. The fences
separating the back gardens have disappeared, and tram-
pled paths lead through a wilderness which blossoms unexpectedly behind the oxblood façades. Three doors away,

another squatted house – 61 Western Avenue – marks the end of the squatters' estate.

'There was a whole fucking street here once,' says the other man sitting at the table. His name is Roz, and his shirtless body is heavily armoured: tattoos crowd his chest and arms; his ears, nipples and eyebrows are pierced, and there are thick, waist-length ropes of hair rooted in the thin soil of his cropped scalp. Yet his face is unadorned: in contrast to his body's profusion of protective decoration, it seems naked, and makes him look surprisingly vulnerable.

There is a woman sitting beside him. Her name is Shay: she has long, red hair and delicately pockmarked skin. 'What's really sad is all these gardens – you get foxes here, and all kinds of things,' she says. 'You know, we don't get just pigeons – we get wood pigeons. We wanted to get a fight going to save them as a wildlife thing – if they're going to build a road, the people who live here should get something to compensate.'

There is a shout from the side of the house, and Glaswegian Don goes to answer it.

'They are going to get something – they're going to get another road,' says Roz, grimly. He does not meet my eye, and I sense he does not trust me. 'Another fucking road.'

'There was a beautiful little note on the door of a house down there – it said, Goodbye to my little house,' says Shay, sentimentally.

'It just fucks everybody, doesn't it?' adds Roz, more robustly. 'All the local businesses, all the local people – it fucks everybody for the sake of the road.'

There used to be four or five squatted houses on the Westway, a stretch of the A40 which lies to the east of Western Circus. The Westway's elevated carriageways, which carry traffic between White City and the Marylebone

Road, were built in the sixties, but the section that connects
White City and Western Circus was built at the same time
as Western Avenue, and many of the houses built beside it
have now been marked for demolition. The squatted houses
were knocked into one, and the walls were decorated with
flowing murals which stretched from one house to another.
The bailiffs 'killed the Westway' in the winter: Shay says
her mother – who lives there – was crying her eyes out the
day they repossessed the houses which her daughter's
friends had squatted.

Don sits down again, rips three Rizlas from a packet,
and tears open a cigarette. 'Have you got a flat, or a house,
yourself? Do you mind me asking what you pay for it?'
He pastes the papers together, and spills the tobacco on to
them; his glasses slip towards the end of his nose, and he
looks at me over the top of them. 'I've done most of it,
meself, at one time or another – rent, Housing Associations,
been on the dole and got the Social to pay, but the best
times I've had have been in squats. It was, like . . . a nice
wee community here, and it's getting smaller and smaller,
as places get evicted.'

The squatters have succumbed to the emotion that
afflicts everyone on Western Avenue: nostalgia. Mr Jackson
laments the passing of the days when everyone owned the
houses they lived in; the squatters' golden age began as his
was ending – when the houses fell empty. Mr Jackson's
memories stretch back forty years; theirs last no more than
twelve months, yet they feel Western Avenue's decline just
as keenly as he does, and they blame the same agency for it
– the government.

Bleary late-sixties Bowie drifts across the garden from a
speaker set up in the downstairs window. With a lit match,
Don tickles a piece of hash the size and colour of a sheep's
turd, and crumbles dope on to the tobacco.

'The other week, the cops arrived . . .' He pauses to seal his spliff with a deft lick of his tongue. 'Left us alone for about an hour . . .' He twists shut the end of the spliff. 'And then it was like . . .'

' "You're going to get arrested!" ' Roz interrupts with an imitation of the police – loud, self-important and aggressive.

'Aye, you're going to get arrested . . . When your man here turned up, right?' Don nods in Roz's direction, '. . . we had local cops coming up to see who was hanging around. Then we saw a couple of cops in the garden, and they wisnae locals – they were Special Unit, or something to do with the travelling community, Criminal Justice Bill boys. They were special boys, and we saw them through the window, walking through the garden, and it was like, they asked us . . . ' "What are youse doing here?" ' Don lights his spliff, and then answers his own question with exaggerated patience: ' "These live here" – and then it was, "How long have youse been here? What are youse doing here?" They just wanted to ask questions, and it was, like . . . "Oh, we've spotted some New Age travellers . . ." '

'New Age Travellers!' This time, the accent Roz has adopted is copper-plate English – the voice of a 1930s BBC broadcaster.

'They were nae local boys, man.'

'They were absolutely petrified that we were going to set up a site here,' says Roz.

'They're looking for party houses,' adds Don. 'Houses for people who are a bit over the top – and I'll give you our due, we party a lot, but it's no noisy enough to annoy our neighbours, the straight people.'

Suddenly, a bottle of wine is banged on to the table.

'FUCKING HELL!' A man dressed in black jeans and a T-shirt tips his head back and stamps his feet in the dirt. 'FUCKING CUNTS!'

Everyone is still. The man in black has cropped hair, and a lop-sided face – his mouth breaks to the side as he speaks, and he is almost spitting with indignation; he looks deranged.

'Listen, listen, to this – the fucking . . . I wanted to go to Brighton, so I went to the cash-point, right? I've got more than £300 in my account, but the fucking machine wouldn't give me more than £50 – so I rang the bank, yeah? And the fucking phone swallowed my money.' He rang the operator, and asked for a refund; they said he couldn't have one. 'So I said, "All right, how much is this going to cost you then?" And I put the phone down, and . . .' He mimes gripping the sides of the door of the phone-box for leverage, steps back and plants his boot into the phone.

'Been having a bad day, have you? We all have bad days,' says Roz, maternally.

'At least you've got some money – we're all fucking skint,' says another of the new arrivals. His name is Techno Dave, and he has cropped hair, round glasses, and large front teeth which draw his tanned face forward. He slumps in a bean-bag at the end of the table.

'Yeah, and I've been working fucking hard for it, 'cos I wanted to go away today.' The man in black finds a corkscrew to open his bottle of wine; he is slowing down. He looks at me suspiciously, and takes a slug at his bottle of wine. He sits down at the table, and lowers his head into his hands.

'You see, a lot of people don't want to go off and live in a little flat on their own,' resumes Shay. 'They don't – it's death. We realize that we need people. We need each other to live a decent life.'

'A commune, an' that,' says Don.

'Recently, there's been a community type of feeling here – we look after each other. A house without people is dead.

There are so many people who are miserable – all they've got is bills in their heads – and just grief, like, really,' says Shay, plaintively.

'It's what they've been conditioned to believe,' says Roz. 'Kids haven't got the imagination to come up with anything other than what they've been conditioned to fucking see, think and believe by the bloody media, and society; I find it really, really sad. I feel sorry for the people. I just feel sorry for them. They're sad fucking people staying in one place . . . Me, I don't know where I'm going, where I've been, or where I come from.' It is his proudest boast.

There are now perhaps ten people in the garden, and the air is thick with the scent of dope. The squatters are uncertain what to make of me: some of them are used to media attention, and perhaps they think that I am too unobtrusive to be a journalist. They know I am not just another visitor to the squats; if I were, they would probably welcome me without reservation. Although they are wary of me, they also see in me an opportunity to put their case: they understand the power of the media, and they blame it for fostering legislation which restricts their way of life. In particular, they resent the Criminal Justice and Public Order Act of 1994, which was designed to restrict the freedom of travellers, squatters, free-party organizers and road protesters.

'Any news we get is basically bad – bad press,' says Don. 'If you're on the up and up, any publicity is good publicity – when you're in our situation, most publicity is bad publicity.'

'I don't know, Don, that fuckin' . . . newspaper article last week was all right,' says a Scottish girl. Her name is Leanne. I have seen the article she is referring to: it was about the squatters and the decline of Western Avenue; it was not unsympathetic.

'The *Sunday Telegraph*?' says Don, his voice rising in disbelief.

'I know they're wankers and all that, but it wasnae fuckin' . . .' says Leanne, less certain now.

'They're the same as the *Sun* – they're right-wing shits.'

'I know they're right-wing shits, but they're on our side.'

'Ha! Ha! They are not on our side, mate,' says Don, fervently.

He is right, of course – the *Sunday Telegraph* is not on their side; few people are.

'It's all this propaganda in the newspapers . . . you know – dirty squatters, we don't have a life,' says a woman called Jenny. She is perhaps thirty years old, yet she has the eager, dirt-smudged face of an overexcited child. 'Man isn't meant to live alone – he wasn't meant to live in a tiny little room on his own, do you know what I mean? You look at primates, where we come from, and orang-utans . . . they're not meant to live on their own, in little boxes. We're an ethnic minority. You can't name us a group, we're not – whatever . . . They're scared of people like us, because they can't control us. In the last five years, I've lived with people who are individuals – and I'm not putting anyone down who's not an individual, but a lot of people put us down . . . There's bad bus people, there's good bus people, there's bad people in council estates, and houses, as well . . . The other day, right, a friend of mine got stopped by a police car to be searched, and I asked the police officer if I could say goodbye to my friend, and he asked me what I do for a living, and I told him, and he said to me, "I'd be ashamed if you were my daughter, you're an embarrassment to your profession." ' Jenny's profession is a respectable one, even by the standards of the police: she is a nanny. 'And do you know what he did? He opened up the back door and tried to trip me up, so I'd hurt myself. It really hurt my feelings. I wasn't being mouthy,' she adds, plaintively. 'I hadn't sworn at him or anything. Why don't they like us? Because it's forced into them not to like us. It's all this propaganda in the newspapers – like you know, if I told people I lived in a squat, they wouldn't think we were, like, intelligent human beings . . .'

'If you tell them you're a traveller, they think you have parties all day and shag each other's women,' says Roz.

'Yeah, they think we sit on a bean-bag all day smoking dope and shagging each other.'

'Well, don't we?' says Leanne; and everyone laughs.

'No one ever asks you if you have a choice. They always presume there's something wrong if you're living like this.'

'There isnae choice, man,' says Don.

'I have a choice. It is my choice to live the way I like. It is my choice.'

'You've got a fucking right to live that life!' Jenny is shouting again.

'There isnae choice, you know what I mean? They could fuck you tomorrow – they could cut your dole tomorrow.'

'The dole makes us greedy, Don,' says Jenny. 'If the dole had never been here, we wouldn't have chosen it . . .'

'If they can cut your dole tomorrow, they can . . .'

'Has anyone got a FUCKING hammer?' The man in black lifts his head from the table. 'I'm going to go and trash that fucking phone-box.'

Outside, the tarmac seems to be softening in the summer heat. The pavement feels spongy. I walk back to my car, which is parked in a side-road above Western Circus. On the Westway, beside the boarded-up houses which were once squatted by Shay's friends, there are vans stocking newspapers, flowers and cold drinks parked in the lay-bys;

salesmen move from car to car, working the queues of stalled traffic.

\-   \-   \-

'The city is crumbling, it cannot last much longer; its time is past,' wrote Le Corbusier. He believed that the cities of Europe were ill-equipped to meet the demands of the new age: traffic was like 'dynamite flung at hazard into the street', and pedestrians were 'a sacrifice to death in the shape of innumerable motors'; but it was not just individual lives which were at risk – the eruption of traffic had endangered the future of the city itself. Yet the machine which threatened the survival of the city provided the means of its redemption as well – we did not know how to build houses 'in a modern way', complained Le Corbusier, while there were prototypes all around us: 'Everybody asserts with conviction and enthusiasm: "The motor-car marks the style of our epoch!" Well, then it remains to use the motor-car as a challenge to our houses and great buildings.' The perfection of the car's design was an affront to the 'wretched and selfish individualism' of most modern architecture – and the architecture of the suburbs, in particular.

\-   \-   \-

At dawn, Western Avenue empties every few minutes, and in the unexpected silence, birds sing, improbably loudly, before the city's heart pulses again, and thick, ugly clots of cars flood the road. There are people walking home, from clubs or nightshifts. A woman climbs the hill with a raft of roses pressed to her chest – she has been picking flowers from the gardens.

\-   \-   \-

The beginnings of a light railway had been laid down across Barker's Field, with carriers for soil and material. The plotters salvaged what they could from the allotments, and men were posted at the exits to make sure that none of the workers stole their produce. The plotters had been defeated: it was plain that the work could no longer be stopped, and they turned their attention to the question of compensation instead.

— — —

'I was named after Shirley Temple – my sister told my mum to do that.'

It was the first detail Shirley Buchan chose to reveal about herself as she drew up two stools in the shaded kitchen at the back of her house and began to talk. Twenty minutes later, she has not paused for more than a moment, and I can already boast a detailed knowledge of the Buchan family history.

A greying, matronly woman in a loose blue dress, Shirley Buchan grew up in a working-class family in Wormwood Scrubs: her father was a full-time lorry driver and a part-time boxer, and her mother worked as a cook at the BBC studios in Lime Grove. She has spent most of her life in East Acton, and she now lives in 59 Western Avenue – next door to the house which marks the eastern edge of the squatters' property.

The landscape of Western Avenue is more important to her than to anyone else I have met – except, perhaps, Robin Green. When she was a child, her family always supported Oxford in the Boat Race, and she remembers standing at Western Circus and looking up the hill: the 'lovely sweep' of the wide, tree-lined road as it curved towards Oxford instilled a sense of loyalty towards a city they had never visited. Every Sunday, she used to cycle up Western Avenue:

'There was a proper little path you'd cycle on, and then there was a little green verge before you got to the road. You can see a little further up how it was – the cycle track, the grass verge, one lane, the verge in the middle.' The memory animates her hands, and she marks out the paths in the air for me.

Every summer, she would walk up the road to buy a new pair of sandals from a Czech firm of shoemakers, and she would visit an ice-cream parlour run by a man whose name – she is fairly certain – was *not* Mark Antonio. 'It was lovely ice-cream, as I remember – but that's how old people talk, isn't it? Everything tasted a bit better then.' She is only fifty-eight, but since her two grown-up sons have left home, she has adopted the protective reflex of calling herself old. She recognizes that talking about the past is an indulgence, but it is one she does not begrudge herself. Besides, she cannot help herself – she is lost in the seductive rhythms and textures of her memories.

She had a nickname for Western Avenue: she called it Toffville. She remembers the people who lived in the big houses beside the road with a combination of envy and admiration which is peculiar to the class-conscious English. 'I suspect we didn't know the people who lived here at all – except to think they were a bit smart. You know, you lowered your head when they walked by; you certainly didn't speak to them; you were kind of in awe of them.'

Perhaps it was a childhood aspiration to return one day and live on Western Avenue, and the allure of the road did not diminish when she grew up and left home. In 1973, when she was living in Ealing Broadway and teaching in a nearby school, there was a girl in her class who was 'quite a poor little thing' – and she lived in Western Avenue. Shirley Buchan was intrigued: 'Now, Western Avenue to me still said Toffville – so how come she was living there?

I had a word with her mother, and she told me that a lot of these houses had been bought up by the Department of Transport and they offered them to people, really, for the asking.'

She gave up a secure tenancy to come and live in 59 Western Avenue. Sadly, the road was not the place she remembered – how could it be? Shirley Buchan will never live in 'Toffville', for Toffville is a place defined, in part, by her absence. The mere fact that she was living on Western Avenue showed how much it had changed. And there were other, more tangible changes as well: the traffic had increased to the extent that she worried about the safety of her sons. 'I was thinking, I just hope that living here never means if I hadn't lived here, they wouldn't have died in a road accident – you know, I was worried they would.' Her eldest son used to play a game on Western Avenue: when he brought friends home from school, he would go outside and lie down in the road, as a dare. 'That's called fun, of course,' she says acerbically. 'I can remember absolutely screaming at him . . . Of course, no one could do that now.'

Her sons were her responsibility alone, for she was divorced by the time she reached Western Avenue – and no one else in her family had ever been divorced. 'I always think I was before my time – there was no sexual activity before marriage, and I don't think it would have been a bad idea in my case . . .'

She was nineteen when she married, and she had her first child soon afterwards. 'I was absolutely thrilled with having Martin; I can remember even now, it's like an ecstasy when you've got your baby, and he's just been born, and you think how clever you are. A lot of women tell me that's how they feel – it's just a lovely feeling.'

After nine years of marriage, she left her husband one Friday night and went to live with her parents. 'And I never went back – there was never this to-ing and fro-ing, or anything like that. There wasn't another man, and there wasn't another woman, and in fact my ex-husband still lives in that house.'

For the first time since she started talking, she pauses for a moment. She has been talking with such unself-conscious fluency that I am beginning to wonder whether she is fully aware of my presence. Now, she looks at me in a way that suggests she is considering the wisdom of confiding in me. 'If somebody had said to me, you're not ever going to get married again . . . I have actually got – I have met somebody, a friend . . .' When she resumes, she is less certain of herself: 'I have got a best friend, who I have known for a long time . . . He is my friend. He's married . . . this is my therapy session!' She puts her hand over her mouth. 'I'm just laughing at myself – I don't know who you are, and I'm telling you all my personal secrets . . . You're now going to tell me you work for the *Sun*!'

She knows it would be wiser to say nothing, but she cannot help herself – like her neighbours, the squatters, she is fascinated by the media. 'I worry about talking to the press, because they might misrepresent what you said, and I don't want to say anything or do "something wrong" – you know, in inverted commas.' As far as I can tell, it is the government she is scared of offending: since she lives in a property leased by the Department of Transport to West Hampstead Housing Association, the government, ultimately, is her landlord.

She soon recovers her poise; she draws her hands together in front of her stomach, and begins to tell me about her marriage. 'I couldn't have told you at the time, I might say – but we were having trouble relating to each other. We couldn't really talk to each other – we didn't have much in common. I, for example, wanted to train to be a teacher, and my husband was saying that would be silly – how could I ever be a teacher? I wanted him to leave, and I think it was because I was wishing him dead, and I didn't like myself for that – if only he could just go away, but he said he couldn't find anywhere to live. He was quite happy to see us go, and he never supported the children.'

She was on her own once she left her husband: there were no social workers or support groups – 'or money come to that' – and it was difficult finding a place to live because landlords wanted the security of a husband in regular employment. 'I went out every day trying to get somewhere to live for us – I used to go to East Acton station, and think, "Where shall I go?" I'd always go to West Ruislip, or Ealing Broadway, depending on which train came first, and on this one day, Ealing Broadway came first, and I got out, and there was this big neon sign saying "Cole and Hicks, Estate Agents", and I just said, "Have they got any flats?" And they had this flat in Blakesly Avenue, and it was beautiful – I just couldn't believe it.'

She had no furniture, but she reclaimed the beds from the family house in Neasden, so her boys had a bed each; she slept on the floor. Meanwhile, she started training at a college for mature students in Acton Town Hall. She had begun to fulfil her ambition of becoming a teacher.

Her first job was in East Acton, and she earned less than she had been given as a grant when she was a student. 'When I was teaching, clear money, I was earning £56 a month, and the rent in Blakesly Avenue was £40 a month. So we had £16 a month to live on, and I had two boys, so I got a job at the Caernarfon Hotel, and I worked as a waitress in the evenings – but you shouldn't feel sorry for me, because I really enjoyed it. And the boys used to be on Ealing Common – these are things you couldn't do now, you couldn't leave your children playing on Ealing

Common when you went to work, but I did – and in the
wintertime, it was dark early, and they used to have a torch
each, and they used to play hide and seek behind the trees.
Whenever I came back, they were in such good moods, and
I was in a good mood, because I'd earned money . . . I
remember one Christmas Day, having to serve lunch at the
Caernarfon Hotel, and there were a few residents there –
they were the only ones left, so everyone was in a good
mood, and nearly all of them gave me chocolate or something for Christmas, and I can just remember feeling absolutely euphoric walking back to Blakesly Avenue with the
boys.'

It is a moment recalled with absolute clarity. Life has
not been easy for Mrs Buchan, but she rejects the idea that
people might feel sympathy for her. 'It's worked out quite
well now – I always felt, I know what I'm doing, inside
myself, and you always knew who you could say "I'm
alone" to, and who you couldn't; it's a kind of bourgeois
morality, but they don't ask, and you don't say. Now, of
course, it's not a problem.'

Last year, when she took early retirement, she was
teaching English to Asian and Bosnian children. For most
of her career, she took part-time jobs in the school holidays
and she earned enough to educate one of her sons privately.
'He was going to go to Oxford – and that was because this
road went to Oxford, and our connection with Oxford,
because of the Boat Race.'

She tells me, in exhaustive detail, about her sons, and I
begin to feel uncomfortable. I cannot help wondering
whether they would like me to know everything that their
irrepressibly talkative mother is proud to reveal.

To get her off the subject, I ask her how the area has
changed. 'Well the traffic makes the house shake,' she
begins. 'It never used to – whether it's just weakened the

foundations, I don't know. In the morning, there are some regular big lorries which go up, and you know it's ten past five, because you're just shaken practically out of bed. I sleep in the back of the house now . . . But East Acton has been annihilated – this is the thing. The whole thing has gone – it hasn't got a cinema anymore, it hasn't got a Woolworth's anymore, it hasn't got the little grocery shops where you could get three rashers of streaky bacon . . . The shops, to me, are the greatest change, but I feel that it's more acute for me now – I mean, a lot of my talking always comes back to what am I going to do now, and what have I done about moving. I could be really angry . . . But if the court asked me to go, I'd go – I'm not into breaking the law; I'll stay while I can, but I'll go when I'm told. If you want anger about the road, you should go and see Colette – she's Irish, and she lives up the road, and she's *really* angry.'

There has been a lot of resentment in the neighbourhood against the new arrivals – both the squatters and the homeless people who were given council houses while 'poor old buggers' like Mrs Buchan had to pay their own rent. She does not expect the Housing Association to provide her with another home – in fact, she would rather deny that she is connected to the organization. Since it has only managed the houses since 1990, she does not feel it is part of her 'identity'. 'I'm too proud – it's like the money situation, the work situation; I don't ask, I just go and work. I mean, I could be a cleaner – that's my gift. If you come from the working classes . . . there are a lot of people who wouldn't know how to clean a floor, do things like that or be a flexible person; I think I could – I'll find work. Also, people won't work for less money than they're used to – I will; I'll just work twice as long.' She is not boasting – she is simply stating the facts.

With the superannuation money she received recently, she is willing to buy her own house, and despite its disadvantages she wants to stay on the road. It seems incredible to me, but she is attempting to buy 76 Western Avenue – a house which lies more or less opposite hers on the eastbound carriageway. Her dedication to Western Avenue is heroic – she is even willing to extend a cautious welcome to the squatters who have moved in next door. It upsets her to see litter in the driveway she shares with number 61, but she does not object to their presence: 'I mean, I just think they've all got their story, and they're all trying to live life through to the end. So what the hell? Why shouldn't they live there, if the houses are there?'

Her brother said it would be better not to talk to the squatters: he was confident they would not mean to hurt her, but he was concerned that she might catch them unawares and then 'they might do something they're going to regret' – as though they were not quite in control of themselves. Of course, Mrs Buchan is too sensible to listen to her brother's advice: 'I do talk to them – I usually say hello; I just say – I always rub it in – I say, "Look, I've been here since 1973 – that's my house, and that's my garden. Do what you like over there, but don't come over here." I wouldn't treat an ordinary neighbour like that – I tend to be very schoolteacherish. But there is one who has been quite nice.' The words 'quite nice' are carefully chosen.

At Christmas, she was going away for two or three days, and she asked the 'quite nice' squatter to make certain that no one came near her house. Two days later, she got a card through the door: 'Really, a most unsuitable card!' she says, with a *moue* of appalled delight. 'There's this man and woman kissing, and the woman has little dots coming out of her mouth' – she draws her finger upwards from her mouth to demonstrate – 'and it says: "Take your tongue out of my mouth, I'm kissing you goodbye." This man, who is Portuguese, I think, said, "It's a joke"; and I said, "Well I'm not going – I'm staying here."' She did not object to the sexual connotations of the card – it was the suggestion that she might be leaving Western Avenue which she did not like.

Her old neighbours who lived in 57 Western Avenue used to complain ferociously about the squatters. 'They weren't the toffs who used to live here – they were people who had bought the house because it was cheap,' she says, with exquisite cattiness. 'Well, they had things stolen, and they blamed the squatters. And there hadn't only been squatters – there had been gipsies, as well, and they are nature's thieves. I mean, that's how they live – nomadic people do live like that, by getting their cattle to eat other people's grass. That's their culture.'

Perhaps she has reason to be suspicious – her house has been burgled no less than eight times, yet as far as Shirley Buchan is concerned, its impending destruction is a more frightening prospect than the arrival of squatters or gipsies. She has watched the bailiffs go about their work with something approaching grief: 'When they board them up, they knock them to pieces – they knock all the sinks out, they break all the windows, just to stop them being squatted. And I was sitting here in the front room, hearing this crashing and banging, and breaking glass. It was like a death. I don't know if you were around at the time of the hurricanes . . . you saw these great trees falling, and even though you know they're only trees, there is this terrible sense of bereavement you feel; I feel the same with houses.'

Not surprisingly, she resents the way she has been treated by the Department of Transport. 'To me, they haven't looked at anyone like an emotional being – you're just like a unit, really. You're just like one of their things –

they put you in there, now they'll take you out of there, and now they're getting on with their work, and there you are, stuck.' It is difficult to believe that Shirley Buchan will be 'stuck' for long.

'I LEAD AGAIN', says the sign posted inside her front door. As she shows me out, I ask her what it means. 'Well,' she begins, 'I had a big National Union of Teachers notice on the back of the door, which said "FAILED AGAIN"; I've taken my driving test four times now, and the last time I took it, I said to the NUT rep, I want to get one of those signs and stick it to my door. So it's been "FAILED AGAIN" for years . . . Only last week, Martin and Andrew and some of their friends came here, and I wasn't here, and they cut this new sign out – funnily enough, though I've spoken to both of them a few times, I keep forgetting to ask who did it . . .' As I step outside, and the door closes behind me, it seems to me that Shirley Buchan is still talking.

– – –

Roz arrived in London in his van on Christmas Eve, and moved into a squat. The police pushed the vehicle on to the road, so it became an obstruction, and they were legally bound to take it away and impound it. The vehicle contained every single thing he owned; he didn't even have a spare pair of socks. He had no choice but to move into the squatted house at 109 Western Avenue.

– – –

Nothing prevented us from mass-producing houses in the way we mass-produced cars, maintained Le Corbusier. In the early 1920s, he produced several prototypes for the mass-production house: the 'Citrohan' – a white-washed cube raised on vertical stanchions with a flat roof and a double-height living-space – was 'a house like a motor-car, conceived and carried out like an omnibus or a ship's cabin'. The functional design was stripped of unnecessary decoration and distinguished by the strict elegance of its proportions. Le Corbusier's whitewashed cubic villa was 'as serviceable as a typewriter'; it defined the concept of a machine house for a machine age.

– – –

'I BREED HATE', says the slogan painted on a lurid yellow TV dumped in the drive of 107 Western Avenue. Racked in a metal grille beside an abandoned white transit van in the drive is a stack of black-lettered signs: 'TODAY, THE ENGLISH GOUVERNMENT OUTLAW THE TRAVEL-LERS, RAVERS AND SQUATTERS. TOMORROW IT WILL BE THE BLACKS, JEWS, ASIANS AND NON-WHITE TORYS. FIGHT BACK!'; 'YOU DON'T HAVE THE RIGHT TO REMAIN SILENT. MAKE SOME FUCKING NOISE!' The house is empty. Two toy Gremlins in the front porch stick their tongues out at me.

– – –

In January 1923, the committee formed to represent the plot-holders of Barker's Field announced that it had accepted the council's offer of £250 compensation. The plotters' 'finest half-hour' came when those who had been awarded large amounts offered 'to forego varying sums to be divided out amongst their less fortunate brethren'. The Chairman commended all those who had given up part of their award for the 'fine spirit they had shown'.

– – –

On the pavement outside 109 Western Avenue, Roz is loading bags into an old car.

'How's it going?' I say.

'Badly, mate – it's going badly.' He hardly looks up from his work. 'Go on, go inside . . . look what they've done.'

He gestures towards the house.

By now, I know what to expect: in the hall, a powerful fist has punched through the floorboards so they rear drunkenly upwards; in the kitchen, the units have been ripped from the wall, and the sink is a shattered, dirty-white skull; a twisted metal pipe careers crazily away from the wall, and dribbles tamely on the floor. Somewhere in the house is the sound of running water.

Roz appears behind me, with his friend, Nords, who has just come out of prison after serving a three-month sentence for driving offences. They came back from a festival two days ago to find that the house had been destroyed. As usual, the degree of violence is startling: upstairs, the bath has been upended, the sink is reduced to a jagged splinter of bone, and mattresses, chairs and carpets have been tipped out of the windows – they spill on to the lawn behind the house. In the bedroom facing the road, there are giant letters sprayed on the wall: L.F.T.C. 'Live – for – the – Crack,' says Roz, his arm at full stretch to trace each letter. He is more animated than I have ever seen him. 'I AM INNOCENT', announces another wall.

There are mattresses and sleeping bags in two of the downstairs rooms, surrounded by debris flaked from the ceilings and the walls. On Tuesday night they slept on the floor because there was nowhere else to go. 'Look at this – a beautiful fireplace destroyed.' Roz points at a bare patch of plaster surrounding a naked hearth. 'This is the only squat that hasn't got a possession order on it – 61 and 69 will be gone in a week, so they're taking the chance to get us all at once.' I ask him who did it, and he shrugs: it could be anyone.

Downstairs, the floor of the sitting-room is painted bright red. 'THE HOUSE OF UNEARTHLY DELIGHTS' says the slogan on the wall. The squatters' graffiti and murals are day-glo bright and ugly, and their apocalyptic slogans anticipate the destruction of the houses. In a sense, they are suitable tenants for the condemned road – yet even they are shocked by the destruction wreaked, presumably, by the bailiffs.

We step over the splintered floorboards and stand on the patio to survey the debris littering the garden. 'What sort of an attitude do they expect young people to grow up with when they're confronted with this sort of thing?' says Roz. He sounds like a Tory politician, yet it is nice to think he is entitled to claim the moral high ground. 'There was a sixteen-year-old girl made homeless from here – yeah, Leanne.' I knew Leanne was young; I did not realize that she is only sixteen. 'It's all right for us – we're going back on site, but what are they going to do? We can't afford to set up another squat – we haven't got the time.'

He is used to living without electricity, but the others aren't. He has given up on his impounded van, but he hopes to get his girlfriend's car on the road, and go to Ireland.

'Me and Roz are travellers – "new age travellers",' says Nords. He puts inverted commas around the words; his weariness at the way they are presented in the media is, by now, familiar. 'So we're used to living in a large community: the kids are safe, there's never any trouble, and if you run out of food, then someone will always feed you, so we'll always muscle in and help if we can. People who've been squatting a long time are used to having four walls around them' – he boxes himself in with lines drawn in the air – 'and a fence, and being able to say this is their space, like anyone else who lives in the city.'

'THE CRIMINAL INJUSTICE ACT, 1994 IS DEATH OF BASIC HUMAN RIGHTS. NO RIGHT TO SILENCE, NO ALTERNATIVE LIFESTYLES, NO JUSTICE / NO PEACE', says the sign propped inside the gaping doorway to the garden. Black shreds of insulation cling to the walls, and lace the edges of the cratered floorboards. An upturned sofa lies on the steps outside – it was thrown through the doors, shattering the glass and splintering the wooden frame – yet the garden is beautiful still: there is a luxuriant grape-vine growing over a trellis on the patio, and in the flowerbeds there are rose bushes, irises, pear trees and fir trees. 'Those rose bushes have been here for twenty or thirty years,' says Nords.

– – –

'I presume the Western-avenue will eventually be completed at a reasonable time before the crack of doom, and will not be burnt up, like many other useful and beautiful promised things, before we have had a chance to enjoy it,' wrote a columnist in 1925. Work on Western Avenue had been delayed, for the bridges which would carry the road above the railways had yet to be built.

– – –

It is a miracle I am still alive: if I'd driven my car for a day longer, the brakes would have locked and the car would have flipped over, crushing me inside the wreck. Or so my mechanic tells me. His name is Tommy, and he used to work at Mercedes-Benz until someone dropped a battery on his back. Now, he walks with a limp, and works from home. The way I treat my car makes him smile.

5. The Peace Place

It is a mid-week afternoon in early July. The dry air is laced with the sweet stink of dope, and there is music playing, louder than usual. Subservient to its percussive demands, Jenny tracks back and forth in front of the house, pounding the earth and flailing her arms; she throws her head back, and raises her hands to the sky, calling down the rain to wash the dirt from her tangled hair. Beside her, dressed in silver hotpants, Leanne seems to be moving to a different rhythm: she is walking on the spot, and pushing herself hard; her legs and hips grind in a regular, robotic motion. I pause for a moment in the protective shade of number 69. There are perhaps thirty people gathered in the garden which stretches between 61 and 69 Western Avenue; some sit in armchairs they have dragged into the garden, or lie in the long, pale grass; others are dancing on the bib of dried earth behind the house.

Don is sitting in his usual place, at the table with a bottle of cider in front of him. I sit down. He seems happy enough to see me. 'It's getting busier and busier in the house – there's more and more people staying here now. It's like, we've got . . . nine. Eight minimum – sometimes ten or eleven.'

I do not recognize them all – some of the squatters evicted from The House of Unearthly Delights, at 107 and 109 Western Avenue, have moved in to the last remaining squatted houses on the road. 'These people . . .' He gestures around the garden. 'Maest of them are hippies, like myself, but people get a bit pissed off – leave the people alone until

you need to knock the house down, and give us an honest
answer as to when we need to move out, and we'll move
out. Don't lie to us because there are people who are in a
mood for confrontation.' Then he gets to the point: 'What
we need is a wee bit of your weight behind us – we need a
wee bit in the *Big Issue* or the *Guardian* to encourage them
to give us some time till they actually need the place.'

I have no 'weight' to put at their disposal – and I say so;
Don shrugs – he is not particularly surprised. Jenny dances
over to the table.

'Have you got £5 for me? I had a friend who spoke to a
journalist, and got £20 for it.'

Her eyes are wide, and her tanned, dirty face is streaked
with sweat. She has been at a festival, and she has not slept
for days.

'You should talk to Baggsie.' Don gets to his feet and
gestures to a man sitting opposite me. 'He's the most
articulate of the lot of us.'

Baggsie has black hair which straggles to his shoulders,
and his front teeth are jagged and discoloured. 'Sure, man,'
he says, obligingly, 'it's no skin off my nose talking to you.'

Beneath a dusty, broad-brimmed hat, his eyes are startlingly blue. Jenny dances away again; her legs are caked
with mud as high as her knees.

Baggsie stands up, and leans his weight on a walking
stick: his leg is in plaster. 'Let's find some shade.' He
hobbles down a path which runs through the undergrowth
at the back of the garden. We sit down on the thick stones
which border a flowerbed. The air which filters through the
trees is cooler here, and the music from the house is muted.
Baggsie's real name is Steve; the nickname, which comes
from his surname, has followed him around for years. 'It's
not even any good as a name for hiding behind,' he says,
casually, as I settle my tape-recorder on a stone between us.

'Everyone knows it – including the Old Bill, I'm sure.' Like all the squatters, Baggsie is conscious of the attentions of two agencies – the media and the police – but he does not exaggerate the importance of either: 'I've got nothing to get paranoid about, which is quite sweet,' he says.

Baggsie has been squatting around 'the west end of town' for five or six years. Eight or nine months ago, they were hounded from house to house in Shepherd's Bush, and they ended up 'bouncing out' to Western Avenue. 'It's been peaceful; communal; calm – quite our little peace place . . . It's a lovely group, it really is – a lot of people who like each other, a lot of people who look after each other, and a lot of people who didn't know each other until they came here.' Of the sixteen people now living in 61 and 69 Western Avenue, Baggsie knew only one of them eight months ago. 'People could do exactly what they wanted and there was enough room for it all. We'd got 109 and 107, and if you wanted to listen to this sort of music in the middle of the night and dance, you could head up there, and if you wanted to calm down, you could head down here, and we'd just be sitting around, we'd have a little fire going, you know, guitars, flutes, whistles, and a little bit of quiet music at the end of the night . . .'

It is plain where Baggsie would like to be: he belongs in what he calls the Peace Place – number 69 – rather than the House of Unearthly Delights, where techno played all night, until the bailiffs put an end to the squatters' parties. Baggsie likes nothing better than getting up in the morning and seeing the fox cubs playing in the gardens behind the houses. Sadly, the foxes' appearances are rare these days – since people have been evicted from the party houses, the garden at number 69 is not as peaceful as it used to be. Yet he would never refuse anyone a place in the house.

Baggsie is a stagehand, and he works on shows at the

major London venues, installing the PA and lighting rigs.
Yet he is now facing a lean period: his leg is in plaster
because he ripped a ligament, and he will miss three weeks'
work – a shortfall in his earnings which would 'decimate'
him if he was paying rent, for he does not get sick pay, and
he does not want to sign on; he prefers to earn his own
income.

Yet even if his income were guaranteed, he would choose
to squat, for he likes the freedom it gives him. Ideally,
he would squat in the winter and then live in a van in the
summer – a routine which has evolved naturally over the
years. When he finished school, he was programming pay-
roll computers for a living, and he would work a split-shift:
finish at 2.30 on Thursday and not start again till 12.30 on
Monday. At the weekends, he would go to a festival: first,
he bought himself a bike; then a car; then the car turned
into a van, 'because it was useful to crash in', and soon he
was living in it permanently.

The thought of spending my life travelling across England moves me for reasons I cannot easily explain. It is
partly Baggsie's character which makes his old way of life
seem so attractive: he is describing a state of mind as much
as a way of life. 'I'd still be travelling if I could. Most
serious travellers have been driven out of England – you
find them in Spain, in France. Italy looks after them. Not
this country, unfortunately.'

Perhaps it is because England has always been such a
densely populated place that the travellers arouse such
antagonism. The demise of the countryside has seemed
imminent throughout the century – as early as 1904, H.G.
Wells foresaw a continuous 'urban region' stretching from
the Scottish Highlands to the English Channel. Few people
are willing to relinquish what remains of England's lanes
and fields to the travellers. The countryside is jealously

guarded not only by the people who live and work on it, but by the millions of others who remain attached to a sentimental vision of England as 'a green and pleasant land'. When it drafted legislation restricting the travellers' freedom, the Conservative government was responding to the instincts of most of the population.

Baggsie has one thing to say about the Criminal Justice Act – it is proving effective. Yet there is still hope: he has heard a rumour that it does not apply to boats. It is still possible to live like a traveller on the canals and waterways of England, and Baggsie is saving up to buy a narrowboat.

His thoughts have emerged unhurriedly; occasionally, I prompt him with a question, but most of the time he leads the conversation himself. His accent is difficult to place – like his friends, he is rooted in the fertile earth of the squats, with their indiscriminate mix of cultures, classes and nationalities. When I ask him where he comes from, his reply takes me by surprise: he was born locally, in Park Royal. As a baby, he was a chronic bronchial asthmatic, and his parents were told to leave the city if they wanted 'to have a kiddie in six months' time'. They moved to the Midlands, where Baggsie grew up.

It pleases me to discover that Baggsie was born in the area, like his neighbour, Mrs Buchan. Coincidentally, they are the only two people I have met who were born on the road and live here still – and they now live next door to one another. Their lives could hardly be more different, yet Baggsie and Mrs Buchan have certain qualities in common: both are cheerfully self-reliant; both are irrepressibly talkative.

Five yards from where we are sitting stands the remains of a wooden shelter, built by a former occupant as a garden retreat: it is invisible from the house, and ringed by carefully planted shrubs and flowerbeds, but little remains of it now, for the squatters broke it up, and burnt the wood on their fires. They burnt the fences which separated the gardens, as well, and they plundered the abandoned houses up and down the road. 'When they first trashed the houses, the gipsies started coming in – as soon as the bailiffs had evicted a house, they'd be in there, stealing all the copper piping, and everything,' says Baggsie. 'Now there's guys from up and down the squats do it. As soon as the bailiffs go in, we go in, take out all the pipes, and that pays for . . . Well, it pays for a party.'

'FIGHT FOR YOUR RIGHT TO PICKET, PROTEST AND PARTY', said a sign outside 107 Western Avenue, but only one activity rouses much enthusiasm amongst the squatters: they like to party, and they have little energy left for picketing or protesting. Why should they? Since they are due to be evicted from the road any day now, they have little stake in its future. Besides, Western Avenue is hardly worth saving – Baggsie says he would like to open up their gardens for the locals to 'come and moon around in', but there are no real plans to disrupt the roadworks: protests require planning, and the squatters on Western Avenue are more concerned with securing the necessities of life – drink, drugs, food, a place to sleep.

'I don't know whether we're an underclass,' he says, thoughtfully, 'but we're a counter-culture, that's for sure.' If so, they are a curiously bland counter-culture, for they have few real ambitions – no artistic goals, no defining philosophy, no vision of remaking society. 'WE WANT TO BE FREE TO LOVE', says the graffiti on the abandoned squat at 107 Western Avenue, but the rhetoric feels second-hand and uninspiring. The travellers amongst them dream of being allowed to live in peace on the common land of Britain, but the others seem content to drift in the blood-warm shallows that fringe the rapid currents of mainstream life. Yet Baggsie has one quality that sets him apart from most of the others I have met: he is motivated by an open-minded enthusiasm for new people and new experiences. 'Yeah man,' he says, suddenly, 'I see so many things, and I love it all.'

It seems to me that Baggsie is not by instinct an outsider, but he is forced to behave as if he were: since his way of life is deemed anti-social, he might as well act anti-socially. He talks freely of confrontations with the police, but there is nothing aggressive about Baggsie – quite the opposite, in fact: he is disposed to like everyone – he even has friends in the police. But outwitting authority is part of the game he has been playing for most of his adult life, and it is a game he enjoys.

Sadly, the rules have begun to change: he does not know how the new laws will affect squatters, but in order to be reasonably secure, they are considering occupying churches or schools – buildings large enough to accommodate twenty or thirty people. 'Then there'll be enough of us to defend it, if need be.'

One morning last week, Baggsie opened the door to find a couple of workmen standing on the step with a sledge-hammer. 'I asked them what they wanted, and they said they shouldn't really tell us, but the score was they were given a list with a few house numbers on, and told to go and try it on – knock on the door, if there was nobody there, break the door down . . . Basically, you'd come home from work, the door would be broken down, they'd have smashed the toilets, smashed the sink, smashed the bath . . .'

The squatters say they want nothing more than to be left in peace, yet they are forced to fight endless campaigns in order to secure temporary havens. Ironically, it seems to me that there are easier ways to live.

We walk back through the garden; as the day cools, the party is grinding down. Jenny is lying on her back on a mattress under the window, cocooned in the music; her arms weave for a moment, and then she is still. In the back garden of 67 Western Avenue, a pile of beer cans four feet high lies beneath the boarded-up window of the house.

– – –

The first time I took acid, I walked on to the motorway bridge which ran above the M3 close to Winchester. Beneath us, the headlights on the road wove a neon cradle of unguessable depth and seductive softness; I wanted to step inside it, to test its strength, and the thought scared me. It was 1987. Ahead of us, the M3 curved around the hill on which the city stood, before it narrowed to four lanes beside a chalk hillside called Twyford Down.

– – –

It is a perfect summer evening. In the squatter's gardens, the trodden paths which wind through the overgrown brambles are soft underfoot, and the air is heavy with the blown scent of cut grass – a reminder of the tidier world which lies beyond the squatters' estate.

A van parked on the fringe of the road has spilled its passengers on to the bib of earth behind 69 Western Avenue. Sipping beer, the travellers sit around the table, waiting for the evening to begin: most of them are bare-chested, and their tattooed skin is etched with dirt; some wear olive-green fatigues and heavy boots; red-eyed, with sun-slapped red faces, they look like the dregs of an exhausted army captured in the middle of a long campaign.

A mist of spray drifts over the table: dressed in his sunburn T-shirt, skinny Don is watering the garden. Baggsie is asleep under a tree, and Techno Dave is playing with a rope clamped in a dog's jaws – neither can shake the other loose, and the dog's lean, muscled body swings backwards and forwards a foot above the earth, a pale lantern in the gathering dusk. Dave's arms are as fibrous as the rope itself; he throws the dog away, and it squirms on its back in the dust.

Techno Dave tells me that the squatters' community has begun to disintegrate. 'Some people have got more money than others, and that's caused a bit of friction, and some people have lost things, and that shouldn't happen with friends. A few of us got really out of it the other night, and lost some money – that shouldn't happen, either.' Dave drains a can of beer, and throws it on to the pile of rusting metal cans behind the house.

Apparently, a hundred and fifty people are coming later for a party – Don does not want them to, but it is too bad. Don is pissed off because food has been stolen from the fridge, but Techno Dave is excited by the garden as a venue for a party. 'You could put a few light wheels in the bushes . . . here – and here.' He shapes a spinning light in his hands, places it carefully in a rose bush, and then springs across the garden on steel-spring legs to position another.

It seems that 109 and 107 Western Avenue were not trashed by the bailiffs, or the builders: they were trashed by one of the squatters – a woman called Debbie, who used to live in the house. 'She'd argued with someone, and they'd accused her of stealing stuff – it got quite nasty, and when they went to Glastonbury, she came in with a couple of people and trashed the place. She had no right to do that.' Dave is indignant. 'She said it was her house, but it wasn't her house – me and Chris broke it, and anyway it's a squat: it belongs to whoever is living there at the time.'

It is sad to think that Roz's righteous anger was

misplaced – sad, too, that the squats should have descended
into squabbling and violence, although it is unlikely they
were ever as carefree as everyone pretended.

The dog that Techno Dave was playing with has found
a new playmate – another Staffordshire terrier, but a
smaller one. The puppy belongs to Shelley, a black woman
with prominent teeth who is wearing a squashy, multi-
coloured velvet hat. Shelley lives on a site behind Allen Way
– she used to live on the seventh floor of a block of flats in
West Kensington, but she is being taken to court for £3,000
rent arrears, and her children have been taken into care.
She used to own another dog – the mother of her puppy –
but it was stolen at Glastonbury. Now, the bigger dog
shakes the rope, and the puppy is thrown across the garden.

– – –

My car breaks down again: it will go forwards, but not
backwards. I cannot afford to have it fixed, which means
I always have to take a passenger to push the car backwards into a parking spot or to reverse it in the crowded
streets around Shepherd's Bush. I buy a bike instead. From
now on, I will cycle through the traffic to visit Western
Avenue.

– – –

By 1927, Western Avenue was known as the 'Road to
Nowhere'. 'Stretching away from Acton across the fields of
West Middlesex . . . is probably the finest bit of road in the
world ever dedicated to lonely moonlight walks for lovers,'
wrote the *Acton Gazette*. The road was complete, but until
the railway bridges were built, the isolated stretches of dual
carriageway were of little use. The dream of a twelve-mile
track providing an escape from 'the madding congestion of

the greater London suburbs' had died: Western Avenue carried 'no more traffic than a country lane'.

— — —

In her back garden one afternoon, Mrs Buchan is sprayed with 'anti-vandal paint' by the bailiffs. 'They're the heavy people – the bailiffs, not the squatters; I'm going to get out because it's going to get heavy round here.'

We are sitting in her kitchen, in the fading heat of a weekday evening. Her case has gone to court, and her house will be repossessed on 17 August. 'The girl from West Hampstead Housing Association, bless her assertive heart, was saying I had to find somewhere and what had I done about it? I'm negotiating buying a house, but the survey report was so catastrophic I was scared of buying it. Then, just before the hearing began, this woman from WHHA said would I accept a self-contained flat in Camden? And I said yes – it just came out yes; I don't really want to live in Camden, but it just came out yes.' She draws a bubble from her lips to demonstrate how it came out; she seems transfixed by the enormity of what she agreed to do.

She went to see the flat she had been offered – a one-bedroom, self-contained flat in the back of a block behind the Euston Road. 'It was the most beautiful flat, but do you know, I couldn't make up my mind! And the woman said you have to tell me by three o'clock this afternoon – and to have that flat would have completely changed my life! It was an enormous decision, and I had to make it by three o'clock.' She knew that if she lived in Camden she would always want to come back to west London. 'I just think you grow roots, that's the trouble – and I'm happy here, really.'

In the end, she decided not to take the flat; instead, she is hoping to buy a house near Acton Town station – another familiar landmark in the geography of her much-loved west London. She has reluctantly accepted that moving is inevitable – 'in the end, of course, the world is bigger than I am' – but she has not accepted her house's fate: it makes her feel ill to watch the neighbouring houses being sealed up, one by one. 'They push the windows out and they leave them hanging. It's like a bomb has gone off inside . . . I'd hate them to do that to my house; I don't want anyone to touch my house.' The thought makes her shiver.

She harbours a dream that the road might still be saved by the 'agitators' she has heard about. 57 Western Avenue – the boarded-up house next door – has a loft, and she sometimes imagines there are people living in it; when the time is right, they will act. 'Apparently, they hide themselves up in trees or something, and then suddenly swoop . . .' she says, vaguely. I cannot tell whether she is serious or not – if so, it is a peculiar fantasy.

I walk up the hill past the squatters' houses and climb the footbridge which arches over the road. A lorry pauses under the bridge, and the metal vibrates beneath my feet. I feel as though I am standing on the back of an animal which has braced its frame against the bridge's fragile struts. Baggsie once talked about 'dropping' this bridge on to the road: bring the bridge down, he suggested, power it up and you'd have a stage for a festival – difficult, he conceded, but not impossible, and well within their capabilities.

The lorry's broad back slips from beneath my feet; I steady myself by clutching the whip-thin metal of the handrail. I do not believe it is within the squatters' capabilities to bring down the bridge, and I know there are no activists hiding in the boarded-up houses on Western Avenue. Mrs Buchan's house will not be saved.

▬ ▬ ▬

The invention of the car had shattered the city's notional limits, said H.G. Wells: by the end of the century, he believed that London would encompass an area the size of Ireland. 'The London citizen of the year 2000 AD may have a choice of nearly all England and Wales south of Nottingham and east of Exeter as his suburb,' he wrote. Wells believed that the car would disperse the city across a wider and wider area – a process which the post-war avant-gardes were intent on resisting. They believed that the city's salvation lay in the creation of an architecture appropriate to the spirit of a mechanized age: 'We must invent and build ex novo our Modern City like an immense and tumultuous shipyard, active, mobile and everywhere dynamic, and the modern building like a gigantic machine,' wrote the futurist, Sant'Elia. Le Corbusier believed the 'beauty of the machine' was 'a new formula' which, if correctly applied, would 'give results of a permanent order'. Having fixed the proportions of the individual house, he began to consider the structure and design of the machine-age city.

▬ ▬ ▬

At 221 Western Avenue, the fence enclosing the back garden has been kicked over, and water bubbles from a pipe sealed inside the house. The weeping willow next door has grown so thick its branches almost fill the garden. For a moment I can smell cut grass – until the traffic resumes again, and the sickly sweet scent of petrol thickens the air.

▬ ▬ ▬

The bailiffs come to 69 Western Avenue one Monday morning in July to find the squatters waiting for them. 'They outnumbered us like the fucking Zulus at Rorke's Drift,' says Don.

The team sent to repossess the house included two policemen, two bailiffs and several workmen. 'They always prepare as though there's going to be a riot,' says Baggsie. There was a riot, of a sort: Baggsie had already been out to buy a crate of extra-strong cider, and by the time the eviction began at 9.00 am, the squatters were 'well gone'. The eviction was another excuse for a party, and when the bailiffs began breaking the windows, the squatters asked if they could join in. 'We got the workmen out of the house and then started lobbing bricks,' says Baggsie. Meanwhile, 'PJ' provided accompaniment on the banjo, and the bailiffs 'did not know what to make of it'.

We are sitting in the long grass at the back of 61 Western Avenue, at a low table which bears a coconut carved into the shape of a monkey. The setting sun slants across the garden, and Baggsie, Don, Techno Dave and Shay are smoking, drinking and talking. Although only 61 Western Avenue now remains habitable, little has changed in the gardens behind the houses.

'There was a serious rainfall last night,' says Don. 'I was just lying awake, thinking of conversations we'd had. People are splitting up, going separate ways. Fucking sad, man, fucking sad.'

'Was it raining last night?' says Techno Dave.

'Too fucking right,' says Don. 'Nice weather.'

'For a frog.'

'Yeah, frog weather.'

It is the hottest summer I have ever known in London. Every night, after the dry, baking heat of the day, the city is treated to a brief, tropical downpour. The squatters have started sleeping in the gardens: behind 67 Western Avenue there is a shack with a low bed, a canvas tent and a rough tepee made from carpets hung over the metal frame of an old swing. The shelters remind me of a description of the homes in Leadville, Colorado: 'Tents; wigwams of boughs; wigwams of bare poles . . . cabins half roofed; cabins with sail-cloth roofs; cabins with no roofs at all – this represented the architecture of the Leadville homes,' wrote a traveller called Helen Hunt Jackson, who visited the town in 1879. Western Avenue was once a frontier town as well; now that the rush to colonize the land has been put into reverse, it is a frontier town again – and its most recent settlers will be among the last to leave.

The contents of the house are arranged on the lawn: a fridge, a cooker, two armchairs, two black-and-white TVs and a scattering of plastic chairs. The speakers that once stood on the window-ledge of number 69 are half-hidden in the long grass behind number 67.

'It was sad moving out – emotional,' says Don.

'Yeah, but it just looked like a corpse once we'd got everything out of it,' says Baggsie.

At first, the squatters thought they would rescue the fridge to try and sell it, and then they thought they might as well take everything else, as well.

'It was a good atmosphere there; good times,' says Don.

He has heard of sixty houses in Plumstead which are like the houses on Western Avenue – 'trashed, rehabbed, and squatted'.

'I don't want to go to Plumstead,' says Techno Dave.

'Yeah, but if you had sixty squats together, man . . .'

Don wants to stay until the apples are ripe so he can sell them, but I do not believe he will do it: many schemes are conceived in the long summer afternoons in the squatters' garden, but few of them come to anything. Recently, life has become harder: there are guards on the skips behind the supermarket where they used to scavenge for food, and the houses and gardens have been stripped of anything of value; it is time to move on. Don has another plan – and it is one which sounds more realistic: 'Find out when we're gonnae get fucked oot of the house – and then party, man.' Later, he might go to Cornwall to pick strawberries and save up enough money to buy a car; then he will drive to the south of France.

Jenny arrives, drunk, trampling through the long grass in heavy boots and shorts. She has just been for another interview for a job she thought she had already secured – she is going to Ireland to look after the children of a family who spend their summers there. 'Rich people always think you've got the money for fares,' she complains. "Just come and meet the kids again,"' she mimics her employer's upper-class accent. 'I've already met the kids four times.'

On the tube coming back to Western Avenue, she met a guy called Tom, who asked her where she lived; as the doors of his train closed, he told her he had got beaten up and robbed by people who lived in a squat on Western Avenue. 'Yeah, I remember Tom,' says Techno Dave. 'He was a smackhead and he left needles lying around – we came back from a rave once, and found two needles lying on the floor downstairs, so the boys walked him upstairs and said, "Pack your bags, you're out . . ." He was a dirty bugger, as well – used to shit in a plastic bag, and leave it lying around. You know, we had two kids in the house . . .'

I walk over to number 69 with Baggsie; we sit on the table behind the house, and he picks at his cast, which is coming off his leg tomorrow. 'Full marks to the surgeon – I can't feel any bruising, can't feel any pain . . .' He looks at the house, and the thought of the eviction makes him smile:

'It was just hugely enjoyable, turning their preconceptions right upside down.'

The dried earth is sprinkled with shattered glass and fragments of lead from the windows, which are now sealed with plywood boards. 'When they're doing an eviction nowadays, it just costs so much money – I mean, it's been read in Chambers on the Strand, so that's going to cost a few thousand, and then there's the cost of getting everybody together on the right day. It must be getting up to a five-figure sum, just to get one house . . . It would be cheaper just to come round and ask us.'

An old computer has been set up on a table in the garden behind number 67: as the squatters moved their belongings across the more or less imaginary boundary separating 67 from 69, each one pretended to log on to the terminal. The wiring is in place for a sound system: at the last minute, when the bailiffs come, they will unplug it and disappear. We wander back through the garden; someone has pinned an eviction notice on a tent behind number 63. 'The way things are going,' says Baggsie, 'I wouldn't be surprised to see eviction notices stuck on here, here, and here . . .' He gestures at the shelters dotted round the wilderness. I let myself out through 61 Western Avenue. The sitting-room which opens on to the garden is unpleasantly warm; suspended from the lampshade is a ring of flies, which tilts and turns in the still air like a child's mobile. The sofa has burst, and its stuffing spills across the floor.

– – –

On the flat summit of the hill between Western Circus and Gipsy Corner, the back gardens of the abandoned houses are wildly overgrown: spilled rubble clutters a semi-circle of grass outside the back doors, but further back the plants and trees have grown up thickly – the fringe of a forest on the edge of the territory marked out by the car.

This is the land which was once Barker's Field – a fact which might explain the richness and resilience of the gardens. If the cars were re-routed, nature would quickly reclaim the land; the trees and grass would rupture the tarmac, scale the central reservation and spiderish footbridge, and absorb the houses. Seventy years after their crops were uprooted, the plot-holders have received compensation of a kind: on Barker's Field, and in the squatters' gardens, nature is resurgent.

6. Oxblood Junction

'I enjoyed my time at the Scrubs – if "enjoy" is the right word: it's a bit like saying did Christ enjoy the Crucifixion?'

For eight years, the Reverend Gerald Arnott served as the Roman Catholic chaplain at Wormwood Scrubs, Western Avenue's neighbourhood prison. 'The job satisfaction is high. You always know that you're needed. People always say "do you make any converts?" – well, you don't make converts, necessarily, though some find faith; some have time to think for perhaps the first time in their lives, on some of the fundamental issues of life – where they're going, and what's at the end of it all. There's so much suffering – particularly at Wormwood Scrubs, where you have one of the main life centres in the country. You get guys coming in there for the first three or four years of their life sentences – you get to know all the stars, as they call them.'

It is a Sunday afternoon. Several months have passed since I first called at the Rev. Arnott's house, which stands opposite the Johnsons', on Barker's Field. He was about to watch a rugby match, and he suggested that I call back.

The Reverend Arnott is a friendly man, with a pleasantly unrevealing face, dressed in the uniform of an off-duty priest – dark trousers, pullover, and a jacket. Something in his scrupulously polite manner suggests that he regards talking to me as an act of Christian duty, but he is approachable – he has to be: it is the main requirement of his work since he left the Prison Service and became Aids Pastoral Care Co-ordinator in the Diocese of Westminster. 'The only thing I can do is make sure that people know that we're there, and if they want to come to us for counselling or advice or if they just want to come to a place of safety, confidentiality, where we can help them cope with the problems of anxiety, depression, grief, guilt – whatever; we will try and care for them.'

He answers my questions with a measured calm, saying little more than is strictly necessary. A crucifix hangs on the wall behind his head. He came to London in 1953 as a bank clerk, and left to train for the priesthood in 1961. 'But that's another book,' he says, politely deflecting my curiosity about his vocation.

His career in the Church started with four years' service at Westminster Cathedral. Then his long-running association with west London began: he worked at a church in East Acton, and later at another in Acton High Street before he went to Wormwood Scrubs in 1976. In 1984, he left to become a senior chaplain to the Prison Service. Although he had sixty-five prisons to look after, with a chaplaincy in each, he was based at the Young Offenders' Institute at Feltham. He is accustomed to the fact that people are curious about his work – 'As soon as they hear you've been a prison chaplain, their ears prick up' – but I do not ask him about his experiences in more detail because I know he would not tell me anything.

When he left the Prison Service eleven years ago, he was no longer entitled to a 'quarter'. He decided to buy a house, and he needed to find one large enough to accommodate himself and the nurse who acts as his housekeeper. During his service in the parishes of Acton, he had often visited Western Avenue; he knew the road, and liked it, and the houses beside it lay within their budget. 'I don't mind telling you we got this house for £45,000 eleven years ago, at the height of the property boom – £100,000 wouldn't buy you

a decent house like this anywhere else. The room sizes are
simply marvellous, and there are no cracks anywhere in the
walls. They were built by the Goldsmith's estate, and they
were great houses, with wonderful foundations; the sadness
is that they are all going to disappear.' He indicates the
room we are sitting in: it is simply furnished, with a dining-
room table and bookshelves, but it is light and spacious.

At the Inquiry in 1989, Gerald Arnott had suggested
that a tunnel should be built through the hill, from Western
Circus to Gipsy Corner, restoring what he calls 'this lovely
road' to its original condition. He was told it was not
possible because the water table was too high – to which he
replies that if you can tunnel beneath the Channel, then
surely you can tunnel beneath Western Avenue. 'A project
like this is about people's lives being destroyed – that's
really the problem, and you can't put a price on that, and
say it's cheaper this way than that. One always gets the
feeling it's not the prime consideration: what is it doing to
people's lives?'

His own house will remain untouched, yet he is concerned by the fate of his neighbours, who were once his
parishioners. He is also dreading the inconvenience of the
next few years – 'the dust and the filth' which the roadworks will entail. As he shows me to the door, a small dog,
a terrier, ricochets between his feet, like a balloon tied to
his shoes. On the far side of the road, the charred façade of
the house flanking the Johnsons' stands as a warning of the
destruction to come.

– – –

The ground floor of the car showroom used to be made of
glass – its wraparound windows displayed ranks of stationary cars to the passing motorists. Now, it is sealed in

oxblood metal plates. 'Our Other Main Depot is Twice as Big', says a sign on the top of the building.

– – –

Outside the subway, Mrs Jackson is resting on the low wall fronting one of her neighbours' houses. She stands, cautiously, and rests her weight on my arm; she has been ill and she is very frail. Then some of her old energy returns: 'The gipsies have gotta go – all, all, gotta go!' She gestures up and down the row of houses, as if she were brushing the unwanted tenants off the road. 'All the people who donna own their houses, they gotta go, because the council donna own them – the Department of Transport do, and they're going to sell. All gotta go!'

– – –

In 1922, Le Corbusier exhibited plans for 'A Contemporary City of Three Million Inhabitants' – a vision of the city rebuilt for the machine age. Three years later, he exhibited the 'Voisin Plan for Paris' – the result of applying his theories to the capital of France. Le Corbusier envisaged launching a 'frontal attack on the most diseased quarters' – entire districts, such as Le Marais, would be demolished to make room for a grid of skyscrapers. The 'flattened-out' city would disappear, and Paris would rise to its feet, 'open to light and air, clear and radiant and sparkling'. Le Corbusier thought it was appropriate that the Voisin motor company had funded the scheme: 'The motor has killed the great city; the motor must save the great city,' he wrote.

– – –

'This is the lowest I can go,' says William Conlin. 'I have to have some sort of standards, you know.'
    He has moved from a self-contained flat to a room in a

shared house which the council declared uninhabitable, but
he is not complaining. 'I just think, well it could be worse –
I could be selling the *Big Issue*, you know what I mean?'
He laughs contentedly. 'I like this place – it's OK.'

He flicks off the overhead light, and leans over the table
set up in the middle of the room – William has converted
the spare room in his new house into a darkroom. He now
lives in The Approach – a side-road which joins Western
Avenue above Western Circus, between the pedestrian footbridge and the first of the railway bridges.

The glass in the front door is shattered, and the Housing
Association has posted a sign on the front window asking
people not to squat the house, for it has been allocated for
people in need. When I knocked on his door, William
opened the window above my head and shouted down. 'It's
lovely to see you again,' he said, as he led me upstairs. The
house was cold and smelt damp: the floorboards were bare
and uneven, and the walls unpainted; upstairs, the spare
room was stacked with rotting newspapers, and a leather
harness hung on a coatrack beside a locked door. I asked
William what it was for, and he told me his housemate
owns a pit-bull: it is a muzzle and lead for the dog.

William drew up a stool for me in the darkroom and
busied himself with a sheet of negatives. The doors and
windows of the unfurnished room are sealed with cloths
and tapes. He turns on the enlarger's carefully focused
beam for a minute, and then drops a sheet of paper into
one of the trays of liquid ranged behind him. He says he
likes having people to watch him work, and he is happy to
talk at the same time.

The traffic is worse than it was in his flat beside Gipsy
Corner, for the road runs parallel to his new house and its
strip of garden. 'It narrows to four lanes just out there
because of that bridge, and the traffic is sitting there most

of the day – there's a big jam one way in the morning, and a big jam the other way in the evening . . . Sometimes there's a big jam both ways.' He laughs unrestrainedly, and the noise is startlingly loud in the darkened room. 'Where I was before, I had the back of the house, and if you sat out in the garden, you wouldn't hear any traffic. But here, I mean . . . The guys wanted to do a barbecue, but I don't think there's any point because it's not pleasant to sit out in the garden. And that's what a barbecue is about, isn't it? To sit there, and relax.'

Imperfect though it is, they must enjoy their garden while they can, for half of it has been set aside for the new road; having consumed his old flat, the road will now encroach upon his new one. Yet William believes there is much to be grateful for – he likes his housemates and his neighbours, who are from Thailand, and his work is going well. 'I'll show you what I'm working on – it's really interesting.' He transfers the developing image from one tray to another, turns on the overhead light, and unclips a photograph from a line spanning the far wall. He passes it across the table: it is a portrait of a dreadlocked black man; it is still damp.

'This guy is a poet, right? He's a Rasta man, you know? I'll tell you what it is . . . basically, he tells biblical stories – parables, so there's a message in every story or poem, you know? Anyway, the portrait I did of him he got published, so he came back to me for another portrait . . .' The story takes a long time to tell, for he is concentrating on choosing the next image to print from a pile of contact sheets. The poet showed the photographs to some friends of his, who liked it, and decided they wanted William to illustrate the sleeve of their next record. 'I really want to do that record cover – I'll do the business cover, right? They've already given me a copy of their single, and it's really good. It's the business. I'm not crazy about the lyrics, but the music is definitely bang on . . . So things are looking up.'

He flicks the light off again, and a wash of red light floods his face. It is no surprise that William spent his compensation money on a new camera. I ask him about the other Housing Association tenants. 'No one became homeless, but quite a lot of people went private, and quite a lot of people got flats up in Gunnersbury Lane – but that's due for demolition as well, so it's all short life. We just seem to be moved on and on from one problem place to the next. But it's the best you can do – you can't give everybody a penthouse, can you? No one suffered major hardship.'

There is only one thing he does not like about his new home: his bedroom is full of dust. 'Somebody said to me the other day, you should get one of those bicycle masks, those Ventilair things . . . Jesus, man! Start walking around in one of them . . .' He drops the photographic paper in its developing fluid, and leans over the tray as the image emerges; he seems content.

– – –

The squats are sealed, and a frosting of glass coats the grass, so it crunches underfoot. There is a medley of junk scattered across the squatters' wilderness: the computer terminal, a tartan skirt, a leather briefcase, an unused tampon, a ski, a sink, a washing machine, five televisions, a pair of crutches and a yellow hula-hoop. 'LEGALISE FREE-DOM', says the first of the slogans scratched into the fresh oxblood paint. 'ENJOY LIFE – FUCK THE SYSTEM'.

– – –

Four years after the plotters had been evicted from their land, work finally began on the railway bridges beside

Barker's Field. The bridges were completed by August 1928; Western Circus had been connected to Gipsy Corner at last. 'We are entering upon a new concrete age,' claimed the *Acton Gazette* in a lovingly detailed account of the technical achievements embodied in the road's construction. Western Avenue – once known as the road ending in a field – was now 'one of the finest thoroughfares in the London area'.

– – –

A stencil is beginning to appear on the house-fronts beside Gipsy Corner – a cartoon sketch of an alien's oval head, with slit eyes and dotted nostrils: 'SPACEMAN – INTER-GALACTIC CHRIST', says the slogan beneath it. Under-neath the branches of the willow tree in the back garden of 223 Western Avenue, the earth is cool and soft. If I wanted somewhere to sleep on Western Avenue, then this is the place I would choose. It is September. In the back garden of a neighbouring house, a crab apple tree has spilled its fruit across the garden; inside the house, I can hear running water, and the grass beside the back door is pulpy under-foot. Slumped against the garden fence is a yellow plastic bag marked 'Clinical Waste'. It is easy to imagine disease spreading in these conditions. The unbroken line of dark-red armour plating which seals the abandoned houses from Western Circus to Gipsy Corner earns the road a new nickname – the Oxblood Junction.

– – –

There are guard dogs and security guards patrolling the lane behind Joan Shaw's house, and she is horrified to see that many of the houses owned by the Department of Transport are being sealed by the bailiffs. 'It's horrendous!

They're smashing up the inside, smashing the windows, and boarding them up. I gather that there have been a lot of squatters on the other side of the bridge, and they wanted to stop that . . . But I mean, it's crazy – even if they are squatters, then so what? These people need homes, and it's better they have them – at the end of the day, that's what it's all about. Why should we deprive them, when they're there for the taking?'

Work has begun at Gipsy Corner: on the westbound carriageway, the gardens have been cleared of trees and shrubs, and the houses stripped of their fittings. Spot-lit, and sealed within a corral of metal fencing, the buildings look like macabre show-homes, on display to the passing cars.

Joan Shaw finds it strange to watch the houses on the opposite side of the road being demolished, but she understands at least why it is being done: she does not understand why the houses surrounding her own are being vandalized. 'It would be different if they were in bad condition, you could understand it – you know, close them up – but they were in good condition, and I gather this place down here, which they've just boarded up, had just been refurbished; I cannot for the life of me see why it was necessary to do that. They say they're going to rebuild the houses and re-sell them, but you can't turn round and say that, after you'd smashed up sinks, toilets, pipes, the lot, and torn all the carpets and tanks out . . .'

She has written letters of complaint to the council and to a newspaper, but she recognizes it will make little difference. She is losing patience with the authorities, and her grudging respect for the squatters is partly due to the fact that she has heard exaggerated reports of their attempts to delay the beginning of the roadworks. 'They're the people who are doing it – I mean, you've got to admit, you know, we've done nothing about it, we've allowed them to get away with murder.'

I do not tell her how little the squatters have done.

One morning, someone told her there was a Compulsory Purchase Order on her front gate; it had been there for several days, but because they never use the front door, they had not seen it. 'So I came straight back in, out the front and yanked it off the gate. I thought, cheek of them! It wasn't just that, it was the whole thing . . . Oh, I suppose I can't say it's really affected me – I just think it's very sad that the place is such a mess, and there's so little you can do about it. I can't imagine what it's going to be like.'

They are losing half their front garden, and they are not satisfied with the money they have been offered as compensation. From her perspective, there is one piece of good news: the gipsies have been given Notice to Quit; most have left already. I walk past the fences and gates that seal the back entrances to the houses on Western Avenue: 'NO PARKING – GATES IN USE', says each one, almost without exception. It is not just the Shaws who have found the entrance to their home blocked by other people's cars and lorries. The back of 276 Western Avenue – which is home to a gipsy family – is open to the road, and the lawn has been replaced by a concrete platform on which a lorry and a Mitsubishi jeep are parked. Through the latticed windows, I can see a giant television set playing to an empty room, but there is no answer when I knock at the door.

I cross the junction at Gipsy Corner. The back of the building site has not been sealed. I stand in the passageway that separates the Greens' house from its neighbour, and watch the cars passing behind the metal grille; the tyres hiss through the junction, which is silver-slick with rain. On the far side of the road, every fourth or fifth house is sealed behind the bailiff's metal shields.

– – –

Three or four workmen in hardhats are loading a lorry parked beside the Westway, and two others are crossing the raked earth of the site towards the open gate. It is dusk, and they are carrying a bone-white bath, its plumbing still attached. The roof and the side of one house have been removed to reveal a bedroom wall decorated with a series of murals – the squat art Roz remembered with such fondness: there is a red-eyed alien, a butterfly, and the spreading golden rays of the sun. 'FUCK YOU', says a sign on the wall of a neighbouring house. The white-helmeted head of a workman emerges from between the rafters. 'MERRY XMAS CUNT', says the slogan on the wall beneath him.

It is the beginning of October, and demolition work has begun on the Westway. The houses that line the approach to Western Circus are stripped of doors and window-frames; reduced to brick skeletons, they are uncluttered, and oddly beautiful.

– – –

'Well, we might as well be in Timbuktu.'

When I drew up outside the Greens' new house in Hayes, Mr Green was waiting in the front garden. Despite the meticulous directions Robin had given me on the phone, I got lost several times after I left the M4, for Hayes is composed of one apparently identical street after another – 'inter-war suburbia of a rather nondescript type', as Robin had put it.

Mr Green drew steadily on his pipe and waited impassively while I parked the car. He did not react as I walked towards him, and for a moment I wondered whether I was interrupting him in the observance of a regular ritual. Then I remembered that Mr Green takes my visits seriously – having considered what he had to say, he had come out to the road to meet me.

'You see, our daughter lives in that house over there,' he said, pointing across the road with his pipe. 'It was her who wanted us to come and live here. She found this house for us.' The Greens like to call themselves 'the Neighbourhood Watch', because they sit and watch their daughter's family come and go on the other side of the road. It is their only contact with the local community. 'As for the rest . . . well!' Mr Green takes his pipe from his mouth, and looks at it sternly: the implication is clear – the natives in Timbuktu would make them feel more at home.

Courteously, Mr Green invites me inside their new home. Although there is one downstairs sitting-room, as opposed to two separate rooms, the house is remarkably similar to the Greens' home on Western Avenue. The Greens complain that the house is smaller, but it feels lighter and more spacious to me – an impression I attribute to the calm which prevails in the residential neighbourhood. Since the Greens did not notice the traffic on Western Avenue in the first place, it is not surprising that they do not appreciate it absence.

Typically, Mrs Green is making the best of things. 'The family were more upset about the move than we were,' she says, stoutly. As always, her hospitality is scrupulously exact, and she serves tea and cake before she sits down. 'Edwina was crying and Christopher was crying, because they were brought up there; I just shut it all out, and we've been so busy, as well.'

She says Hayes is like a country market town: she walks to the bottom of the road, gets a bus into town and discovers everything she needs – banks, shops, building societies, and so on. 'It's a marvellous place for buses,' adds Mr Green. It is not only Robin who takes a keen interest in public transport; Mr Green's enthusiastic appreciation of London's buses has survived the move from Western Avenue.

Ironically, Heathrow's air traffic troubled them more when they lived on Western Avenue: they couldn't sit out in their garden in the summer because of the planes flying overhead. Now, although they are much closer to the airport, the planes don't affect them 'one iota'. Robin, who clattered down the stairs a minute ago, has an important qualification to add: they have not, as yet, 'endured all weather patterns as regards Heathrow'; there may be days when the planes are noisy.

Robin gestures towards the sliding doors which open on to the narrow garden at the back of the house. 'This particular property, with its aspect to the south, looks over bungalows, and the land falls slightly down to the M4 and Heathrow, so the horizon is much more open from the rear elevation of this property, and therefore much more exposed to noise sources than my sister who enjoys the benefit of being screened by two-storey semi-detached houses. Still, I'm not particularly sorry to have left Western Avenue – notwithstanding the proximity of the Nestlé coffee factory, which sends out huge roasted coffee bean aromas now and then, depending on the direction of the wind, the environment is a lot better out here.'

Two weeks ago, Mr and Mrs Green went back to look at their old house, and were shocked by the damage. Robin was not surprised – not only had he known what to expect when the bailiffs took possession, but he had helped them by draining the water from the taps and disabling the electricity. For Robin Green, observing the rituals of government procedure is a kind of religious practice.

Perhaps I should have anticipated how he would engage with his new neighbourhood, but I had forgotten the extent of his obsession with bureaucratic procedure. 'It's a bit of a challenge,' he replies, when I ask him how he has settled in the area. 'It's a different situation getting up in the morning, and not having to be on automatic pilot. It's stimulating having to find your way around the area, and I'm still learning about it. My life hasn't changed much, but what I'm surprised about is the difference in the service delivery achievements of this borough, compared to the London Borough of Ealing. It's a poorer borough, in some respects, yet the council tax bill is twenty per cent higher than in Ealing. The educational facilities seem to be well endowed, and the children accordingly well adjusted, but the mainten-ance of public streets and open spaces compares unfavour-ably even with the darkest corners of East Acton. I was astonished to find grass growing up between the tiles in the tennis courts on the local park! I'm not obsessed with the piles of broken glass everywhere, but the prevalence of litter on the streets is indicative of a wider inattention to detail – my experience of local councils, and the way they operate, tells me it is symptomatic of deeper problems in the running of the council.'

I had not asked him to assess the performance of his local council, but he finds the subject irresistible. Within weeks of arriving in Hayes, Robin has assessed the emotional maturity of the local children, and delivered a verdict on the state of the local tennis courts. Plainly, he has settled well in his new neighbourhood – better than his parents, at least.

'I find it lonely,' says Mrs Green, abandoning the pre-tence that the move was an easy one. 'I go shopping every morning, because I'm not content. I haven't settled down yet. We've been spoiled, that's our trouble. We go off to

Ireland, and it's as different as chalk and cheese. Everyone talks to you wherever you go – then you come back here, you can pass dozens of people in the streets, and they don't even say good morning. I went out the other morning, and I said to Freddie, I said hello to several people, and they said nothing. It takes a lot of getting used to.'

— — —

Three years ago, the Parkers collected a cat for their children from the Cats Protection League. Two days later, the Cats Protection League came and took it back. The Parkers were told they were not allowed to keep a cat, because they lived on Western Avenue. They live 500 yards beyond Gipsy Corner, in the last house that will be affected by the redevelopment. When the flyover is built, it will encroach upon the bank that separates them from the road.

— — —

Outside Mrs Buchan's house, there are workmen mapping the fencing that will seal the abandoned houses from the road. One is digging holes for fence-posts in the churned earth; he is working with his bare hands. Parked in the lay-by where the travellers' vans once stood, there is a recovery vehicle and a caravan for its two-man crew: one man is sleeping, curled up in a bed under the window which faces uphill; the other sits at the other end of the caravan, drinking tea and staring at the oncoming traffic.

— — —

There is a blue Volvo parked in the Johnsons' drive, beneath the hanging basket on which I banged my head when I first visited the house ten months ago. The neighbouring houses have been gutted and pinned behind metal fences. I ring the doorbell, and a man opens the door; I do not recognize him. I ask if Mr Johnson is in, and he closes the door in my face; it opens a moment later.

'Who are you?'

I explain, and he opens the door wider. Mr Johnson is standing behind him. Cautiously, he invites me inside. The door opens directly into a gloomy, unlit sitting-room. There are papers spread on a table in the front room. The window overlooking the road is sealed roughly with a tarpaulin. It seems incredible that they are still living here. The other man stands close to Mr Johnson, as though he has been hired to protect him.

'I can't talk to you now,' says Mr Johnson. 'I'm busy. The council are trying to find us somewhere to live, but they keep offering us crap.'

I write down my number again, and Mr Johnson promises to call me; I do not believe he will.

I cross the road, and walk down the hill towards Gipsy Corner. The houses that stand above the traffic lights are derelict, and their gardens piled with rubble, yet there are two yellow balloons flying above the door of 201 Western Avenue, and a dull light glows in the hall: this must be where Colette lives. I ring the bell, and a middle-aged woman opens the door. I have time to notice that she has dirty-blonde hair, but little else, as I tell her that I would like to talk to her about the road. She looks at me sullenly.

'How much are you going to pay me?'

Nothing, I say.

'Well, you can piss off, then; go and write your own fucking book – go and write it yourself.'

She slams the door in my face. Mrs Buchan had warned me that she was angry.

- - -

By 1927, nearly 130 miles of arterial roads had been completed, and another 73 miles were under construction. 'The roads are anybody's and everybody's now,' wrote *The Times*. 'They are bare, open, shadeless and shameless, as shiny as steel and as hard as the rigours of commerce . . . They suggest power and purpose: and power and purpose have their charm, no less than the gentle, casual air of the old roads. And the steely surface, in sunshine or in rain, can take on lovely colours of many shades. It reflects trees and clouds almost like water. It lures, as the surface of a river lures, to embark upon it and see the world.' But the article conceded that for those with 'eyes to see and love the beauties of the English countryside', there was 'a deep and apprehensive interest in the question of their threatened destruction by the pick and shovel of the arterial road architect'.

— — —

I am standing inside the remains of a house on the Westway: its walls are represented by knee-deep lines of bricks and there are mountainous piles of debris on the cratered earth – torn squares of lino, rafters, office chairs, an Ali Baba laundry basket, radiators, doors, carpets and an upturned bath. It is the middle of November. Two workmen are dancing on the pavement further west: one is black, one is white; both wear luminous green overalls. Inside the site, a yellow earth-mover, swivelling awkwardly on the rubble beneath its tracks, sends its hinged arm crashing through the remnants of a house.

— — —

'I wish I hadn't spoken to you now. How do I know that you are what you say you are? You could be anyone.'

I was surprised when I realized it was Mr Jackson on

the phone. 'I got a letter this morning,' he said, belligerently, without bothering to introduce himself. He went to
find it, and when he came back he seemed distracted. As
he read the letter through, he hardly seemed aware that he
was talking to anyone else. The letter was from a firm of
solicitors offering to act as his agent in negotiating compensation from the Department of Transport. He is adamant
that he will have nothing to do with them, for he is
convinced they will cheat him – if they have not done so
already. I suddenly realize he thinks I have something to do
with the solicitors. It takes me ten minutes to convince Mr
Jackson that I am, in fact, a writer.

— — —

Snow is falling, as thin and mean as rain, as I cycle past the
first building site on the Westway. It is the beginning of
December. The bulldozers have cleared the white-ribbed
ground: the wooden fences conceal nothing other than a
strip of flattened earth 100 yards deep and 600 yards long.
It is hard to imagine there were ever houses here.

They have fenced off the houses in Mrs Buchan's block.
In the thick, grey afternoon light, the fence seems to go on
for ever; standing at Western Circus, and looking up the
hill, I cannot see where it ends. I cycle to Gipsy Corner, and
climb over a pile of discarded roof-beams to enter the site
beside the road; a nail drives into the heel of my boot. The
roof has been lifted off each house, and their chimneys jut
into the dusky, dark-grey sky. Snow falls though the rafters,
and softens the profiles of the houses.

Although it is only four o'clock, it is almost dark, and
the lamp-posts are invisible – the flat lozenges of the street
lamps seem to be suspended from invisible threads. Patches
of pink, yellow and blue wallpaper are exposed inside the
houses, but everything else is muddied, black and grimy. In

the Greens' house, the floorboards have been taken up, revealing the foundations which divide the house into a series of shallow pits. The house is no more than a geometric puzzle, a series of interlocking boxes: with its structures revealed, its pretensions to being worthy of affection are destroyed.

— — —

Western Avenue was opened to through-traffic from Western Circus to Hanger Hill in September 1929. Three days later, the road claimed its first victim when a pedestrian was knocked down by a car. The lack of proper lighting was said to be the cause of the accident.

— — —

When the land currently occupied by the condemned houses becomes a grass verge beside the road, William plans to come back and plant a tree where his house used to stand. 'Where one builds, one plants trees,' wrote Le Corbusier, quoting a Turkish proverb. 'With us they are uprooted. Stamboul is an orchard: our towns are stone quarries.'

— — —

Before she left Western Avenue, Mrs Buchan rented space to store the contents of her house in a depot in Ealing – they gave her a key, she said, so she could go and stroke her furniture whenever she wanted.

— — —

Four years ago, the Reverend Gerald Arnott was called out to give the last rites to one of his neighbours. She was found in an empty bath by her handyman, who was 'like a son to her'. She had been there since three o'clock the day before – when she had tried to get out, she had found she could not move, so she had pulled the plug out of the bath and waited for help to arrive. She was French, or Belgian, and she insisted that everyone should call her 'Madame'. She had lived on the road for sixty years. Madame died the following day with hypothermia; three months ago, Gerald Arnott conducted the funeral of the handyman who had discovered Madame dead in her bath.

— — —

The Greens' house has been destroyed: all that remains is a pile of bricks which marks out the space it once occupied. In the half-light, they are clean, pale grey and look newly minted, like freshly turned earth on a grave. It is 16 December; almost a year has passed since I first came to Western Avenue. Balanced on top of the fence-post at the entrance to the next site is a doll's head with flowing brown hair and a cocktail of blood and dirt smeared on its mouth – a voodoo icon, guarding the site against the clamorous ghosts of the people who once lived here.

PART TWO: 1996

The act of design is opposed to the record in stone of human habitation.

Richard Sennett, *The Conscience of the Eye:*
the Design and Social Life of Cities

A legitimate complaint against suburbia is that it spreads itself too widely. As the motorist drives out of town along his concreted highway, his hopes of green fields are frustrated mile after mile, and when the single ribbon of highway breaks away ... into deep bastions of residential development, the motorist sees with alarm a future England that has become, in effect, one enormous built-up area.

J. M. Richards, *Castles on the Ground*

7. Cloud City

Buffeted by contradictory currents and half-submerged in Western Avenue's sluggish tide, the cars slop through the narrowing banks of the junction. They are stationary for seconds at a time – I could cross the road by stepping from the crocodile-snout of one bonnet to another.

It is February, the second month of a new year on Western Avenue. My breath hangs heavily in the air, as do the fumes expelled by the slow-moving cars at Western Circus. The buildings beside the eastbound carriageway measure the traffic's advance as it edges towards the centre of London, yard by yard, house by house. The houses seem so solid and securely rooted it is difficult to imagine the road without them, but Western Avenue's southern boundary was once lined with similar buildings, and it is now stripped bare. To the west, it is fringed by a stretch of empty, rutted land; to the east, the arm of an earth-mover extends through a gap in the fencing on the Westway, and rears upwards, poised as if to drag the cars off the road. I am waiting for signs that the work is about to begin.

– – –

For the time being, Western Avenue ran across open fields: to the west, footpaths bracketed the road as it climbed towards Gipsy Corner; to the east, beyond a broad stretch of parkland, stood the 'forbidding walls' of Wormwood Scrubs prison ('an imposing pile, standing, however, a sufficient distance away, and well removed from all other buildings', added a local guidebook, in a flurry of nervous gentility); to the south lay the village of East Acton – the high-water mark of the tide of brick and tarmac soon to engulf the land.

In 1928, the *Acton Gazette* published an enthusiastic appreciation of a 'fine house' which was being built at Western Circus: it was, it said, a 'distinct acquisition to a district which already boasted considerable architectural beauties'. Within a year, the house was sold to a doctor called William Hunt – the first settler had arrived on Western Avenue. Soon afterwards, the Borough of Acton received an application from a developer called Charles Peppiatt to build four pairs of semi-detached houses, in brick, with tile roofs, on Western Avenue's northern boundary; following amendments to the specification of the drains, the application was approved. (Etched in white on an oxblood transparency, the architect's plans are still preserved in the council vaults.)

Soon, the hillside above Western Circus was cobwebbed with the brick and timber frames of half-built houses, and adverts for 'charmingly situated and well-built villas' began to appear in the local newspaper. In 1930, Dr Hunt's neighbours began to arrive on the road. The new residents gave names to their houses, and the titles they chose are indicative of the spirit in which they began life on the edge of the city: one house was called Bienvenue and another Westernville – as though it alone commanded the western approach to London.

– – –

Le Corbusier's 'Contemporary City' was structured around two 'great arterial roads for fast one-way traffic'. Built on immense reinforced concrete bridges, and approached every half-mile by subsidiary roads, the arterial roads run from north to south, and from east to west. Traffic circulates freely within the Contemporary City, enhancing its cultural and commercial life and liberating its citizens, who no longer live 'like hunted animals'. The arterial roads intersect in the Central Station, which stands at the heart of the Contemporary City amongst the skyscrapers which house the city's business district. Where most utopias envisage a public assembly – a parliament or public square – Le Corbusier had positioned a transport terminus. His philosophy was simple: a city made for speed is made for success.

– – –

A long-winded graffiti-artist has gone to work on the hoarding outside Mrs Buchan's house: 'THIS IS A DIRTY EXHAUST AREA – A Local'; 'GO AWAY, DIRTYS!'; 'IF YOUR EXHAUST IS CLEAN, WHY NOT SIT IN YOUR GARAGE AND RUN YOUR ENGINE?' Each slogan runs on for ten or fifteen yards. It is dusk – the end of a metallic winter's day in March. The headlights of each car light up the back of the car ahead, but pools of darkness lie between them. As the drivers climb the hill at walking pace, they spell out the messages, word by word: 'NEVER . . . IN . . . THE . . . HISTORY . . . OF . . . POLLUTION'; then the traffic leaps ahead, and the last words – 'HASSOLITTLE-BEENDONEFORSOMANY' – pass in a blur.

At Gipsy Corner, they are skinning the car showroom: the building's massy flesh has been removed, revealing the brittle yellow skeleton which lay beneath it.

– – –

The queues of cars which besiege London today began their vigil in the twenties. Car ownership was not to match the levels enjoyed in America for many years, yet by 1927 the idea

of banning cars from the centre of London had already been
proposed, and *The Times* was complaining of the 'unmeasured millions of loss caused by the traffic delays of today'.

No one doubted that Western Avenue would become a
busy road, but no one saw anything to fear in the prospect.
In fact, they welcomed it: the 'enterprising traders' who
opened shops at Western Circus were said to have 'great
faith in the future possibilities of what is likely to become a
great artery for traffic', and the cars which would bring
prosperity to Western Avenue were not seen as a threat to
the road's future – it would remain a pleasant place to live.
'Trees have already been planted at the side of the footpaths, showing that the road is to be of the nature of a
boulevard,' said the *Acton Gazette*.

The shops at Western Circus were completed in 1930,
and an estate agent, a bank and a tobacconist soon opened
for business. Later, a hotel was built on the southern side
of the junction, and a firm of undertakers set up nearby. In
1931, Mrs Enid Leslie opened the Cake and Candy Shop at
26 Western Avenue; her advertising boasted that she used
'only the best and purest ingredients'. She soon had competition when a woman called I.V. Morgan opened a cakeshop, The Mascot, on the other side of the road.

In 1931, more than sixty houses were built beside Western Avenue, and the building that would later become the
bingo hall opened as a 'picture theatre'. A new cinema was
opening every three or four days in Britain. Eighty per cent
of the films they showed were from Hollywood, and it has
been suggested that the settlers in the suburbs saw, in the
legends of the Wild West, a reflection of their own lives on
the expanding frontiers of Britain's cities. America's frontier
towns promised prosperity, and so did Western Avenue; the
West threw up fragile communities, devoid of history,

composed of immigrants to the area – and so did the
suburbs and the arterial roads.

The allure of clean air and open spaces which had
prompted the exodus to suburbia persuaded a new breed of
industrialists to desert the city as well. Charles Colston –
the managing director of Hoover – believed that a 'factory
in the slums quickly becomes a slum factory', and in 1931
he chose a site at Perivale for his company's new factory,
claiming that it was 'magnificently placed for road and
rail transport and for the housing of our workers'. Land
for playing fields – then considered an essential amenity for
the workers – was readily available, and the new factory
would overlook Ealing Golf Course, which would 'never be
built on': Colston's 'factory in the country' would remain
just that. The American fashion for single-storey factories
'prominently placed along the highways and dramatically
floodlit at night', had been imported intact to Britain, and
Colston employed Thomas Wallis – the leading architect of
'daylight factories' – to design the Hoover Building.

Even the prospect of industrial development was treated
with equanimity: the new factories which had begun to
appear beside the road to the east of Gipsy Corner, were
'pleasant looking structures, with gardens that would do
credit to private villas', said the *Acton Gazette*. So long as
'no objectionable industries' were permitted on the border-
land between houses and factories, there was no cause for
concern. Western Avenue, it seemed, was promised both
peace and prosperity.

– – –

The Contemporary City was predicated on the destruction
of the suburbs: to facilitate its construction, the centres of
our 'great cities must be pulled down and rebuilt', and 'the

wretched existing belt of suburbs must be abolished', wrote Le Corbusier.

Though he called the suburbs 'one of the greatest evils of the century', Le Corbusier recognized that the aspirations which drove people to desert the city and colonize the surrounding countryside were legitimate: the congested city was 'so antagonistic to the fundamental needs of the human heart that the one idea of everybody is to escape . . . To live where there are trees and to look out on grass. To escape forever from the noise and racket of the city.' Yet suburbia was a poor compromise: its residents relinquished the benefits of life in the city without finding what they were looking for – the clean air and open fields of the countryside. 'Millions of city dwellers have moved out to the country,' he wrote in 1936. 'The result is a vast, sprawling, built-up area encircling the city – the suburbs . . . Yet all this only makes a life of very little real freedom – front doors side by side on the edge of the road, windows overlooking each other, neighbouring roofs shutting out the sky, and an occasional tree which has survived this onslaught . . .'

Instead of allowing the city to expand, interminably, into the countryside, Le Corbusier proposed to make better use of the land that lay within its existing frontiers: to reduce the congestion in our cities, he said, we must increase their density. The twenty-four skyscrapers which stand at the heart of the Contemporary City occupy only a fraction of the land once claimed by buildings in the city centre. The reclaimed land at the feet of the skyscrapers is converted into gardens, and the city becomes 'an immense park' – terraces stretch out 'over lawns and groves' and the geometrical façades of the buildings form a trellis against which the trees are 'displayed to advantage . . . Here is the

CITY, with its crowds living in peace and pure air, where noise is smothered under the foliage of green trees. There are gardens, games and sports grounds. And sky everywhere, as far as the eye can see.'

The 'essential joys' of sun, trees and air were available within the precincts of the Contemporary City: the park is not in the city, one observer pointed out – the city is in the park. In Le Corbusier's vision, the exodus from the city had been stemmed.

– – –

It is the end of March. The shops at Western Circus have begun to close. They are demolishing the bingo hall which dominates the junction; the tiles have been removed to reveal fragments of sky embedded within the roof-beams' angular cage. On the Westway, the eastbound carriageway is reduced to two lanes, both of which are clogged with traffic. They are digging up the road to re-lay the central reservation. As the cars move slowly towards the centre of London, redundant road-signs warn of impending delays; faintly luminous in the dusk, green-jacketed workmen patrol the closed-off lanes.

– – –

On 19 October 1931, three men died in a 'motor-cycling tragedy' on Western Avenue. John Herbert Harbridge, who had been riding on the pillion of a motor-cycle driven by his son, was killed instantly; his body was found in the middle of the road near Gipsy Corner. His son, John William Harbridge, and Albert Waight were thrown on to the 'greensward' by the force of the collision; both died in hospital. In November 1931, an out-of-work labourer who 'had no place on this earth to go' was fined for camping on

a road in west London with his wife and five children – he
had not yet embraced the implications of living in an age of
speed.

- - -

A residential zone housing the Contemporary City's
600,000 'citizens' surrounds the grid of skyscrapers at the
city centre. To the west a great park obtrudes into the city;
to the east lie the warehouses and industrial quarters, and
on the horizon, beyond a 'protected zone' of woods and
fields, lie the garden cities where the workers live in communal housing projects.

The Contemporary City was structured around the
whitewashed cube of the 'Citrohan' house: the city's apartment blocks were 'really so many Citrohans stacked up
around courtyards into communal units that looked like
large filing cabinets', writes the architectural critic William
Curtis. The accumulation of perfectly proportioned cells
satisfied Le Corbusier's desire for a harmonious and
ordered urban architecture, for 'the repetitive and tranquil
framework created thus from innumerable cells would lead
up to great architectural schemes, far removed from our
wretched corridors of streets'. The car had inspired the
creation of the individual 'cell', which in turn had structured the design of a city predicated on the destruction of
the suburbs and shaped by the necessity of accommodating
the car. His plan was greeted with what he called 'a sort
of stupor': the 'shock of surprise caused rage in some quarters, and enthusiasm in others'. Yet it made little difference: the city continued its haphazard advance into the
countryside.

- - -

The population of Western Avenue was doubling every year. Building work began at Gipsy Corner in 1932, and in1933, the Greens' house was sold to a man called Ernest Edward Stevens. To the north and the south, side-roads breached Western Avenue's broad banks and flowed into the surrounding countryside. The flood-plain was spreading across the fields of Acton.

The Hoover factory – 'A Fairy Palace of Commerce' – opened for production in 1933. 'It might almost be the palace of some oriental potentate,' declared the *Illustrated London News*, describing the 'gleaming palace in dazzling white and red' which stood a 'few miles only from the heart of the empire's capital'. Its walls were 'almost all glass' and it was 'set like a glittering gem in the midst of the green lawns and gay flower-beds'. According to the architectural historian Wendy Hitchmough, the Hoover Building echoed the design of the tombs at Mastaba: massive Egyptian pillars adorned with coloured caps and bases divided the building's front into fifteen bays, and at night, it was dramatically floodlit.

To the modernists, the factory was the cathedral of the machine age: 'Nothing in the world is more beautiful than a great humming power-station,' Marinetti had written in 1914, and Le Corbusier had called the American grain elevators and factories the 'magnificent FIRST-FRUITS of the new age' – adding, in his hectoring fashion, that 'THE AMERICAN ENGINEERS OVERWHELM WITH THEIR CALCULATIONS OUR EXPIRING ARCHITECTURE'. Le Corbusier contrasted the clutter of suburbia to the austere perfection of the American grain silos.

Although Wallis's design reflected the belief that the factory was the 'architectural opportunity of the era', the Hoover Building was too gaudy both for the modernists and for those of more traditional tastes and expectations. 'Sanity may come tomorrow, Ornament is in today,' ran a poem in the Architectural Review mocking Wallis's design:

> What the country needs is beauty,
> Art's the thing for industry
> Who'd suppose such curves and zigzags
> Could conceal a factory?

J.B. Priestley was equally sceptical: 'Years in the West Riding have fixed for ever my idea of what a proper factory looks like: a grim, blackened rectangle with a tall chimney at one corner,' he wrote in 1933. Travelling down the Great West Road, which was built at the same time as Western Avenue and was sometimes known as Wallis Avenue in honour of the man who had designed many of its most striking buildings, Priestley felt as though he had 'suddenly rolled into California', for a parade of 'decorative little buildings', adorned with 'glass and chromium plate and nice coloured lights', marked his progress out of the city. The buildings 'seem to my barbaric mind to be merely playing at being factories. You could go up to any one of the charming little fellows, I feel, and safely order an ice-cream or select a few picture postcards. But as for industry, real industry, with double entry and bills of lading, I cannot believe them capable of it.'

Priestley did not believe that the new factories could adequately replace the declining industries of the north, but others were seduced by the sheen of modernity. In 1934, the *Acton Gazette* welcomed a tobacco factory which was being built on Western Avenue, describing, approvingly, its tower of Portland stone and its windows which stretched the 'whole length of the front elevation on both storeys, ensuring ample natural light for the employees'. Elsewhere, a two-storey factory lined with an 'elaborate system of neon lighting' and a factory of 'steel and brick with a white stone frontage' were nearing completion. As Le Corbusier put it, 'it is the age of steel, and the glitter of steel fascinates'.

– – –

It is the end of April. Measured by the changes on Western Avenue, the year is passing slowly. As I cycled up the hill this morning, I kept pace with a fluorescent yellow car, shaped like a cartoon thought-bubble. As we passed the site where Mrs Buchan used to live, the driver rummaged at his side, and the car changed gear; I stood on the pedals of my bike. For the last six months, my car has been parked outside my flat, while a gritty amalgam of London's air has condensed upon its enamelled skin. I tried starting it this morning, but nothing happened: the battery has died. Once, it would not go backwards; now, it will not go forwards either. I cannot afford to have it repaired, and I do not know how to repair it myself. Every time I pass it in the street, I feel guilty.

There is an almost-new car parked outside the Johnsons' house, but the curtain-draped façade reveals nothing – other than the fact that the Johnsons have not left their home. On the approach to Gipsy Corner, three houses remain standing, but only one is still occupied: Colette's house is shouldered upright by derelict buildings. The frontage of 203 Western Avenue has been bitten away to reveal a staircase which ends four feet above the ground. At Gipsy Corner, a wall has been built across the back of the site where the Greens used to live, sealing it against casual visitors. Barring the eviction of Colette and the Johnsons, the road is ready for redevelopment, yet nothing seems to be happening.

– – –

On London's 'newer exit roads', the number of accidents
was rising steadily, and in 1933, a survey concluded that
ribbon development was 'dangerous to life and limb'.
'When our new arterial roads are built, houses should not
be built all along them,' said a letter to *The Times* on 19
August 1933. The author compared the Great West Road
to two roads which had just been built outside New York –
the Hutchinson Parkway and the Bronx River Parkway:
'Nowhere could driving be more comfortable or safer,' it
said.

The parkways were the creation of Robert Moses –
America's greatest road-builder, whose career had begun in
1924, when he became President of the Long Island State
Park Commission. While the construction of Western
Avenue was under way, Moses had created a series of
public parks and bathing beaches on Long Island and begun
building a network of roads which tied the city to its new
pleasure-grounds to the east.

'New York City has led the way in the development of
an outstanding system of express highways and parkways,'
noted a team of British urban planners. 'These are so good
it would seem almost essential that England should study
them.' The 'parkways' were designed exclusively for the use
of private cars: Moses deliberately built low bridges across
the roads to seal them to buses and coaches, and commercial traffic was barred. No building was permitted beside
them – instead, they were bordered by lawns and trees; they
were themselves 'attenuated parks'. The parkways were
compared to the great European road-building schemes of
the same era, yet there was one crucial difference between
Moses' roads and Mussolini's *autostrade* and Hitler's auto-
bahns: the parkways were not conceived for military
purposes, but for recreation.

To Le Corbusier's acolytes in the Modern Movement,

the parkways were works of art: aerial photographs revealed the 'great sweep of these early highways' and the 'graceful sequence of their curves', wrote the architectural critic Sigfried Giedion. But the parkways were not simply static patterns scratched into the earth's surface: Giedion rhapsodized about the sensation of travelling 'up and down hills, beneath overpasses, up ramps and over giant bridges', with 'the wheel under one's hand'; driving on the parkways was like 'sliding swiftly on skis through untouched snow down the sides of high mountains'. Moses had devised a setting in which man and machine were united with the natural world. But Giedion's appreciation of the parkways was not merely an aesthetic response. He believed that modern science had uncovered a new principle in nature – the unity of space and time. It was a discovery which was explored in the work of great contemporary artists: as Richard Sennett puts it, 'what Einstein calculated, Picasso painted'; and what Picasso painted, Moses built. Like a cubist painting, which views objects from several points of view, none of which has exclusive authority, the parkways could not be appreciated from a single point of observation; their beauty was only apparent from the ever-changing perspective afforded by the car as it traversed a landscape animated by its own momentum. The car's motion was an integral part of a design which united man, machine and nature in a fluid, mutating composition. The parkways were not only the finest creation of the automobile age: they embodied the spirit of modernity. They counted amongst the greatest scientific and artistic innovations of the era.

– – –

In 1930, Le Corbusier had flown over Rio de Janeiro in a plane piloted by Antoine de Saint-Exupéry. Seeing Rio from above, he was struck by its position on a narrow strip of land between the sea and the mountains, and he sketched an extension of the city in the form of a 'highway, flying from mount to mount and reaching out from one bay to another'. Stacked beneath the surface of the road were fifteen floors of apartments for residential use. The perspective afforded by the aeroplane – the second great invention of the machine age – had revealed another means of accommodating the car within the city's fabric.

– – –

In 1935, a law was passed prohibiting the kind of roadside developments still under way on Western Avenue. It was regretfully concluded that planners had 'been outpaced by ill-directed private enterprise' – the 'development of roads for residential, commercial and industrial purposes' had been 'fostered and accelerated to an almost embarrassing extent by the new arterial roads'.

Osbert Lancaster dubbed the houses beside roads like Western Avenue 'by-pass variegated', and mocked their haphazard design: 'If an architect of enormous energy, painstaking ingenuity and great structural knowledge had devoted years of his life to the study of the problem of how best to achieve the maximum of inconvenience, in the shape and arrangement under one roof of a stated number of rooms, and had had the assistance of a corps of research workers ransacking architectural history for the least attractive materials and building devices known in the past, it is just possible, although highly unlikely, that he might have evolved a style as crazy as that with which the speculative builder, at no expenditure of mental energy at all, had enriched the landscape on either side of our great arterial roads.'

– – –

There is no reason for me to stay in London babysitting a road which shows no signs of changing, but I cannot afford to leave the country unless I sell my car. When I jump-started the car today and ran the tired engine, one of my neighbours came out to complain about the noise and the smell of its exhaust. With the engine pitched as high as it would go – if it stalled, I would never start it again – I drove my car to Westbourne Grove, to deliver it to Tommy. He did not even smile when he saw the state it was in.

– – –

By 1938, the map of Acton had been transformed: a black grid had been cross-hatched into the white spaces which had stained the map ten years earlier. Only road junctions and railway bridges interrupted the parade of buildings on Western Avenue, and a river delta of side-roads had worn tracks through the land surrounding it. Some of the roads were given names which echoed the district's semi-rural heritage, like Taylor's Green and Yew Tree Road; others were simply called The Fairway or The Crescent – like countless other streets across the country, for the 'very spirit of suburbia', wrote J.M. Richards, one of its few champions, was 'a kind of rural-romantic make-believe'.

Most critics despised the wilful nostalgia of suburban design. 'Why are you . . . living in an imitation Tudor house with stained wooden slats shoved onto the front of it to make it look like what is called a half-timbered house?' wrote the design critic John Gloag in 1934. 'Those slats have nothing to do with the construction of the house. They are just applied as ornaments. The house does not look like a real half-timbered house and it never can. It has been built in quite a different way from a real Tudor house. Why do we live in this sort of half-baked pageant, always hiding our ideas in the clothes of another age?'

Suburbia had rejected the Modern Movement and its plea for a new architecture of concrete, steel and glass. J.M. Richards argued that the suburban semi-detached house was every 'Englishman's idea of his own home', and its architecture reflected the desires and insecurities of its inhabitants: its myriad gables and porches allowed them to express their individuality, while its nostalgic appropriation of the style of earlier eras provided a reassuring counterpoint to the uncertainties of modern life.

The preponderance of Tudoresque styling in suburbia was rooted in a wish to escape. In 1938, the writer and broadcaster Anthony Bartram recalled that he used to receive many letters claiming that 'the suggestion of those quiet old days gives us the restful atmosphere we seek in our homes: this is self-deception, because of course the old days were far from quiet, but it is not surprising. These are insecure and frightening times, and I believe that economic depression and fear of war are the chief promoters of the Tudoresque.'

Suburban architecture was an attempt to create a self-sufficient retreat in a dangerous world – in Richard's phrase, 'an oasis in which every tree and brick can be accounted for'. Yet even he was forced to admit that the attempt was bound to fail on the arterial roads: 'Who could carve a lonely enclave out of a foreign world – and contrive within it a self-contained landscape – if so uncompromising a reminder of the outer world's foreignness as an arterial highway tore noisily through the midst of it?'

In the backwaters of East Acton, suburban life was finding its rhythm; but on Western Avenue, the traffic was beginning to beat an insistent, disruptive tattoo.

– – –

There was a crucial flaw in Robert Moses' designs: the parkways were so popular that they were soon clogged with cars. Moses' solution to the congestion was simple: he built more roads. By 1936, he had built a hundred miles of parkways in the state of New York, yet as each new stretch opened, it soon became congested. In the space of four years, the number of cars in the city had increased six times over – New York was strangling on its traffic. Moses' response was characteristically ambitious: he devised a cross-town highway network linking the city to his Long Island parkways – a road network that had no precedent anywhere in the world.

– – –

In the summer of 1938, a black-bordered poster appeared in the window of a red-brick villa at Western Circus: '100,000 KILLED AND 3,000,000 INJURED ON THE ROADS OF GREAT BRITAIN SINCE THE WAR', it announced. The death-toll on Western Avenue had risen steadily throughout the decade, and the bitter harvest of accidents and injuries had earned the road a new nickname: the 'Avenue of Speed and Death'. According to the local paper, the stretch of road between White City and Gipsy Corner had become a 'veritable death-trap': ambulances paid it almost daily visits, collisions between cars were common, and 'reckless speed merchants' endangered the lives of both pedestrians and motorists; people had begun to ask whether the road was a 'highway – or a dieway'.

Soon, the poster began to appear in the windows of houses elsewhere on Western Avenue, and its residents petitioned the Ministry of Transport: they wanted a speed limit of twenty-five or thirty miles an hour imposed on the road. The Ministry admitted that a speed limit was an 'ingenious provision' which would save lives, but it would also nullify 'the whole object of constructing a road free from congested traffic'.

The request was denied – a decision which was greeted with anger in East Acton. An impromptu protest meeting was called: 'The time for talking is over,' announced the mayor. 'You must act.' He knew the protesters would be orderly, but he also knew they would 'do their duty in no half-hearted way' – a diffident and peculiarly English call-to-arms. Mr T.H. Foley of the Pedestrians' Association was more outspoken: 'We have had months of terror, death and injury . . . We must stir the dictators to a recognition of our rights!' The council had never before recommended that its citizens break the law, but Councillor O'Day conceded that the residents of East Acton would have to do something 'drastic': nothing short of blocking Western Avenue would persuade the Ministry to take any action.

At 5.45 pm on 21 July 1938, the protesters gathered in The Approach – the most dangerous point on Western Avenue. Led by the Reverend Race Godfrey and Mrs Godfrey, the procession filed across Western Avenue, turned to the right to cross the side-street opposite The Approach, and then crossed the main road again, forming a moving 'hollow square'. Within five minutes, the tailback on the road stretched beyond Western Circus.

The protest had immediate effect: the next day, the Minister of Transport arranged for two footbridges to be erected on Western Avenue – one beside Gipsy Corner, and the other beside The Approach. Yet the demonstrators were not satisfied: they believed bridges would do more harm than good, for they would only encourage motorists to drive faster than they did already. They had heard of plans to 'wall off' certain roads, forcing pedestrians to use bridges and subways, and they 'must insist upon their right to cross on the level'.

A week later, a thousand people gathered in The Approach to block the road again. The demonstration was of 'national importance', argued Mr Foley – if the people of East Acton accepted pedestrian bridges, and allowed Western Avenue to become a 'speed track', then bridges would be introduced elsewhere, and pedestrians and cyclists would be pushed off the road.

– – –

It is the end of July. The trees that once stood in private gardens blossom inside their wooden stockades. I no longer expect to find the work has begun – something has happened to delay it.

While it stood outside my flat, my car had begun to disintegrate: as well as a new gearbox, it needs two new tyres, a new battery and new brakes. The repairs will cost so much money that I will have to sell the car to pay for them.

– – –

By 1938, there were 250 factories in Park Royal employing 20,000 people. The spreading suburbs of north-west London were the era's 'Silicone Valley', and it was the new roads which laid the foundations for their economic success. 'It is transport which has made West Middlesex the favoured area for industrial development,' noted the *Economist*, in 1937, adding that 'the advantages of the area could be seen at Park Royal'; the railways had played their part in the industrial estate's dramatic growth, but it was the arterial road which 'was perhaps the greatest attraction'. Yet the car had already begun to undermine the security of the world it had helped to create. Throughout the summer of 1938, the protests continued on Western Avenue.

– – –

Moses' control of a series of apparently innocuous public
committees had secured him enormous power in New York,
and he soon began reshaping 'the face of the greatest city
in the New World' to accommodate his fifty-mile network
of urban highways. What the *New York Times* called the
next 'masterpiece out of Robert Moses' atelier' was revealed
in 1937: the 'West Side Improvement', which began in the
northern suburbs and followed the Hudson River to the tip
of Manhattan, was described by the *Daily News* as 'the
most beautiful drive in the world'. Moses was an artist
whose work stood comparison to Leonardo da Vinci.

– – –

'One of the performers of the Western-avenue play is
reported as saying that the parades are causing repercussions over a wider field,' began the letter to the *Acton
Gazette*. 'Mussolini's march to Rome has produced repercussions over a very wide field, and it started in much the
same way as the Western-avenue parades. Hitler's rise to
fame has had wider "repercussions", and he started his
career not on a main thoroughfare but in alleys and backstreets.'

Mr Arthur Forrester could not tell when obstructing the
King's highway ends and mob rule begins, but he knew one
thing: mob rule invariably ends in fascism. Still, he had
faith in the decency of the English character: 'I doubt if
there are any budding Mussolinis or Hitlers strutting the
stage in Western-avenue,' he concluded. 'When a Scotland
Yard official says, "Now, you good people, get home to
bed" – they will. Yours etc.'

– – –

During the thirties, Le Corbusier reprised the theme of a
motorway city in a series of plans for the reconstruction of

Algiers. 'Plan Obus' envisaged an elevated highway snaking along the coast, linking the suburbs with the city centre. Shops, walkways and apartments were slotted into the space beneath the surface of the viaduct, creating accommodation for up to 180,000 people – almost a city in its own right.

— — —

The girders of the hated footbridge were rising above Western Avenue. In September 1938, in a mock-ceremony held before a crowd of 500 people, a woman from East Acton demonstrated the difficulty of 'pushing a perambulator up its steps', and the footbridge was christened Pons Asinorum – 'the Bridge of Fools'. The bridge was such a curiosity that it had became a tourist attraction. It was not much used, but it was regarded as one of the sights of west London, and the *Acton Gazette* claimed that it was 'quite usual to see people from other districts coming to look at it'.

Mrs Barker, who lived in The Approach, regarded the Bridge of Fools as a 'disgrace'. She could no longer let her dog play in her garden because 'hooligans' had begun to congregate on the bridge to throw stones at it, and the traffic was so loud that some people were thinking of leaving; others had begun to keep their curtains drawn at the front of their houses. Less than ten years had passed since the first settlers had arrived, and yet their expectations had already been crushed.

Torchlight processions held up the traffic every evening for a week in October 1938. The demonstrators were accompanied by a dog with a red light attached to its collar, and four 'bearers' carried a coffin at the head of the parade; a man's soft hat was placed on top of the coffin. 'We want crossings, not coffins', said the demonstrators' placards.

The demonstrations continued well into the new year: 'We deserve a little praise for our determination,' said the Secretary of the East Acton Association in June 1939.

— — —

My throat hurts as I cycle up the hill beside the road: for the last few days, I have had flu, and my lungs are raw; or perhaps I have just forgotten how thick the air is on Western Avenue. I leave my bike chained to one of the spindly legs of the Bridge of Fools, and climb its gently angled steps. It is strange to think that such an unexceptional piece of street furniture should have aroused such antagonism, yet I am beginning to understand why the residents of Western Avenue resented it so much: it was a clear statement of their place in the new order created and sustained by the machine.

Le Corbusier would almost certainly have understood their confusion and resentment. In the introduction to *The City of Tomorrow* – the book in which he expounded his vision of the machine-age city – he described his reaction when the traffic returned to the streets of Paris after the comparative lull of the summer months: 'In the early evening twilight on the Champs-Elysées, it was as though the world had suddenly gone mad . . . once you had crossed your threshold you were a possible sacrifice to death in the shape of innumerable motors.' As he surveyed the 'fury' of the traffic, Le Corbusier lamented the passing of the time when the streets of the city were the property of its people: 'I think back twenty years. The road belonged to us then; we sang in it and argued in it, while the horse-'bus swept calmly along.'

Yet as he witnessed the 'titanic reawakening' of the city traffic, a kind of 'rapture' descended upon him: 'not the rapture of the shining coachwork under the gleaming lights, but the rapture of power . . . We are a part of it.' 'We are a part of that race whose dawn is just awakening. We have confidence in this new society which will in the end arrive at a magnificent expression of its power. We believe in it.' Marshall Berman calls the passage 'a modernist parable': one minute, Le Corbusier is dodging the traffic in the street, and the next, he 'lives and moves and speaks from inside the traffic'; he had surrendered to the intoxicating power of the machine, and had been reborn in the flood-waters of the traffic – a prophet of the new age.

Le Corbusier's lament for an imaginary urban paradise was intended to dramatize the fact that there was no point resisting the machine. However much we might regret it, its advance was inevitable, and if we were to profit from its potential to enrich our lives, then we had better acknowledge its power to disrupt and distort them as well. The boomtown spirit which had galvanized Western Avenue had not embraced such far-sighted concerns: the car had been allowed to invade the narrow streets of the city, and then, to compound the error, houses and factories had been built beside the few roads that were designed to carry through-traffic.

To Le Corbusier, it was evident that there was 'no longer any place for the city street with its heavy traffic running between rows of houses': the 'first necessity in the development of the future city' was the abolition of streets like Western Avenue. But the residents of Western Avenue had not yet embraced the 'realities' of the new age – they thought that they were living on a traditional city street, flanked by houses, and they believed that the road belonged to the people who lived beside it. They were wrong – and the battle they fought against the traffic was one they were bound to lose.

It is midday: the traffic is flowing freely, yet the cars

passing beneath me are travelling at no more than twenty
miles an hour. Ironically, the speed limit the residents
desired is in place; it has been imposed by the cars themselves. There is new graffiti on the hoardings above Western
Circus – 'HESS': the last two letters are jagged lightning
bolts – a deliberate imitation of the insignia of the SS; next
to it is an advertisement for tights.

— — —

In September 1939, the protests on Western Avenue were
suspended, pending the resolution of a greater crisis. Le
Corbusier had claimed that 'man is capable of perfection',
yet the new age had ended in unimaginable circumstances.

I find a biography of Le Corbusier in a library in
Kensington; there is a black-and-white photograph of the
architect on the centre pages, and someone has drawn a
swastika on his cheek. Clearly, the principles that structured
Le Corbusier's utopia had much in common with the
practice and rhetoric of the authoritarian regimes of the
thirties. The Contemporary City, which was governed by
its technocratic elite of 600,000 citizens, proposed a vision
of society which was as dangerous as it was seductive.

Yet Robert Fishman, the author of a book on twentieth-
century utopias, argues that Le Corbusier's desire for social
order transcended 'the anti-democratic spirit so prevalent
in Europe between the wars'. Fishman excuses Le Corbusier's flirtation with Mussolini and, later, with the Vichy
government, by pointing out he was so intent on seeing his
plans realized that 'he had reduced politics to a simple yes
or no . . . he was willing to support any regime that said
Yes.' What's more, the rule of Le Corbusier's elite was the
'opposite of authoritarian domination by force', for its
power was primarily imaginative, and its authority rested
on its ability to 'discern and promote the well-being of the

whole'. The triumph of an ordered administration, Le Corbusier believed, would be to liberate its citizens from its control.

In other words, he sought libertarian ends, yet the means he endorsed were, undoubtedly, authoritarian. As the mayor of Algiers pointed out, anyone who implemented Le Corbusier's city plans would have to be 'an absolute dictator with the property and even the lives of his subjects at his disposal'. Le Corbusier readily acknowledged the charge: 'France needs a Father,' he once said. 'It doesn't matter who.'

The demolition of Paris envisioned in the 'Voisin Plan' was brutal, but Le Corbusier claimed it was justified because 'town existence and life itself are brutal: life is pitiless, it must defend itself, hemmed in as it is on all sides by death'. More convincingly, he argued that to do nothing would prove, in the end, a more destructive choice: 'THE GREAT CITY OF TODAY IS DESTROYING ITSELF,' he reiterated; it was 'using up and slowly wearing out millions of human beings'. *The City of Tomorrow* is guilty of many excesses, but its response to the spectacle of a city gorged with cars is clear-sighted and eloquent. 'At what rate do the trees which border our present streets wither and die?' wrote Le Corbusier. 'What sort of curve would the nervous system of an inhabitant of the great city show during, say, the last ten years? And his respiratory system?'

Le Corbusier drew inspiration from the example of the last man to have attempted to rebuild Paris: Baron Haussmann, Prefect of the Seine in Napoleon III's Second Empire. Haussmann had demolished 20,000 buildings, including entire areas of Paris, in the course of building 'les grands boulevards'. But Le Corbusier believed that Paris could accommodate traffic in the 1920s only because Haussmann had 'cut it about' so ruthlessly sixty years earlier, and it

now required another dose of his 'powerful medicine'. 'We
cannot agree to a merely *convenient* solution,' he insisted;
'if you are dying of heart disease, you do not spend your
time doing five-finger exercises on the piano'. The machine
age had only just begun – and what would Paris or London
be like in fifty years' time, if the car continued to advance
its claims?

– – –

Osbert Lancaster had only one good thing to say about
roads like Western Avenue: the thought of their destruction
did much to reconcile him to the prospect of aerial bom-
bardment. Between 1924 and 1939, London's population
had grown by a third, but its built-up area had more than
trebled, and even George Orwell conceded that 'the new
towns that have swelled up like balloons in the last few
years' were not particularly attractive places: 'The newness
of everything! The raw, mean look! The kind of chilliness,
the bright red brick everywhere . . .'

Yet in 1941, Orwell offered a reasoned appraisal of the
arterial roads: 'The new red cities of Greater London are
crude enough but these things are only the rash that accom-
panies a change.' Orwell relished the unanimity of a world
where 'the sharp distinctions of the older kind of town,
with its slums and mansions, or of the country, with its
manor-houses and squalid cottages, no longer exist'. Priestley, similarly, welcomed the new England 'of filling stations
and factories that look like exhibition buildings': 'After a
social revolution, there would, with any luck, be more and
not less of it,' he wrote. The emerging country of 'arterial
and by-pass roads' contained almost every luxury, yet it
was, he said, an 'essentially democratic' world – a world
where the old distinctions of class and income were rubbed
smooth by the mass media of radio and cinema; a world

which copied its style from America and mimicked its aggressive egalitarianism, as well. There were to be no servants in the houses beside the arterial roads, and the labour-saving devices in the purpose-built homes would foster 'an England, at last, without privilege'.

Priestley disliked the fashion for detached or semi-detached houses which ate up 'miles of good countryside, or meadow and heath and woodland, making the town go straggling on and on and on in the dreariest fashion'. But he recognized that the new houses represented the possibility of a better life to many thousands of people: they were a 'kind of sign-post pointing to a sunlit main road of life', and he concluded that we should be content 'to make the whole country hideous if we knew for certain that by doing so we could also make all the people in it moderately happy'.

What Priestley called the cheapness and the 'rather depressing monotony' of the suburbs and the arterial roads attracted scorn and criticism from several quarters. 'From dreary towns the broad, mechanical noisy main roads run out between ribbons of tawdry houses, disorderly refreshment shacks and vile, untidy garages,' wrote Thomas Sharp in 1932 in a book called *Town and Countryside*. 'The old trees and hedgerows that bordered them a few years ago have given place to concrete posts and avenues of telegraph poles, to hoardings and enamel advertisement signs. Over great areas there is no longer any country bordering the main roads: there is only a negative semi-suburbia.' The arterial roads, which were designed to offer an escape from the city, had brought the city with them – or a pale imitation of the city. Driving down the A11 from London to Southend was like 'motoring through a continuous loosely strung-out town', wrote C.E.M. Joad in 1931, in a pamphlet called *The Horrors of the Countryside*. 'There

were no signs of civic life, no churches, chapels or meeting
houses, but equally, there were no signs of rustic pursuits,
no farms, no ricks, no animals.' The people who lived
beside the arterial roads, Joad concluded, possessed 'none
of the advantages which town dwellers lacked', yet 'lacked
most of those which town dwellers possessed'.

In 1938, the senior resident medical officer at the Royal
Free Hospital wrote an article in *The Lancet* defining what
he claimed was an increasingly common condition: he
called it 'the suburban neurosis'. Mrs Everyman – who lives
in a 'small semi-detached hire-purchase villa on the wonderful new Everysuburb Estate, adjacent to one of our great
by-passes' with Mr Everyman, a clerk in a Brixton business
house – had become a frequent visitor to Dr Stephen
Taylor's out-patients department, complaining of sleepless-
ness, headaches, back-ache, a swollen stomach, weight
loss, and so on. Dr Taylor's response to Mrs Everyman's
'miserable little story' was simple: it was modern life in the
suburbs and on the arterial roads which caused her apparently rootless anxiety and depression. We had 'allowed the
slum which stunted the body to be replaced by a slum
which stunts the mind'. His professional verdict was brutal:
since we had 'let matters go too far in the jerry-building,
ribbon-development line to institute an entirely satisfactory
scheme of prophylaxis', all we could do is hope that the
'rotten little houses' would collapse like 'a pack of cards'.

▬ ▬ ▬

It is September. In the day's bitter sump – the in-between
hours of early evening – I turn on the television. Two
people are playing the local news game. I watch, distract-
edly, until I hear a name which flicks at my nerves: Western
Avenue. They are discussing the reconstruction of the road.

It is a moment before I understand the meaning of the

report: the funding for the work has been withdrawn. At first, it seems as if the entire project has been cancelled, and the houses have been destroyed for no reason, but then I realize it has not been cancelled – only delayed. Under the government's Private Finance Initiative, the work is now to be funded by a private company, which will be reimbursed with a 'shadow-toll' paid by the Department of Transport for every car that uses the rebuilt road.

The houses had been demolished ahead of schedule, but the scheme will still proceed: Western Avenue is to become one of Britain's first private roads. The vision that inspired its construction has died, but a new spirit is at work: the road will be rebuilt for profit.

– – –

In 1941, someone suggested that the Bridge of Fools be torn down to help the war effort, but there was no need: thanks to the number of cars laid up by rationing, there was no shortage of scrap metal. There was now so little traffic that it was possible to cross Western Avenue in relative safety once more. The proprietor of the garage at Western Circus complained that the war had brought business to 'vanishing point'.

Colonel Hellard had envisaged his 'fast exit from London' running to the heart of the city, yet Western Avenue splintered into a web of side-streets at White City, and the plan to extend the road to the centre of London was abandoned when the war began.

– – –

The great arterial roads that structured Le Corbusier's Contemporary City were 120 metres wide – the same width as the broadest street Haussmann had built in Paris. He had built the Avenue Foch three times as wide as his architects suggested, for his ambition far exceeded their scope. 'When Haussmann was transforming Paris, he once remarked bitterly that no architects were living to match "les temps nouveaux",' writes Giedion. Le Corbusier's dilemma mirrored Haussmann's: Giedion believed Le Corbusier was equal to the challenge of the time, but there were no 'directing officials' of Haussmann's stature to implement his vision.

Although Paris would never be rebuilt as Le Corbusier hoped, Giedion believed that New York had found a man capable of responding to the challenge of the *temps nouveaux*: Robert Moses combined the attributes of Le Corbusier and Baron Haussmann, for he possessed both the imagination to envisage the reconstruction of the city and the ruthless pragmatism required to realize his vision. So far, the roads Moses had built had clung to New York's shoreline, but Giedion believed that they were only a rehearsal for a far greater scheme: the construction of urban highways that would 'pass through the city as the early parkways passed through the landscape'. The parkway was 'the forerunner of the urban highway which can weld the automobile . . . into the actual organism of the city, so that they are a constituent element of the whole'.

– – –

My newly repaired car seems to have moss growing inside its window. Ashamed of its appearance, I park outside the gates of the Renault showroom. I still have not left the country: I don't seem to have the energy, or the curiosity, or whatever it is that takes other people abroad; I don't have the money either – or the initiative to travel without it. Of course, no one wanted to buy my car.

The roof of the Renault showroom is shaped like a seashell, borne aloft on slender struts. The walls are glass, and the floor on which the cars are displayed is made of gleaming white tiles. The bonnet of each car is open, and their engines are moulded from a rich, soft metal. They are beautiful machines.

PART THREE: 1997–98

The wider ownership of the car that has come since the 1960s has finally transformed the nature of the city. The old certainties of urban geography have vanished, and in their place is this edgy and apparently amorphous new kind of settlement . . . a soup of shopping malls, hypermarkets and warehouses, drive-in restaurants and anonymous industrial sheds, beltways and motorway boxes.

Deyan Sudjic, *The Hundred Mile City*

If I were asked to condense the whole of the present century into one mental picture I would pick a familiar everyday sight: a man in a motor car, driving along a concrete highway to some unknown destination.

J. G. Ballard, *A User's Guide to the Millennium*

A large proportion of London's public domain, including almost all its streets and squares, are now dominated by the motor vehicle. These are places designed to respond to the needs of traffic and marred visually by its signage. Grand spaces like Parliament Square, Piccadilly Circus, Trafalgar Square, Hyde Park Corner and Marble Arch have all been overwhelmed by cars. The situation is even worse in local centres such as Hammersmith, Shepherd's Bush, Brixton, Dalston or the Elephant and Castle.

Richard Rogers, *Cities for a Small Planet*

8. The Automobile Works

'We're very much on our own here: we're our own little entity – one block of flats in the middle of all these industrial warehouses, and people forget that we're here.' Anna-Marie stubs out a cigarette in the ashtray on her kitchen table. The kitchen doors are open: framed by the metal stanchions of Anna-Marie's balcony, the city stretches towards its north-western horizon.

Wendover Court is a narrow block of flats that stands half a mile to the west of Gipsy Corner. Its prow is tipped towards Park Royal, and its central stairwell is a single white pillar inlaid with stained glass – a characteristic emblem of thirties design. It is one of the landmarks guarding the approach to central London: to the east stands the compacted city; to the west lie the outer suburbs and the plastic warehouses of the industrial estate.

When I arrived at Wendover Court this morning, two men were digging holes in the lay-by in front of the building. The noise of the generators and drills washed through the hallway and slopped against the doors and windows of the first-floor flats. I climbed to the third floor, where I pushed through a heavy swing door and walked on to the balcony which runs across the front of the building. The whitewashed wall broke below my waist; the drop to the road was dizzying, and the blustering wind which ricocheted along the balcony was so strong it threatened to unbalance me. Below, the road swung to the west and climbed towards Park Royal. The skyline is thick with illuminated logos: I could see a clothes warehouse and an office equipment superstore; further west lay the ceramic shell of the Renault showroom; a garage and a Happy Eater stood on the opposite side of the road. The cars flowed past the building at sixty or seventy miles an hour.

I met Anna-Marie on the balcony on the fourth floor. She was dressed in black, and her made-up face seemed ghostly white in contrast. Thanks to the whip-crack echo of the passing cars, she had to bend towards me to hear what I was saying. She held up her keys: she was going to collect her son from school, but she would meet me in half an hour – more, if the traffic was bad. 'People used to say you could leave your car on Western Avenue, go and have breakfast, and when you came back it would still be in the same place because the road was so chock-a-block,' she explained, later, as we settled in the kitchen at the back of her flat.

She lights another cigarette. Anna-Marie is thirty-two years old – an attractive woman, with red hair cut short and a wide, full mouth. Her father is British, and her mother Croatian; she grew up in Sibelic, a town on the Dalmatian coast. She came to England in 1983. Unprompted, she tells me that it 'was not a case of economic migration': she's British, and she came back because she was feeling independent; she just wanted to. Her accent is fading but still distinct: it thickens her words, so that each one carries a faint echo of a central European childhood.

She moved to Wendover Court in 1986 – 'just before Thatcher's boom'. True to the spirit of the time, she bought the flat, although she was only twenty-one. Property values were reasonable then, she recalls, but a year after she moved in, they went sky-high. 'I mean, when you buy your first property, you just want to buy, but now you can't sell it for the life of you – you just can't sell it, because nobody wants to live here.' Her mouth turns down in an extravagant gesture of disgust. Her face – impassive until she began to talk – has become animated, and the pitch of her voice has risen; she speaks quickly and insistently. 'My next-door neighbour, as well, who bought it two years after I did, and spent an absolute fortune, and he can't sell it, and I can't sell it, and two doors away they can't sell it – nobody can sell it! You can't say – "Oh I'm going to move this year," because you can't sell it – you just can't sell it, and that's it, and I don't care what people say, you just can't sell it . . .'

Suddenly, a train rattles past on the tracks behind the flat, and the noise is so loud that we cannot speak for a moment. Anna-Marie raises her eyebrows disdainfully: see what I have to put with? Yet when she talks again, she is calmer. 'It is very difficult living here. You don't know many people, people are coming and going, and then you have the big freight trains, and they go on for ever – you know, you have twenty-five or thirty wagons behind the locomotive, and it's, like – dard-dup darp-dup dard-dup . . .' She does a passable imitation of a chattering, swaying train. The railway lines carry passenger trains, freight trains and tube trains, and between six in the morning and midnight they are rarely quiet.

Still, Anna-Marie says the road irritates her more than the railway. 'It's the main cause of all the people's aggravation. It's intimidating, you know? I walk my dog, and there are like, three lanes of traffic, all staring at you – you know, you feel like you're on a catwalk. It makes you phobic. Three lanes of traffic, every day – imagine that! You're living on this busy commuter road, and it is hard – you just get really peed off. When you have, like, the huge lorries rattling along this road, the whole house shakes – and I'm talking really shakes, you know, and it's ah-ah-ah . . .' She sets her teeth rattling. 'And you think, one day, that's it . . .

But it's not so bad,' she adds, abruptly. 'I don't know where you live . . .'

Behind the shopping centre on Shepherd's Bush Green, I say.

'Shepherd's Bush!' She seems pleased – we are practically neighbours. What's more, Shepherd's Bush is not exactly an urban paradise. 'Well, that's not so bright, is it?' she says, with evident satisfaction. She is bored of the condescending incredulity of outsiders like myself, horrified by the conditions in which she lives, and she is pleased to point out that Shepherd's Bush is not much better than Western Avenue. 'It's always busy down there! People always say – "How can you live here?" But you know, once you get here, you completely don't know. You wouldn't know! Would you know that you are on the road?' She looks at me expectantly. She is right: it is surprisingly quiet in the flat – when she closed the glazed front door behind us, the noise of the traffic died to almost nothing. But it is impossible to ignore the trains which pass intermittently on the tracks behind the building. 'No, you wouldn't know,' she concludes.

Anna-Marie lived in Hounslow and in Richmond before she came to Western Avenue. 'I'm a west Londoner – it's me,' she says, with conviction. 'I can't live anywhere else. I thought, yeah, west is for me, because it's very cosmopolitan and there are lots of people from eastern countries, and lots of different cultures – you have Indian, you have Chinese, you have Polish . . . I mean, if you told me to go to east London, I'd die – and I would not go across the river!' She shudders extravagantly. Once, she drove along Eastern Avenue, and hated it so much that she will not tolerate comparisons between the two roads. 'I could not live there – at that I draw the line! It looks awful – it looks

so derelict. It's an awful area! There is a distinct difference
between west and east in London, and it's so obvious its
unbelievable – well, you know, don't you? Shepherd's Bush
is not far away.'

Again, she appeals to our shared experience, yet her
loyalty to west London is stronger than mine. All of London
was strange to me when I arrived; I ended up in Shepherd's
Bush because I had friends living there, but I would never
think of myself as a 'west Londoner' – or a Londoner of
any sort. It was a year before I felt comfortable travelling
on the tube, and it was two years before I went to the East
End. Even now, the city defeats my attempts to know it
better: in the rush-hour – at most times of the day, in fact –
I can get to Bristol as quickly and as easily as I can get to
Greenwich, on the other side of the city.

There is a map of the Dalmatian coast pinned to the
door behind me. It must be beautiful there, I say, inno-
cently. 'Yes, and then to come here and live on the main
road! Oh my God, don't tell me, I do regret it a lot, I just
think – "What have I done?" ' she wails, extravagantly, and
then collects herself; she lights another cigarette. 'But people
live in worse circumstances than this – I mean, really, if
people want to classify people by where they live then it's
the wrong idea, I think, because you can be intelligent, you
can be articulate, and you can live in a downright dump
. . . So where you are does not necessarily mean what you
are – but it's annoying when you have friends over, and
they say, "Oh my God . . ." '

She didn't see the flat when it was bought: her husband
– her *ex*-husband – saw it, and she was not consulted. 'But
it seemed not so bad, I thought, "Yeah, it's going to be a
couple of years . . ." But you end up living here for ten
years, and then you think – "Shit! shit!" I would never,

ever have bought the bloody thing.' Her anger flames like a
struck match, a sulphur-flare of resentment which crackles
briefly and then dies.

I tell her that I wouldn't have chosen to spend more
than a weekend in Shepherd's Bush, and yet five years have
passed, and I am still living there. In London, people settle
wherever they happen to find themselves. Calmer now,
Anna-Marie agrees: 'It's very hard to have a place in
London anyway, so if you have your flat and you bought it
by working hard for it, then everything is good; you just
have to be happy with what you have. That's my philo-
sophical attitude towards it.'

The doors to the other rooms were shut when I came
into the flat, and I had assumed they were empty; it seemed
too small to harbour someone else undetected: I was wrong
– a woman suddenly walks into the kitchen, and puts a
mug down beside the sink. Now I come to think of it,
Anna-Marie's son must be somewhere in the flat as well,
though there is no sign of him.

'This is my mother,' says Anna-Marie. 'She just came on
holiday – she's in transit.' Then, as though she were know-
ingly reviving an old argument, she says, mischievously,
'She always says to me, "Oh how can you live here, how
can you live on this road?" '

'Where? Here?' Her mother seems surprised. She is a
handsome woman with long greying hair. She is dressed in
a tracksuit.

'Yes, here.'

'Well, it's not very nice . . . hindsight.' Her accent is
thicker than her daughter's. She gestures towards the back
window. 'At home, we have the sea, and the mountains.
It's all right, you know, living here for a short while, but
we like the countryside and the sea . . .'

Surprisingly, Anna-Marie seems to agree with her. 'I

mean this place – you work, you come home, you go back to work, you come home again. You can't be bothered to do anything.'

'It's too much rushing!'

'If you come from a country which is, like . . . quiet and leisurely, then everything irritates you. I mean, it took me forever to get used to it – you know, London offers so much variety, and that's why you come here, because you want to see all the different things in life, which you don't have in your other countries, but when you live here, you think . . .' The passage of another train silences us for a moment. Her mother's presence seems to have reminded Anna-Marie of the benefits of life in Croatia. 'See that?' she says, when it has passed. 'We can't even open the back door. It does make you go a bit crazy.'

We walk out on to the balcony, and Anna-Marie points out the landmarks on the horizon: to the west, the Guinness Brewery; further north, Wembley Stadium. It is April, and summer has come early; the sky is a pale, bleached blue, and the air is warm and dry. From the east, the railway lines converge on Western Avenue, pinching Wendover Court in the apex of a narrow triangle scored by road and railway. On the far side of the tracks, the industrial estate begins. Hemmed in on all sides by the city, it is hard to imagine life beyond its boundaries – harder still to imagine life in Croatia. 'I can't see myself going back,' says Anna-Marie. 'Money. It's always money – I'd like to do lots of things, but I can't.'

I follow her inside.

For most of the last ten years, she worked as the manager of a shop in Oxford Street. She is not working at the moment, as she has been through a difficult divorce and she needed time to rest. 'I had a very bad life, these last two years. I'm getting back on track now – I'll try to get back on track, if this area doesn't get to me. But it won't. That's why you try to isolate yourself a little bit – make this flat look a little bit like home, a lot more like home than some other people make it, because if it's your home you have to make it better.' The walls in the hallway have been stripped to bare stone; it looks as though the redecoration has stalled.

Her mother reappears in the kitchen. She has something to tell me: 'I quite like it here,' she says, earnestly. She is regretting her criticism of her daughter's home. 'I'm only joking, it's quite nice – a little bit different, but quite nice, I think. When I talk to English people, I always say I don't like it here, but it is quite nice. It's quite acceptable. It would be nice if it was bigger.'

'She's an old-age pensioner – she needs her garden, that's what she needs,' says Anna-Marie. Her mother laughs. Soon, she will be returning to the sea and the mountains.

— — —

William's house in The Approach is empty. The windows are sealed with grey metal plates, gridded like an insect's eyes, through which I can see the polished wooden floor of his bedroom. It is the end of May: the Labour government has just been elected. Rain falls intermittently, and a hot wind gusts across the garden. My face is gritted with sweat. A storm is due.

— — —

The next works to issue from Moses' atelier were fashioned with a blunt instrument: 'You can draw any kind of picture you like on a clean slate and indulge your every whim in the wilderness in laying out a New Delhi, Canberra or Brasilia, but when you operate in an overbuilt metropolis, you have to hack your way with a meat ax,' he said, candidly. After the Second World War, Moses began driving six expressways through the heart of New York. He was fulfilling the modernist prescription for reshaping the city around the car, but the work had only one real precedent, and he was willing to acknowledge the debt. 'Let it be said to Baron Haussmann's eternal credit that he grasped the problem of step-by-step large-scale city modernisation,' Moses wrote.

– – –

Anna-Marie once saw a van hit the central reservation outside Wendover Court at seventy miles an hour: it flipped over, skidded across the road and on to the pavement – '. . . and the guy just walked away. You know, nothing happened to him.'

– – –

When Helen was a child, anyone who needed a job would walk along Western Avenue, calling at every factory beside the road until they were offered work. Helen is a slim and rather delicate woman with straw-blonde hair cut in a Cleopatra bob. She grew up in East Acton, and has worked at the Renault showroom for the last fifteen years.

Helen is sure that her parents would hate the way Western Avenue has changed, but she feels you have to move with the times; besides, some of the changes have been for the better. 'It feels cleaner,' she begins, tentatively. 'People used to put up with a lot of discomfort in their working conditions, but we've got a workshop, and it's spotless; you'd never think it was an oily, dirty workshop. Standards are a lot higher now – people's rights are more to the forefront.' We are sitting on a sofa in the showroom,

chaperoned by the business-like figure of the general manager's secretary. Linda has already warned us that we must
not take too long, for there is work to be done.

Renault established an assembly line on Western Avenue
in 1926: 'Automobile Works', says the legend on the 1935
map of Acton. In 1961 the Acton works became a parts
store and a service department, and in 1995 the refurbished
showroom opened in its current form: 'Oh, it's lovely!'
interjects Linda. 'I can't tell you the difference compared to
what we had before – there was no air-conditioning, it was
all old and a little bit decrepit; every year, the roof would
leak, and such-like.'

There are no factories on Western Avenue anymore.
Beyond Wendover Court, the road frays into a series of
slip-roads which lead towards a collection of low-slung
sheds – retail hypermarkets selling designer clothes, office
equipment, and cars. Linda believes that few of their customers are passing drivers, but she likes to think that the
showroom is a nice, new-looking site which might draw
people in. 'I think it is quite an impressive building – but
then am I objective?' she asks, rather coquettishly.

There is no reason for her to be objective, yet her role as
a representative of the company constrains her in other
ways – or rather, it constrains me. We have been talking
for only five minutes, and I have already run out of questions. I feel self-conscious in the pristine surroundings of
the showroom. There are men and women in business suits
seated at desks around the room, but I would not know
how to begin to speak to them. Linda, in particular, is keen
to help, yet the functional atmosphere discourages personal
recollections of any sort – Helen remembers little more than
the fact that the girls who lived in the mock-Tudor houses
on Western Avenue used to come to school by taxi. She
seems puzzled by our conversation. It is, I suppose, a

strange departure from office routine to be asked to talk to a journalist about the street on which you happen to work. We watch as a salesman walks across the showroom, his heels ringing, his hands low and held in front of his knees, as though he is pushing a wheelbarrow ahead of him. 'Maybe they've considered business concerns above residential concerns,' ventures Helen.

On my way out, I cross the forecourt where the second-hand cars are displayed; a Renault banner hangs loosely in the still air. On the far side of the road, there is a billboard advertising Honda vans – on Western Avenue, commercial franchises compete for space of more than one kind. I find myself face to face with a middle-aged man dressed in a crumpled linen suit; he is holding a set of car keys, and his face is damp.

'You don't know how you get out of here, do you?' he says.

He has driven off the road, and cannot find his way back on to it.

– – –

Anna-Marie's mother-in-law is the author of the *Colombo Directory* – a written map of the capital of Sri Lanka, like an A–Z of London, but without the illustrations. She walked the city, noting the layout of roads and landmarks, and tracing routes through the city's streets. 'Station Passage: off Justice Akbar Mawatha, opposite Elephant House, alongside Slave Island Railway Station,' reads one entry.

– – –

The Green Belt had frozen London within its pre-war limits, but the forces that had powered the city's expansion were still at work. London vaulted its ring of encircling fields and resumed its outward surge. By the fifties, the population of Greater London was stable, but the ring fifteen miles from the city centre was growing faster than any other part of Britain. 'By the end of the century, Great Britain will consist of isolated oases of preserved monuments in a desert of wire, concrete roads, cosy plots and bungalows,' warned the *Architectural Review* in 1955, dubbing the new Britain 'SUBTOPIA'. The campaign against suburbia had not relented, but if the wartime commitment to rebuild Britain's cities was to be honoured, then the slums must be demolished and their inhabitants rehoused – and where were they to go, if not to new housing on the city's periphery?

Legislation was in place to monitor the development of every acre of land in Britain when the Conservative government launched a slum clearance programme in 1955. There was only one way of rehousing the urban population while containing the spread of Britain's cities: the era of the 'high tower' had begun.

— — —

Pauline Harper has, perhaps, one unspoken aim in life: to restore Wendover Court to the condition it was in during her childhood. It is an impossible dream, and she knows it. Ten years ago, when the residents 'clubbed together' to buy the freehold of the building, Pauline Harper became the managing director of the Wendover Court holding company. Now, she struggles to maintain the way of life she inherited from her parents, but she gets no thanks for it from her fellow tenants: 'People are very good to criticize in life – they're not so good to express any gratitude,' she says, wanly. 'It's a bit like an albatross, really, around my neck. You do it, really, I suppose, for your own benefit. But it is a big effort.'

We are sitting on the grass in a park in Ealing on a bright afternoon in July; the weather is as hot as it was in the summer of 1995, when demolition began on Western Avenue. Since 'she does not know me from Adam', Pauline Harper did not want me to come to her flat; in reply to the letter I sent her, she rang and suggested that we meet in Ealing Broadway. She is a tidy, delicate-looking woman with greying hair cut to her shoulders, and a faint, unanimated voice. Yet there is one subject which never fails to excite a response from her: the decline of Wendover Court, where she has lived all her life. 'I feel sad to see it lose a bit of its . . . former glory. I mean, someone once wrote and said it was a luxury block of flats – I don't think it was ever that, but we did have community spirit; now people are dropping rubbish in the common parts, and leaving the lift gates open.'

As she talks, she tucks her dress over her stockinged legs repeatedly. She works as a chiropodist in Ealing Broadway, but only part-time, for she has decided she would rather not be the richest person in the graveyard. Her manners are courteously old-fashioned; throughout the afternoon, she calls me Mr Platt. I do not know what to call her in return. Plainly, I cannot call her Pauline, but I do not know if she is married, and I do not think she would like to be called 'Ms' Harper.

Her parents moved into an empty flat in Wendover Court during the war, and she is eager to talk about the road as it used to be. 'It suddenly comes back to you: it was fairly busy, but it was a real avenue, with a grass verge, and with all the trees in blossom . . . I mean, it was nice.' Despite the encroaching traffic, the *Acton Gazette*'s 'boulevard' survived until after the war – Pauline Harper's memory of the tree-lined road matches Shirley Buchan's.

Her childhood memories are richly inconsequential: she went to school with her neighbours – all of whom have left the building – and her mother would meet her at the bus stop and guide her across the road when she came home for lunch. After lunch, she would lean over the balcony to see the bus approaching from Park Royal and run downstairs to catch it. She used to be woken in the middle of the night by the trains which stopped to let off steam behind Wendover Court. She remembers gashing her knee on the gravel path outside the building and she used to cross the road on foot, slipping through a gap in the wire fence opposite Wendover Court. From time to time, the gap in the fence would be repaired, and then one of the tenants would go out with wire-cutters to open it up again. 'Years ago, I used to work over the road, and I used to regularly jaywalk through the traffic. I don't know where we got the nerve from to do it. I wouldn't do it now. Horrific crashes along there. Now you often hear the skid, and you just wait for the impact. I mean, there was a lady downstairs who used to permanently have her blanket ready, to rush out and cover people up – it was like a casualty station.'

Car crashes have become a spectator sport at Wendover Court, and Pauline Harper concedes they have become a 'bit blasé' about accidents. Like Shirley Buchan – another woman who had invested heavily in the memory of Western Avenue's better days – she does not drive a car. To me, it seems ironic that she should live beside the main road without enjoying its benefits, but she does not agree: the road is part of the landscape of her childhood, and she could not imagine life without it. Besides, she thinks it is no more dangerous than it used to be, though she regrets the fact that it now runs within ten feet of the building. She was upset when they widened the road, and they lost their 'nice green verge'.

It irritates her that people assume it is unhealthy to live on Western Avenue – her father lived to be ninety-five, and one of her neighbours was more than a hundred when she died. Thanks to her double-glazed windows, she hardly notices the traffic. It is not the noise on the road, but the noise of her neighbours which upsets her. 'Those flats are just paper thin, and you can hear everything – and I mean, everything . . . But that's flat living, isn't it? You can't stop it. I read an article years ago, saying we were, you know, getting like rats in little boxes – and then rats turn on each other.' Since people found they couldn't sell their flats, and started to let them instead, the building has deteriorated; it is a familiar complaint. 'I think, for my old age, I might find somewhere a bit more convenient,' she says. Yet she would be reluctant to leave: for obvious reasons, she has always felt safe in Wendover Court.

Her flat is positioned on the eastern end of the block, facing east, towards Gipsy Corner. It overlooks a riotously overgrown patch of land between the road and the railway – a thick, tangled mattress of brambles, bushes and ferns which looks deep enough to cushion a belly-flop from the top of the building. Her father used to call it his garden. She likes the natural look of it, and in the spring, she often finds birds by her door. The garden is home to a family of foxes as well.

Her father, who died in 1988, worked in an engineering firm at Gipsy Corner. Her mother only died a couple of years ago; she had cancer, and Pauline nursed her through it. 'When you've been through a few traumas, I think you have to reassess . . .' She is half-turned away from me, facing into the park. The trees and benches which make up the park furniture are dissolved in a hazy gauze of sunlight. Her hands are locked over her knees, and her voice is so quiet it is hardly picked up by my tape recorder.

Sometimes living in Wendover Court makes her feel invisible. The building is so inaccessible that local doctors are reluctant to accept the residents as patients, and people have trouble finding it, for it is not marked on any map. By her own account, she has grown old in Wendover Court – she is only fifty-three, yet she seems preoccupied by her age. 'I'm a war baby – but not the Boer War, as some people think,' she jokes, weakly. She has just been on holiday to a place with 'wall-to-wall geriatrics' – the fact that she was the youngest person there was good for her morale.

Occasionally, she says, she dreams of leaving the road, but she does not say it with any conviction. Yesterday, she saw a patient from Portugal whose regular chiropodist was an Englishman who had set up in Lisbon; she thought for a moment that she might do the same. 'He was doing quite well. Sell up and move to Spain, or move to the Dordogne . . . Sounds nice, doesn't it? The trouble is I'd be too attached to my possessions.'

She would also have trouble selling her flat: like Anna-Marie – whom she seems to regard, rather scornfully, as a newcomer – she feels trapped in Wendover Court. Since she cannot, or will not, leave, she devotes her time to protecting the building. It is a demanding job, and she has learnt she has to be perpetually wary: people have tried to put up hoardings in her father's garden, and an advertising pylon was recently erected in front of the building – a flat, silver board like the palm of a giant hand held out to attract the attention of the passing drivers. 'It looked like something out of a concentration camp – a watchtower,' she says. In Park Royal, retail has replaced manufacturing. The buildings which once housed the city's factories now house the consumer emporiums and leisure centres of London's post-industrial economy, and the sky is scribbled with neon signs and hung with advertising hoardings designed to communicate with the motorist travelling at speed through the city's suburbs.

She believes the destruction of the houses at Gipsy

Corner and Western Circus is testament to the incompetence and thoughtlessness of those in authority. She regrets the demolition of the mock-Tudor houses where the 'better-off people – for want of a better word' used to live. 'It used to be beautiful, that road, and that's what's so sad: people used to take great pride in their houses down there, but they've ruined it – and it was all unnecessary. I mean, apart from it being such a blot on the landscape, people's lives were disrupted – and the people who took the decision live in smart places, don't they?'

Still, she half hopes that the day will come when Wendover Court will be requisitioned and demolished by the Department of Transport; then she will be able to leave the road.

An hour and a half has passed, and she is surprised to find herself still talking. 'I didn't think there was so much to talk about! It's surprising how much you remember suddenly, isn't it? You must think I'm a garrulous old lady!' As it happens, I thought she was neither garrulous nor old; I thought she was tired and disillusioned – though still spirited enough to fight to preserve her inheritance. I leave her sitting on the grass, in the sun, with a copy of the *Daily Mail* open on her knees.

― ― ―

On Western Avenue, there is a tramp who walks from Alperton to Western Circus and back again every day – a distance of several miles. Sometimes he breaks his journey to stand beside the road and shout at the traffic.

― ― ―

In 1958 – thirty years after Moses completed the first of his Long Island parkways – an eight-mile stretch of the M6 bypassing Preston opened to traffic. Britain's 'Motorway Age' had begun. Accommodating the car within the city had become one of the primary aims of post-war planning, and a World Congress on Housing and Planning declared that city populations should be contained within limits which allowed for 'reasonable traffic arrangements'. Cities that had already exceeded a population of 700,000 would be required to adopt more drastic measures to facilitate the free flow of traffic within their precincts, for 'traffic is the life-stream of the twentieth century'. Car ownership in London had almost doubled since the end of the war, and in 1959, the Ministry of Transport warned that a 'traffic crisis will soon overtake the Metropolis'.

— — —

No one I have met has ever spoken to The Man, but everyone knows where he lives. The traffic lights turn red, and I step into the road. Ignoring the drivers' stares, I edge between the cars, a metal bonnet warm beneath the fingers of my trailing hand. Twenty yards before the Hanger Lane gyratory, there is a slip-road that allows the westbound traffic to double back and feed into the eastbound carriageway. It is the only turning point on Western Avenue between Gipsy Corner and Hanger Lane. It seals one end of an island scored by cars. I reach the path that runs across the island: to my right, there is a sheer drop to a steep-walled valley – the mouth of the four-laned tunnel, which carries the cars beneath Hanger Lane; to my left, the island is swathed in greenery, yet an observant driver might notice the wooden slats on the roof of the hut where The Man lives.

It was Anna-Marie who first told me about him. 'We call him "The Man" – "The Man with the House",' she said, emphasising the formal nature of his title. 'Kids are fascinated by him – they always say, you know, "Where's The Man?" He has a little tricycle, with a little mesh wire basket on the back, and he collects all this debris every-where, so maybe he makes a living out of that. A bit of a weirdo – but aren't we all?'

Ahead of me, a white metal gate bars the path across the island. I approach it cautiously. It seals a concrete courtyard set below the level of the road. The gate is locked, and the steps which lead down to the courtyard are littered with debris: a stuffed white cat, a brush and a bowl of dirty water; elsewhere, scattered around the island, there is a traffic cone and a deflated dinghy. Like Anna-Marie, who said she always wants to stop and snoop, I want to see more of The Man's house. But the two large wooden doors in the far wall are sealed with a chain and padlock: The Man is not at home. A ticking, scratching noise comes from beneath the blue cloth which hangs in front of the hutch on the far wall; a tray of feathers and a tray of bird-shit are placed in front of it.

Forty feet below, the cars disintegrate as they enter the tunnel. They are travelling so fast that the eye cannot hold them in one piece.

– – –

In total, 250,000 people were evicted from their homes to make way for Moses roads. Marshall Berman, who grew up in the Bronx, remembers with awe 'the vistas of devas-tation stretching for miles to the east and the west' as the construction of the Cross-Bronx Expressway reduced his neighbourhood to 'sublime, spectacular ruins'. Yet Moses' concept of 'step by step large-scale city modernisation' did not stop at road-building. Exploiting the federal funds available for the post-war reconstruction of America's cit-ies, Moses began clearing New York's slums and reshaping the city around the car. Soon, the rest of America would follow his example.

9. The Motorway Box

'We've got energy here on Friday and Saturday, you know what I mean?' Lorraine leans across the counter to speak directly into my tape-recorder. Behind her, in matching uniforms, the staff at the Warner Bros multiplex crowd the popcorn stand like a sixties pop group relishing their first encounter with the press.

It is Lorraine, a striking black woman in her early twenties, who dominates the conversation. 'People go to the club, they come here, they meet friends – girls and guys checking each other . . . Talent and stuff, you know.' For a moment, she is distracted by the woman beside her: 'It's true! Don't look at me like I'm telling lies!' Then she addresses me again: 'The Western Avenue? OK. Being a pedestrian, the Western Avenue is fine. The pollution, you get pollution, yeah, because it's so busy – for twenty-four hours a day that road is busy! – but for a driver now, for a *driver* looking to get to a nice busy leisure park like this, yeah, it's one whole *rigmarole*!' Lorraine delivers the word as though she were auditioning for a West End musical – she is practically singing. 'We need easier access, you know what I mean? Next person!'

Lorraine slaps the counter, and takes a step back. As far as she is concerned, the sole purpose of Western Avenue is to deliver customers to the door of the cinema – a task which it does not perform well. Tanya – a plump-cheeked and exuberant woman – assumes Lorraine's place at the head of the queue. 'This is such a beautiful complex – I don't know why they had to put it here,' she says, sadly.

The Royale Leisure Park stands on the brow of the hill between the Renault showroom and Park Royal tube. It is a loose corral of modern buildings dominated by the grey warehouse of the Warner Bros multiplex.

'It's a bad site.' Jags – an Asian man with wolfish incisors – has been waiting behind the women pressing against the counter; now he comes forward. He is studying business and computing at Middlesex University, and he does not plan to work here for much longer. 'A business graduate working behind a popcorn stall. I don't think so, somehow!' he says, scornfully. Beside him, stands Sheetal – a diminutive woman with startling blue eyes, like a Disney cartoon of an Arabian princess. 'I think it's nice,' she says in a voice so quiet it is barely audible.

Most of the staff are students, though Tanya is a 'full-time mother' as well. They are surprised when I tell them there are plans to rebuild the road: most live locally, but they knew nothing about it. They welcome the news enthusiastically. 'It's got potential, right?' says Jags. 'But because of access, a lot of people don't want to come here.'

In each corner of the foyer, televisions suspended from the ceiling relay trailers for the week's movies. Outside, there are hundreds of cars moored in the ocean of tarmac: a drive-thru Burger King and a Shell garage stand closest to the road; elsewhere, there is a pizza parlour, an English pub, a Mexican restaurant and an American diner; a club – the Zenith Discotheque – and a bowling alley dominate the far corner of the lot.

'It's like a little town, isn't it?' Lorraine has resumed her natural role as cheerleader. 'It's like our little home.' There is a knowingness about her which makes the others – Tanya, in particular – seem innocent and uncalculating.

'When we're here during the days, we use everything. Yeah! Uh-hmm,' choruses Tanya. 'It's fun. We get on.'

'Not all the time,' interjects another woman. Her name is Queenie. She does not look at me.

'At times.' Tanya laughs.

'Some people get on. Some people don't,' says Queenie.

'Well, as with any company . . .' begins Tanya.

'It's a beautiful company!' says Lorraine.

'It's lovely. We work very hard to maintain the standard that you see. And it's very social. The staff are nice, and you meet a lot of people down here. The local people . . .'

'Not all the people who come in here are nice – some of them are blatantly rude and got no manners.' Queenie wants to ignore the impromptu press conference, but she cannot resist the chance to make her point.

'It's true, it's true – we were trying to see the sunny side, but it's true . . .' Lorraine shakes her head in exaggerated sadness.

For the first time, Queenie looks at me directly: 'And the problem is that people who think they've got money think they have got every right to degrade you and diss you, and I don't take none of it. People don't even use simple things like "Please".'

'But because we're getting paid . . . It's a job.' Lorraine is determined to restore the mood of optimism.

'Yeah, we just get on with our job,' adds Tanya, brightly. 'We're always smiling.'

I go in search of the manager. His name is Mr Bywood. When Tanya sees us together, she puts her hand to her mouth in a gesture of horror, and then rushes across the foyer. 'I swear I said nothing bad to him,' she says, earnestly to Mr Bywood. 'Did I? Did I say anything bad?' She touches my arm in her panic. 'Don't write anything bad about the company! Don't you dare!' she scolds. Her loyalty is matched by her lack of confidence in her own judgement –

and by her lack of faith in journalists. She watches me
nervously as I leave the building.

I cross the parking lot and enter the bowling alley. It is
the school holidays, and the hall is crowded with teenagers.
A young girl places a ball in the centre of the polished
runway, and pushes it forward with both hands; it rolls
gently into the gutter five feet beyond her outstretched arms.

Beside the bowling alley is a video arcade – a dark and
humid alleyway, alive with the parrot-squawk of electronic
machinery, and vibrant with simulated danger. Shoot the
terrorists! Don't shoot the hostages! A sweat-stained busi-
nessman, a tearful secretary and the captain of a cruise ship
stumble across the gun-sights of one machine. Nuclear
Threat! Seize the ammunition dump! The video games
replay the stories that Hollywood tells us: the dreams and
images that seep from the grey temple of the Warner Bros
multiplex infest the leisure park.

A kid shoots the living dead, his gun held rakishly flat,
gangsta-style, like they do in the movies. There are two girls
sitting on a step beside his feet. He gouges green bile from
the attacking zombies, and then turns to the girls, stooping
to gather the admiration he has earned, while all around
him, the machines chatter to one another like monkeys
hidden in the branches of a rainforest.

– – –

Twyford Abbey, which stands behind Western Avenue,
near the Guinness Brewery, was a monastery until it was
converted into a mental hospital. While it was part of
the Health Service – before it was 'rationalized' – Pauline
Harper used to treat patients there: 'Do you remember that
book, *Tarka the Otter*? By Henry Williamson? He used to
be in there – someone pointed him out to me. One day he

escaped and he was caught running down the Western Avenue . . . It's sad, isn't it? Poor soul.'

– – –

The elevated roundabout encircling an expanse of grass is bisected by another road which runs on concrete pillars towards the pale-blue horizon; scattered trees blur the edges of the tower blocks which overlook the raised carriageways. This 1960s drawing might have been illustrating a detail of the Contemporary City; it was, in fact, publicizing the route of the Western Avenue extension. The road was to be driven through North Kensington – a 'twilight area' of tenement buildings and terraced streets ruled by the notorious slum landlord Rachman. Corbusian imagery and rhetoric informed the debate over the road's design: the *New Scientist* even proposed that the Westway should be built across London's rooftops. The magazine envisaged two rows of buildings fifty metres apart, each supporting one three-lane carriageway and joined at intervals by cross-buildings, forming 'pleasant traffic-free enclosures for gardens or courtyards'. The 'roof road', it was claimed, would reduce pollution and congestion – life in our cities would become 'civilised and tranquil' again.

– – –

'We've got a really weird person in our other branch. It was seven years ago that he came in – probably more. He was a huge guy. Heart trouble. He'd take three steps and . . .' Tony places his hand on his chest and pants heavily: the man could hardly breathe. Most people store furniture or office equipment in Tony's warehouse, but the man with the bad heart returned with plastic carrier-bags and bin-liners filled with nothing but old newspapers and back copies of magazines. 'Just crap,' says Tony incredulously. 'And he's been paying for it ever since. Never missed a beat. Money arrives by cheque every month – and the cheques have got his name and his signature, so I know they're coming from him. And of course it's got dearer and dearer, and yet still he keeps paying for all this stuff – it's very, very weird.'

The warehouse where Tony works is subdivided into rooms for hire. 'Your lock, your key, your room,' says the sandwich-board propped beside the road. The rooms are like safety deposit boxes, only bigger, and each one contains the contents of someone's house or office. The customers, who are equipped with their own keys, come and go as they like. For ten hours a day, Tony presides over the office, registering new customers and settling any difficulties which arise; it is hardly surprising that he agreed to talk to me.

'The job is as boring as it sounds, but it's a living,' he began, as he sat down at the desk behind the counter in the wood-panelled office. He was hoovering when I walked into reception. He turned off the vacuum cleaner and listened attentively while I introduced myself. He is a solid man with tidy red hair and green eyes, dressed in jeans and a short-sleeved shirt. He looks competent and reliable, yet it soon becomes apparent that he is blessed with an energy and curiosity at odds with his rather stolid appearance. 'It's one of those jobs which you take on, and you think, "Well, it'll do for now, and I'll make up my mind what to do when I'm an adult." And now here I am – nine years later . . .'

There is another junk-hoarder in their Chelsea branch: Tony thinks it is a woman, but he is not certain, it may be a man. 'African. Black. White make-up, thin little lips, a straight wig, a pair of shades . . .' He elucidates the details carefully. Tony's accent is nondescript, but from time to time, his flat London vowels acquire a richer intonation, and I find myself wondering where he comes from. 'Always smells unwashed – obviously it's so much trouble to put the make-up on, he or she never washes. And this woman, man – whatever he or she is – has got rubbish stashed away, newspapers – stuff like that. You know – it's an expensive way of storing newspapers, isn't it?'

I have a friend whose mother once hired a housekeeper for their Hampshire home. It soon became apparent that the housekeeper hated throwing anything away. One day, she was seen rescuing chicken bones from the dustbin. Alarmed, my friend's mother decided to explore the room at the top of the house where the housekeeper sometimes slept. She found it waist-deep in rotting compost. A narrow path led through the rubbish, connecting the bed to the door. Later, they found that the woman's home in the village was filled with rubbish, as well.

I understand why Tony is so fascinated by the compulsion to hoard belongings: it is such a strange impulse – and yet such a familiar one. Tony, whose work makes him something of an expert on the subject, believes you can divide people into two categories: those who value possessions, and those who don't. He places himself in the former category, yet he recognizes that the gap between storing possessions and hoarding junk is often a narrow one. He gives me an example: 'My wife reads *Vogue*, *Harpers* and *Tatler* every month – I used to buy them for her, on a Sunday morning, when I went to get the papers. She reads those three, and we also read *World of Interiors* and *Elle Decoration*, so that's like, five magazines which come in, every issue, every month. In our living room now, there's loads of piles of magazines, and they go from

there into boxes. You pay £3 each, so it's a pity to throw
them out, and OK, there's interesting articles – but you
never bloody go back to them. You know, there must be
several hundred pounds worth of magazines, boxed up and
forgotten about.'

In other words, he understands why his customers might
want to keep their old magazines – it is the fact that they
are willing, and able, to pay to do so which fascinates him.
'You know, where do they get the money? How does that
person have a job?' The question mystifies him: these people
look like misfits, yet they seem to be able to afford to
indulge their obsessions; while Tony, on the other hand, is
obliged to work for a living.

A customer interrupts us for a moment: he signs the
visitor's book and then he's gone. I soon discover why it is
that I cannot place Tony's accent: he is Irish, but he grew
up in England as well as Ireland – so the English think he's
Irish and the Irish think he's English. 'I've been batting
backwards and forwards between London and Dublin all
my life. Yeah, my dad was one of those who came over in
the early sixties. He drove a cement mixer, doing all the
building and stuff that was going on then – he was one of
the "Holloway Road mob", if you will . . .'

The fastidiousness with which he qualifies the phrase
betrays a slight unease about his background – a distance
instilled, perhaps, by his education: although his parents
were 'poor', they sent him to a private school in Ireland,
run by Carmelite monks. 'My dad has got really weird
ideas – he thought I'd get a trade. That's what he wanted
me to do. But the guys I was at school with became
solicitors and lawyers and accountants – so how did he
expect me to become a plumber or a carpenter?'

Inevitably, perhaps, he became neither a carpenter nor a
lawyer: he became a painter. He went to art college in

Dublin, and he has just set up a studio in the basement of
his house in the East End. Unfortunately, his job at the
warehouse leaves little time for painting. 'I don't dislike this
job, but it's what – nine-odd hours a day? More on a day
like this, and it's like . . . your life is sand going through
your fingers, and you're never going to get it back.'

In the long hours at the warehouse, he has begun to
worry that he will never again produce work that he likes.
'I look at my early stuff, and by anybody's standards, it's
dreadful, but I went through a phase before I came over
here, and I kind of like it; I look at them once in a while –
and they're not bad, I don't mind them . . .' He seems
surprised. 'And then I look at the stuff I'm doing again
now, and oh my God, it's like – dreadful again. And you
sometimes wonder – was that it? Was that the little spark
back in '85, '86, '87, and that's all I'm ever going to
produce that I'm not ashamed to show people?'

He did not stay in Dublin for long; at the time, he hated
the city. London seemed to offer everything that Dublin
lacked, and he came to live here permanently almost ten
years ago. London and Dublin are still the twin poles of his
world, as they were in his childhood. He does not like
travelling, which is probably just as well, for his spare time
is pressured by the demands of a seemingly endless list of
hobbies: painting, drawing and photography are only the
beginning, for he is also a woodcarver, a carpenter, a
mechanic, and a fisherman. At the moment, he is repointing
the back wall of his house in the East End, he has a piece
of walnut wood he wants to begin carving, and he soaks up
his spare time at work by filling notebooks with cartoons.
It is hardly surprising that he is fascinated by people who
seem to survive without working: there is so much he could
be doing elsewhere, if he were ever freed from the pressure
of earning a living at the warehouse. It is strange to think

of such an active man presiding over empty space on Western Avenue.

Still, he is careful not to complain. 'It's not the world's worst job. I don't hate coming in here. I'd love to be doing something "artistic" for a living, because I work quite long hours here, and it doesn't give me much spare time, but if I actually stop myself and think about it – you know, two of us, a house, a basement, the food I can eat, the wine I can drink . . . You know, I'm very, very lucky. Well, you can't live your life sort of thinking, "God, aren't I really lucky," but when you do take stock every now and then . . .'

At the moment, he comes to Western Avenue only one day a week – most of his time is spent at other branches. He hates the traffic as much as any of the people who live beside the road: 'You hobble out here at six, and it's straight into a gap in the traffic, and it's slow all the way down to Western Circus – if you keep your window up you start baking, if you wind your window down, you get all the fumes . . .'

Tony must have driven past Wendover Court hundreds of times, yet he has never noticed it. He pays no attention to the buildings on Western Avenue, for he sees little to admire in them. 'It's rather desolate – there's no ornamentation, everything's functional and dust-covered. Down in the East End, they're building flats and stuff at every available little plot, you know, but I don't see the same sort of renewal around here.'

Yet Tony's warehouse is evidence of renewal of a kind. It was empty until eight or nine months ago when his company bought the building and began to convert it into storage space. The factories and warehouses built between the wars are being drawn back into use, and Park Royal's fortunes have begun to revive. Recently, mobile telecommunications firms, companies specializing in business services and film, television and media support facilities have set up in the industrial estate – businesses as emblematic of the 1990s as the 'radio works' and 'automobile works' were of an earlier era. The Hoover Building stood empty for years when Hoover relocated to south Wales. It reopened as a supermarket in 1992, and the newspapers did not miss the significance of the event – the factory which was once a temple of high-tech manufacturing had been reborn as testament to the principal pursuit of the modern era: shopping.

Tony offers to show me round the building. We pass through the double doors beside the office, and enter the warehouse: it is dimly lit, and corridors run between the rows of cubicles. We wander through the metal-walled aisles. Table-legs and chairs protrude through the metal grilles which join the top of the partitions to the ceiling, but no one knows for certain what is kept in the confines of the individual rooms – a fact which fascinates the police. Tony denies there is anything mysterious about the contents of the warehouse: he gets to know people, and he tends to know what they are doing. 'You know, the truck pulls up, and the household furniture starts coming off – sure, there are boxes, and you don't know what's in them, but in seventy-five per cent of cases, you generally get an idea . . .' The warehouse is not a repository for stolen goods, but a storehouse for furniture, paintings, clothes, files, old news-papers – a collection of objects with nothing in common except the fact that their owners consider them worth preserving.

Upstairs, the process of partitioning the room has not yet begun. The concrete floor stretches unbroken for hundreds of yards. The fans hanging from the ceiling are a legacy of the days when the warehouse contained a manu-facturing plant. Tony says he would like to position a bed in the centre of the enormous room and sleep in it, a lamp and a table beside his head.

— — —

Until six or seven years ago, when the Hanger Lane gyratory was fitted with traffic lights, Anna-Marie remembers that the roundabout was like a roundabout in Paris: 'You could just go round and round and round it,' she says. 'You know, lost for ever, lost for months . . .' She seems transfixed by the thought.

— — —

The pattern of suburban expansion which had transformed Long Island was being replicated across America. In 1956, work had begun on a vast programme of highway construction, modelled on the parkways and expressways Robert Moses had built for New York. As whole districts were demolished to make way for urban expressways, and funds were channelled into the suburban developments which the inter-urban highways were opening up, an exodus from America's cities began. In a decade, 19 million people emigrated to the 'automobile suburbs' emerging across the country. Marshall Berman believes America's planners had begun to conceive of cities 'principally as obstructions to the flow of traffic, and as junk-yards of sub-standard housing from which Americans should be given a chance to escape'. The 'automobile suburbs' were spreading so rapidly they seemed to threaten the survival of America's cities – at least in their traditional form.

— — —

Opposite Wendover Court stands a factory called Achilles House. In almost every respect, the building matches the description of the tobacco factory built on Western Avenue in the boom days of the early thirties. Only one detail has changed: the building is derelict, and the windows designed to provide its employees with natural light are broken or sealed with cardboard.

As usual, there is a strange smell in the air around Park Royal – bitter, at first, yet concealing within it a sickly chocolate-sweetness. It was Tony who told me that it was barley from the Guinness Brewery behind Western Avenue – one of the few companies which has remained in business in Park Royal since the boom days of the thirties. In the sixties and seventies, London's manufacturing industry shrank to vanishing point. Drawn by the vertiginous pull of Heathrow Airport, many companies settled in the 'Sunrise Belt' flanking the M4 between London and Bristol. *The Times* noted that the 'human population' of London was falling and the 'car population' rising, and in 1964, bull-dozers began clearing the route for the Westway. The task of remaking the city to accommodate the car had begun, yet the outward movement of people and jobs continued, and the 'art deco' factories on the Great West Road and Western Avenue fell empty.

I try the front door, but it is locked. The manager of the go-kart track which occupies the next-door warehouse tells me that Achilles House has been empty for years: 'Everything in it's been smashed up,' he says, with curious relish, as he chews on a mouthful of smoke.

– – –

In a paroxysm of uncertainty, Mrs Johnson clutches the knuckles of one hand in the palm of the other. 'My God! It's incredible! You see these beautiful houses – the whole lot have gone! What have they done to the people? I don't know what to believe!'

The new government has just announced that the

reconstruction of Western Avenue is to be suspended, pending a review of transport policy. The news comes as a
surprise to Mrs Johnson. She is dressed like a housewife
from an Ealing comedy: slippers, a floral-patterned house-
coat, thick brown-framed glasses; her hair is greying, but
her face is creased with laughter lines. Mr Johnson is not at
home.

'So what are you telling me? They're not doing it at all?
I can't believe it! But they still want us to get out of here!
Maybe they do it later? Is it final?' She slaps her hands
together in a gesture of dismissal. No, it is not final, I say.
'It's crazy – I don't know who to believe!'

I leave her standing on her doorstep, her arms spread
wide in a gesture of bemused supplication.

– – –

Once a day, the staff of the Warner's multiplex walk
around the building's perimeter, checking the outside lights
and making sure that there are no cars parked on the kerb.
Otherwise, they never leave the building: 'You do get a bit
encapsulated, being inside all day,' says the manager.

– – –

It was to be the 'greatest instrument of change that London
had seen for centuries': in 1965 the GLC announced plans
for a network of motorways which would encircle the city
in a cordon of steel and concrete. Construction of Ring-
way One – the innermost of three concentric motorway
rings – would cost £100 million and make 100,000 people
homeless, yet it would foster a city which was socially
and economically mobile. The new roads would 'help the
Leyton housewife who wants to shop in Harrods'.

– – –

The scalloped lawn is tidily cropped and the flowerbeds are well tended, but creepers, ferns and wild strawberries have burst through the broken-down fences which separate 123 Western Avenue from the abandoned houses on either side. Norm and Irene try to keep their garden in good repair, but it is not easy, for the surrounding gardens are running wild.

123 Western Avenue stands a block to the west of Shirley Buchan's old home, below the Bridge of Fools. It is one of only six houses which remain on the hill above Western Circus – and one of only three which are still occupied. Telephone in one hand and cigarette in the other, Norm sits on the terrace behind the house; Irene, who was leaning on a walking stick when she answered the door – 'Go on outside,' she said – has picked her way through the house to join us.

She lights a cigarette from one of the three packets that lie on the table, and we wait until Norm hangs up his phone, stretches expansively and locks his arms behind his head: 'It's a mess, isn't it?' he begins. 'What they've done to this road is a crime – it really is a crime. There's no other word for it – legalized vandalism is what it is. It's very sad. I mean, this used to be a beautiful road – all those gardens down there were very well kept. We used to have a lot of fun here.' He lights another cigarette. 'It's very sad that the faceless men – and I don't necessarily mean the politicians – can wreak such havoc for no end.'

Two years ago, when the bailiffs began to repossess their neighbours' houses, Norm and Irene were uncertain what would become of them. 'I've got to admit that at one stage we were very, very edgy.' Norm is a solidly made Glaswegian with bulky black hair and a stomach as round and firm as a basketball. 'When they boarded these houses up at the beginning, no one would clarify what was happening.

I couldn't find out if they were expecting us to get out or what – you didn't know if a letter was going to drop on the mat, saying "You've got four weeks . . ." '

Outside, the rush-hour is in full flow, but the garden is surprisingly quiet – or, rather, the noise of the cars is smothered by a shrieking chorus of birdsong. The birds are so loud that I thought there must be an aviary nearby, but Irene assures me they are all wild; she is proud of the garden and the wildlife it supports. Two years ago, when the demolition of the neighbouring houses began, their garden became infested with rats. 'They're all living underground in the back gardens, and so on, so when you destroy the houses, you're destroying a habitat – and they move on,' explains Norm. The rats burrowed into their garden shed, and ate all of its contents – including the sunloungers they were given as wedding presents. 'Everything in that shed was demolished – ruined!' says Irene. 'It's horrifying! It's horrifying expecting people to live like this!'

Irene and Norm have been married for eight years. When Irene first moved into Norm's house, she was not looking forward to living beside such a busy road, but it did not take her long to get used to it; now she would miss Western Avenue. The traffic used to drive her crazy, but now she notices it only when it stops. Sometimes, she is woken at night by the unexpected silence.

If the work proceeds as planned, then Norm and Irene will find themselves living in strange circumstances: Western Avenue will advance to within three yards of their front door, and a cul-de-sac will be built across the bottom of their garden, pinning the house to a narrow strip of land between two roads.

'We'll be living on an island, more or less,' says Norm.

'Some island! A traffic island!' Irene laughs, and reaches for another cigarette.

'Well, we don't have any trouble with the neighbours, let's put it that way,' says Norm. 'But at the same time, it's insecure.' The broken glass beneath the windows of the derelict houses acts as a kind of burglar alarm.

They have reason to be wary: their house was burgled one afternoon several years ago; Norm, who had come home early from work, found a cigarette burning on the carpet in the hall – he had disturbed the burglars. On average, he tells me, it takes a burglar two and a half minutes to ransack a house. It does not take the bailiffs much longer.

'We had a man from the Department of Environment in this back garden and he said to me, "The squatters next door wrecked these houses." He was quite taken aback when I said, "No they didn't – your men did."' Norm closes his eyes and dots the air with his cigarette. 'And he said, "Yes, but there's a hole in that roof" – and I said, "Yes, your men did that as well."' He opens his eyes again, and looks at me steadily. 'They'd actually knocked a hole in the tiles, from the loft.' He points to the roof of the next-door house: below the chimney, there is a hole several feet across. 'These houses were never coming down – that is the major factor. It's criminal. Would they not have been better letting them until the road scheme starts – why wreck 'em and board 'em up? What good is that for anybody?'

Norm gestures to the building behind him: 'If you think about it, that's a seven-roomed house in there.'

123 Western Avenue was once home to a family of seven: Norm's son and daughter from his first marriage, Irene's sixteen-year-old daughter from hers, and twin girls to whom they are legal guardians – Irene had nursed their mother before she died. All of their children have grown up and left home except for Irene's daughter. They have no children together, but the certainty with which Irene tells

me that they would have done, had they met earlier in life, is striking.

Norman and Irene did not object to the squatters, they would rather the houses were lived in than left empty. Besides, they enjoyed their company. 'The first day that the squatters moved in, I happened to be home that day, and I heard this noise, and I actually went in; and there was two of them in there, and they tried to tell me that they were there legally.' Norm tips his head back, and closes his eyes again. For a moment, while his memories clothe themselves in words, he says nothing. Then he resumes: 'And I said, "Now, funnily enough, all the tenants of West Hampstead that I know were given keys – they didn't have to smash their way in." I said, "Now, I don't care, you're here, as far as I'm concerned, you can stay here, I won't bother you," I said, "but if you annoy me, make too much noise, cause trouble for me, then I'll cause trouble for you: I'll have the police around here every day . . ."'

He recalls his sternness with satisfaction, but what happened next gives him even greater pleasure. 'And I never had a problem,' he says, with relish. 'I've walked in the front door and said, "That bloody music in that back garden is too loud." "Sorry!"' He raises his hand, imitating the squatter's apologetic gesture. 'No problem – switch it down . . . The only thing was that you could have got high sitting here with the fumes coming over the fence – they were fantastic! They were gay!'

'They were trying to teach us how to mix cocktails!' giggles Irene.

'You could meet 'em outside at night, and they'd say to you, do you want a drink out of the bottle, and all this carry-on – it was hilarious! We were speaking to one of them in the pub one night, round down the Goldsmiths, and he said, "I'll buy you a pint," he said. "You two are not working, I'm working, I'll buy you a drink." And he's squatting next door!'

Eighteen months ago, when she was nursing, Irene injured her back. Since then, she periodically loses power in her legs, and her shoulders have calcified to the extent that one fractured spontaneously earlier this year. Her memory and concentration have begun to decline, as well. 'I need somewhere very peaceful, which doesn't rattle my brain too much,' she says, matter-of-factly. She has been tested for multiple sclerosis, but the results were inconclusive.

Norm's health began to deteriorate four years ago. He has heart problems; he is also a borderline diabetic, and he suffers from stomach ulcers. 'I bet you wish you'd never asked now,' he concludes, more than half-seriously.

'We're sort of both living on a knife-edge,' says Irene. 'Some days I wouldn't be sitting here talking to you – I wouldn't be able to move off the settee, my speech would be slurred, my brain completely flat, and my concentration dead; I can't walk any distance, I can't balance, I can't stand for any length of time.' She moulds the end of her cigarette on an ashtray which stands beside her elbow. It is surprising, given their litany of ailments, that they both seem so content. 'We try and live as normally as we can, with the illnesses,' says Norm.

Irene agrees that they are much more relaxed these days, but when they were demolishing the properties, life was 'hell'. Still, they are conscious that they have suffered little in comparison to the people whose homes were destroyed. 'Moving's bad enough if you're young and healthy and you've chosen to do it – but if you're elderly and unhealthy and you have no choice . . .' Irene does not finish the sentence.

For Norm and Irene, the garden has particular significance: it was here that they hosted their wedding reception.

They had a marquee on the lawn, and patio tables across
the terrace – 'Proper ones,' says Norm, 'Not like this one.'
He slaps the plastic-topped table which stands between us.
'I'll miss the garden when we go,' says Irene. She leans
sideways, and squints through the trees which are shielding
us from the setting sun. 'You could see a church steeple
across there but the trees have grown too high now . . . It's
very peaceful here. I've been fortunate all my life – wherever
I've lived and worked, I've always had a bit of garden.'
When an accident interrupts the flow of traffic and the cars
are held up outside their house, the volume of fumes is
unbelievable, but nothing would drive them inside: they
often sit in the garden until eleven at night. An empty
packet of cigarettes is discarded, and a new one opened;
another long evening is beginning. It is eight o'clock, but
the air is still warm, and the smell of woodsmoke drifts
across the garden.

I leave Norm and Irene on the terrace behind their house
and cross the road on the Bridge of Fools. Beneath me, the
red and yellow trails of the traffic glow richly in the dusk.
When I came to Western Avenue, I did not expect to find
people who felt they belonged here; I used to think the city
was made up of visitors to it, like myself, and it was a relief
to discover that I was wrong. Many of the people who
regarded the road as their home have been forced to leave,
but even now, Western Avenue sometimes seems a better
place than I have ever allowed it to be.

– – –

The receptionist in the Daewoo showroom, next door to
Office World, tells me that the name is pronounced 'Day-
ooh'. Like a music-box fairy, a Day-ooh car spins on a
silver disc in the centre of the showroom. 'How did you get

here?' says the customer survey on the video machine. 'Just passing / Killing time / Planned visit / Been here before.'

– – –

'Get us out of this Hell – rehouse us now', said the banner draped over the houses abutting the carriageways of the Westway. The elevated motorway begins at Marylebone Road: it cuts through Paddington, Westbourne Park and Ladbroke Grove before descending to ground level at White City, where it joins the original A40. The A40(M), as it is called to mark its status as an urban motorway, opened in July 1970. As the longest stretch of raised motorway in Europe, it was an engineering triumph, and yet within weeks, there was talk of an injunction being brought to close it again. Worldwide media coverage of the opening ceremony concentrated on the plight of the people who lived within sight of the road, and the transport minister said, apologetically, that he hoped 'those who use this road will spare a thought for those for whom it is not a blessing'.

The Westway was 'a bad advertisement for the GLC's controversial programme of urban motorways', said *The Times*, yet it still believed that the motorway box was 'an effective solution to London's traffic problems' – and it was modest compared to the networks envisaged by cities like Glasgow and Birmingham. Within a month, the Westway was carrying 47,000 vehicles a day.

– – –

The blue hatchback lies upside down beside the exit ramp of the Hyde Park underpass, its bonnet clamped round a thin strut of scaffolding which bars the façade of a Knightsbridge hotel. 'Result of a pursuit when the bandit went offside', says the caption beneath the photograph – one of a series designed to advertise the work of the Area One Traffic Police. 'That will have been a fatal,' says PC Hewitt, tapping the noticeboard as he walks ahead of me into the canteen at the Euston Traffic Garage.

PC Hewitt and his partner, PC Welsh, have patrolled the elevated carriageways of the Westway for fifteen years. They are a long-established partnership – not merely colleagues, but friends and neighbours as well: they both live in Harrow and commute to work on the road they police in their professional lives.

These days, thanks partly to congestion and partly to the effect of reduced speed limits, there are few accidents on the A40, but crashes are commonplace on the Westway's elevated carriageways and on the Shepherd's Bush roundabout. 'People tend to go too fast for the bends,' says PC Hewitt. His black hair is cropped into thick spikes through which his scalp shows in patches – the hairstyle of an overgrown adolescent, and a bulbous nose interrupts the delta of thread-thin veins which are spreading across the flat plains of his face. 'The camber of the road pushes you out towards the wall, so they lose control and panic, and drive straight into the wall.'

'We've had a lot of nasty fatals up there,' adds PC Welsh – a slight man with rust-coloured hair and a sharper, more self-conscious wit than his rather ponderous partner. They speak of 'fatals' with a familiarity born of long experience: in 1997, there were fifty-seven accidents on the Westway – approximately one a week. It is 2.30 in the afternoon, and we are sitting at a table in the staff canteen as traffic policemen come and go, one or two dressed in leathers and clutching helmets.

J.G. Ballard's novel *Crash* is set on the Westway. Ballard's 'hoodlum scientist', Vaughan – 'the nightmare angel of the expressways' – patrols its exit ramps and elevated carriageways photographing accident victims and dreaming of the death of the actress Elizabeth Taylor in a car crash. Vaughan is obsessed with the 'pantheon of auto-disaster victims' – a roll-call of iconic figures which includes James Dean and Albert Camus. Vaughan adds to their number by concocting imaginary deaths for 'the famous and the beautiful'. More than 15 million people have died in accidents in the hundred years since the car was invented, and Ballard insists that we acknowledge both the dangers inherent in driving, and our acquiescence in those dangers: 'If we really feared the crash, most of us would be unable to look at a car, let alone drive one.'

The introduction of safety measures such as speed cameras and drink-driving laws has dramatically reduced the number of 'fatals' in Britain: the 2 million cars on the road in 1931 claimed more lives than the 20 million vehicles registered in 1982, but the police have learnt that you will never eliminate the potential for human error. 'Obviously some of it you can't help,' says PC Hewitt, 'but it's mainly stupidity, I'd say.' Many of the fatalities are pedestrians – 'tourists, looking the wrong way, and stepping out in front of a bus'.

Most of their energy seems to be devoted to keeping the traffic moving: if a car breaks down on the Westway, they will help the driver change a tyre, or tow it off the motorway if necessary, for any interruption to the flow of traffic can cause a tailback within minutes. It is now 2.45 pm, and the westbound traffic will be tailing back from Western Circus as far as White City; within two hours, it will reach the Westway's elevated carriageways, but understandably, perhaps, they do not like the suggestion that London's traffic is more or less gridlocked.

'It moves,' says PC Hewitt, stoutly.

'You think it's going to grind to a halt, but we do our best to keep it going,' adds his partner.

They avoid Western Avenue in the rush-hour whenever they can. In the last twenty years, since they began commuting to central London from Harrow, they have seen the A40 gradually upgraded. When the flyover and underpass are built at Gipsy Corner and Western Circus, Western Avenue will become a seamless extension of the Westway. The fast exit from London which was first conceived of in 1910 will have been completed in circumstances unimaginable at the time.

Since the houses have been demolished, PC Welsh is certain that the work will proceed: 'All we've got now is pockets of derelict land that will get dumped on and become overgrown. Politically, they don't want to spend money building the road, but sooner or later there'll be pressure from the Road Haulage Association, or from London's Director of Traffic . . . The road will get made. The underpass will get done.'

– – –

Released from hospital after an accident that seemed a private rehearsal for 'the end of the world by automobile', the narrator of *Crash* notices that the highway engineers have pushed the 'huge decks' of the carriageways that run beneath his apartment more than half a mile further south: 'I realised that the entire zone which defined the landscape of my life was now bounded by a continuous artificial horizon, formed by the raised parapets and embankments of the motorways and their access roads and interchanges.' When the motorway box was complete, a million people would find themselves living within sight of its carriageways. The GLC attempted to placate critics of the scheme by devising tunnels and cuttings to ease the motorway's passage, but the Westway had revealed the true nature of the city we were intended to inherit.

10. The Worst Place
in the World

'Axed!' exclaims Joan Shaw. 'The A40's been axed!'

The Ceefax announcement on the giant television screen in the Shaw's sitting-room is blunt: the reconstruction of Western Avenue has been cancelled.

'Well, how about that!' says Joan Shaw wonderingly. She sits down on the sofa and stares at the television. It is 28 July 1997: for as long as she has lived on Western Avenue, there have been plans to rebuild the road; now it seems that years of blight, and the public inquiries, and the demolition of half the neighbourhood, were all for nothing. 'Well, how can they leave it like this?' she begins. 'They must have some . . . After all this time – that it should hit the dirt!' Then a strange thought occurs to her: 'Well, we'll be here for evermore!' She laughs uncertainly, and her dog takes advantage of her distraction to show me his teeth again.

When I arrived at Joan Shaw's house ten minutes ago, I was surprised by her appearance. In the two years since I last saw her, I had formed an image of her which did not match the physical presence of the woman who answered the door; she seemed smaller and more fragile than I remembered. Still, she was as welcoming as ever – her hospitality in stark contrast to the attitude of the small dog, Cassius, clutched beneath her arm. As she walked ahead of me into the sitting-room overlooking the road, he was borne backwards into the house, teeth bared, scrabbling to escape his mistress's hold; each step I took into his territory was noted with an anguished snarl.

Joan Shaw gestured towards the far side of the road, where the fly-postered hoardings seal the empty building sites. White lace curtains blurred the profiles of the passing cars, so they fell past the house in a soft, streaming torrent of blue-grey metal. 'It just seems really weird to look out and see nothing, you know,' she said. She was wearing paint-stained tracksuit trousers and gym shoes, and there were flecks of paint on the frames of her glasses; she is redecorating the house. 'We weren't going to do anything, but we were fed up waiting, and in the end I couldn't live like that any longer. I had the place carpeted again, and all the things that needed doing, you know. We've done the hall, you know, and it's the usual thing, right through again – we do try and keep it going.'

The wallpaper in the sitting-room is green, flecked with gold, and a portrait of an Alsatian and a Golden Labrador hangs in the collection of paintings arranged above the sofa. Both of the Shaw's dogs have died since my last visit; the Alsatian had a heart attack, and the elderly Labrador pined away within weeks. Cassius – a clutch of fur with jewel-bright eyes and jagged teeth – is only a fraction of their combined weight, yet thanks to his remarkable ferocity, he more than compensates for their absence. As I sat down in an armchair, he spasmed with rage. 'Oh come on, you miserable old thing,' said Mrs Shaw. Cassius writhed in her lap in a fit of adolescent fury. 'Woof, woof!' she said, mockingly. A minute passed before he was calm enough to allow us to resume our conversation.

'It's been a bit of a disaster really,' she began, mildly. 'I'm sure if they do go ahead it will be better. We're just a bit worried, because we hoped we'd be able to sell and get out, but we still don't know if it's going to happen or not. They're announcing it this week.' She was surprised when I told her that they were, in fact, announcing it today. At her request, I turned on the television and called up the head-lines on Ceefax. The announcement was brief, but its meaning was clear enough: the A40 is one of several road schemes to be cancelled; the work will not proceed.

After a moment, I turn off the television – a movement echoed, as usual, by a snarl. I feel as if I am intruding on a private tragedy, but Joan Shaw does not seem to resent my presence – in fact, she seems keen to talk. 'Well, I suppose in a way, we're lucky,' she says, speculatively. 'At least, if they're not going ahead, we know they're not going ahead, so we'll be able to say to ourselves, "Well, that's it, you know – we might as well get on with it." I mean, that in itself is quite good, really . . .' Only minutes have passed since she told me that she hoped the work would proceed, and already she has begun to explore the possibility that the announcement is, after all, good news; yet she does not sound entirely convinced. 'To think – thirty-two years!'

The last two years have been the most difficult of all. Last year, there was an invasion of rats on Western Avenue; from their bedroom, the Shaws watched them feeding in the open bags of rubbish left in the garden next door. There was rubbish dumped on the verge beside the road as well. The smell became unbearable, and the weeds in their neigh-bours' front garden grew until they were head high. Then, their neighbour employed a gardener who broke the Shaws' fence and killed the honeysuckle whose scent had smothered the stench of garbage.

Meanwhile, as the houses opposite were being des-troyed, and those around her fell into disrepair – her health began to deteriorate. 'The thing was I'd had a pain – you know, when you're rushing about and doing a lot of things, you get like a pain in your chest. I thought it was just stress.' After the shock of the day's news, she is beginning to gather herself again. Although she seems to me to be diminished physically, her manner is much as I remembered it: unforced, gossipy, casually intimate. 'I was really, really lucky actually. I'd had a really bad couple of weeks – I knew I was low, but I didn't know how low I was. I came home from work one day, and of course, you come indoors, and the first thing you do is you start hoovering. And then I suddenly got a very bad chest pain – so bad that I couldn't breathe, and I must have collapsed on the bed. All I can remember is looking at my watch – I think it was ten to five, and my husband came back after seven, and the hoover was still going . . . It was very frightening – very, very frightening.'

She had had a heart attack, and she was told it was probably not the first. When she thought back over the previous months, she realized her health had been deteriorating steadily. 'I remember I kept thinking to myself – 'stupid scales, they must be wrong, I haven't put on weight, but I can't breathe. I'm going out, and I'm running with the dogs and I can't breathe – What's the matter with me? I know I'm getting old, but you know, you should be able to breathe!' She laughs.

She had been given a warning – next time, she fears she might not get one. 'And that does make you stop and you say to yourself, "Yeah well, that's not how I should do things . . ." But my attitude is, you know, you're very lucky – look at the amount of young people that are dying, you know, look at some people. So, you know, some people don't have much luck – I've been lucky. I always say to myself, No, it's another day, you know. Make the best of it. I've been very fortunate.'

Illness was not the last of their difficulties. Soon after Mrs Shaw had her heart attack, Mr Shaw was made redundant. 'I'd forgotten about it, actually – that bit of it. You get over the humps, and you say, oh well, that's

another one that's gone . . . You know, you have a little bit
of a downer one way, but it goes up the other way.' He is
now working again – self-employed, and earning less than
he used to, but enough 'to pay his way'. In the meantime,
her own job has become steadily more difficult. As she tells
me about it, she begins to speak in a fierce whisper, her
voice pitched so low that I cannot hear half of what she is
saying, and my tape-recorder picks up only an occasional
word.

She believes the management is to blame for a complete
breakdown in the functioning of her department at the
hospital. She used to enjoy her work, until they started
reducing staff, and the arrival of three new managers
further increased their workload. If she had thought it
would get as bad as it has, she would have left months ago.
Then, when she was ill, her GP was told that her hospital
would not see her. She was shocked, for she feels that
overwork had contributed to her illness in the first place: 'It
sounds awful, but that's what made me a little bit – not
bitter, because I'm not a bitter person, I don't bear a grudge
– but it just made me sit up and say to myself, Now,
look . . .'

For many years, the Shaws voted Tory – 'everybody
docs what thcy fccl thcy can gct thc bcst dcal out of, I
suppose' – but she was glad to see the government defeated
in May. Ironically, it was the change of government that
facilitated today's revelation: had the Tories remained in
power, we both agree, they would not have abandoned the
work begun during their administration. It is strange to
imagine what life would be like on Western Avenue if it
had never been started.

'A lot more people would have moved on,' says Joan
Shaw, confidently. 'I don't think the ability to move on has
been there, because people can't sell their houses. She

pauses, as though she is registering the shock of today's announcement with renewed clarity; then she dismisses its implications. 'Well, I couldn't have that – I couldn't,' she says, defiantly. 'I couldn't live like that, thinking, God, I hate it here. I'd have to get out – I'd go into a rented place or something. What difference does it make? As long as you've got peace of mind. To let your life deteriorate to the extent that you just sit around and moan and groan about the state of the place. Some people do make martyrs of themselves! OK, so we all moan about the state of things from time to time, but it's not the be-all and end-all, because at the end of the day it's only a roof over your head.'

Despite the traffic, and the years of blight, and the rats, and the noise, and the neighbours, Joan Shaw is happy living on Western Avenue; what's more, like many people on the road, she resents being patronized by outsiders. 'My family make me die – they think this is THE WORST PLACE IN THE WORLD. My sister says, "How can you live here?" ' She drops her voice again, and adopts a horrified whisper; then, her eyes bright, she announces loudly, 'And I say, "Quite well thank you – because the fact that I am a long way from you helps!" ' She shrieks with laughter. 'I think, yes I would like to get out,' she adds, more calmly, 'but even though we've talked about it, it's never been an actual decision, you know what I mean? I like it here – it's got its pluses. I wouldn't like to be on a road where I knew everybody – I'd want our fence to be six foot six, so I could sit here, read my paper, and not have to say good morning or good afternoon.' She laughs again. 'Which is dreadful when you think about it, but it's what you get used to, isn't it?'

Cassius follows me to the door, tucked under his owner's arm, his feet pedalling frantically in mid-air in a cartoon of frustrated aggression. Outside, the traffic is massing for the evening rush-hour: it is 4.00 pm, and the eastbound traffic coagulates 200 yards before the lights at Gipsy Corner; on the far side of the road, sprung from the city's traps, the cars begin their race to Park Royal. It is a beautiful afternoon: the gardens fronting the houses are blossoming, and there are deep pools of shade beneath the trees which line the pavement. 'SAVE US', says the graffiti on the oxblood façade of a derelict house beside the subway entrance; but Joan Shaw, for one, does not need saving.

– – –

201 Western Avenue is empty. The glass has been removed from the window beside the front door. On the wall hangs a print of Jesus surrounded by a host of angels, his hand held out as though he were soliciting donations. Judging from the letters on the mat, the house has been empty for days. Colette has finally left Western Avenue.

– – –

Robert Moses was ousted from power in New York in 1968. His demise marked the end of America's infatuation with 'urban renewal' and coincided with a growing suspicion of the machine whose interests he had done so much to promote – the car. Inevitably, opposition to urban renewal began in New York – the city that had witnessed the most radical manifestation of the era's thirst for 'step by step large-scale city modernisation'. 'This is not the rebuilding of cities. It is the sacking of cities,' declared Jane Jacobs, an architectural journalist who had inflicted a rare defeat on Robert Moses when she campaigned against his plan to build a road through a park in Greenwich Village.

The 'third stage of automobile consciousness' had begun: the car was no longer regarded as 'an historically

progressive force for change in American civilisation';
appreciation of its merits was tempered by the growing
awareness of the disadvantages of mass-motoring. 'For over
half a century, the automobile has brought death, injury
and the most inestimable sorrow and deprivation to millions of people,' wrote the 'consumer crusader', Ralph
Nader, in a book called *Unsafe at Any Speed*. J.G. Ballard
wrote that Nader's assault on the Detroit motor industry
succeeded for the first time in 'making Americans feel guilty
about their greatest dream image and totem object: the
motor car.'

— — —

'We've been the subject of a confidence trick.'

Behind his latched front door, Mr Jackson's face quivers,
blurring like the image on a badly tuned television. 'It's to
do with compensation, and the lawyers – people pretending
to be lawyers. We can't talk about it because it's in the
House of Lords at the moment.'

Mr Jackson withdraws for a moment. Then, as though
he is rocking backwards and forwards on his heels, his
square face comes into view again: 'Are you Edward Platt?
When were you last here? A year ago, was it?' Longer, I
say. Behind him, I glimpse Mrs Jackson; she looks angry
and confused. I wish I had not disturbed them. 'The trouble
with you people is you always come when we're not
expecting you.'

Mr Jackson asks me for proof of identity, and I show
him the only thing I possess: an out-of-date NUJ card. He
retreats behind the door to inspect it. He still seems to
thinks I am involved in a scheme to defraud him of the
compensation money the Department of Transport is due
to pay to the residents who have remained beside the road.
There is nothing I can do to persuade him that he is wrong

– in fact, I am beginning to think I am only making things worse.

'I thought you came from an estate agents – that's what we thought. Trying to see inside the house . . .' His hand is shaking as he passes back the card. 'And what's happened to all the pictures you took? We thought you wanted them for our death certificate, but we fooled you – we're still alive.' The door closes for a moment; then Mr Jackson emerges again: 'The Western Avenue's finished anyway – it's finished. They're not going to do anything here. They're not going to do anything.'

— — —

One morning, the Shaws woke up to find that the low brick wall at the front of their garden had collapsed – as had the wall in front of the next-door house, and the next, and the next. They soon discovered that every other wall along the road had collapsed overnight, though they still do not know why.

— — —

In 1968, Ronan Point, a system-built tower block in east London, was destroyed in a gas explosion. Its collapse symbolized the failings of Britain's own urban renewal project. In 1971, a philosophy lecturer called David Wiggins, standing for election in London on behalf of a group called 'Homes Before Roads', attacked the planning departments which 'march across town and countryside, building huge roads' and 'destroying communities'. He declared that urban redevelopment, which began with the best of motives, often turned into 'acts of the purest totalitarianism'. The high towers built across London had proved 'as unacceptable to their present recipients as they would be, and would always have been, to the middle and upper

classes', he wrote. Yet Londoners of all classes had reason
to resist the road-builders' advance, and Wiggins hoped
that universal antipathy to the motorway box would heal
the class rivalries which the planners' reconstruction of the
city had fomented.

— — —

'It's an outrageous scandal – that's what I call it,' says
the Reverend Arnott. 'An abominable mess – and criminal
when you think of those beautiful houses that were
destroyed.' It is an unbearably hot Saturday morning; my
clothes are sticking to my skin, yet the interior of the house
is dark and cool.

When I rang the bell, his housekeeper had told me that
he could not see me because he has not been well. I could
see the Reverend Arnott standing behind her in the hall. He
came forward and lifted up the bottom of his shirt to
reveal, briefly, a spreading, purple bruise which coloured
one side of his ample stomach. 'I'm recovering from a burst
blood vessel, you see.' Yet he was plainly keen to talk –
'And you've got things to say, as well,' he said to his
housekeeper, whose name I never discover. After a brief
consultation, they agreed to let me in. The Reverend Arnott
settled in an armchair in the sitting-room at the back of the
house, beside a low table which bears a tray of pills, and
began to talk, forcefully and fluently. He does not look or
sound like an invalid, but perhaps it is his sense of injustice
which has animated him.

He is angry because he had hoped they would sell up
and move to the country in the next few years. If the work
were complete, he estimates the house would be worth at
least £120,000; as it is, he is not certain anyone will even
make them an offer. Not surprisingly, he looks tired, and
his face seems to have shrunk, as though it has been

compacted by the pressure of age and illness. 'I thought they would go ahead with this because it was really on the cards for so long, and so many beautiful houses have been pulled down – they've done the biggest part of the job.'

'It's the accountability owed to the residents here,' adds his companion – a nurse in her fifties, with short blonde hair, cut in a jagged bob. 'They've abused their authority, and let us down badly.' Half of Western Avenue has been destroyed for no reason, and last year's upheavals already seem hard to comprehend. 'Those houses down there were so beautiful – though that's neither here nor there any-more,' says the Reverend Arnott, dispiritedly. His initial burst of energy has faded.

'The future must be saved from the costly and ugly blunders which isolated action in the past has bequeathed to us and which we inherit today, much to our regret,' said John Burns, chairman of the Greater London Arterial Roads Conference, in 1913. 'To the best of my recollection, Western Avenue was the first, certainly one of the earliest, of the great arterial roads to be commenced,' begins a letter to the local paper of 23 March 1928. If they were not going to finish the work, the writer complains, they should never have started it. The pattern has not changed: the abandoned reconstruction of Western Avenue is just another messy and inadequate attempt to cater to the apparently limitless demands of the city's traffic.

Le Corbusier believed it would require the imposition of a dictator's will to restructure the city to accommodate the car, but now the task is impossible – no authority, however brutal, could accomplish it. Robert Moses' reign in New York demonstrated the concept's self-defeating absurdity. He built bridges, tunnels, dams, parks, stadiums, housing projects and, above all, roads – 627 miles of roads, in total, bequeathing to the region a wider network than even Los

Angeles could boast – but the man who had excluded buses
and coaches from his parkways neglected one aspect of the
city's urban infrastructure: he did not build a single mile of
track for its subways or suburban railways.

As the city's public transport system declined, Moses'
vast network of roads were swamped by the volume of
traffic unleashed into the city: by 1955, the expressways,
which had opened in 1952, were carrying the volume of
traffic forecast for the mid-eighties. Within three years,
the traffic had reached levels it was not expected to reach
within three decades; Moses had flooded the city with cars.

As I walk back to the Bridge of Fools, I notice that the
tramp who patrols Western Avenue is standing in the
phone-box beside the Johnsons' house. He rests his forearms on the glass and leans his head on his hands, so he
can stare into the eyes of the oncoming drivers. His saggy
jeans are shiny with dirt, and the skin on his bald head is
furrowed and blackened, like burnt wood. For several
minutes, he is motionless. The heat inside the glass cubicle
must be unbearable.

On Western Avenue, the traffic never stops anymore –
not even at night – and the air is getting worse.

– – –

There is a man who washes windscreens at the traffic lights
above Gipsy Corner. He is a graphic designer, and he used
to live in a squat on Western Avenue. He lost his job and
flat when he had problems with a woman: she ripped him
off, he dropped out. Every day, he cycles to work on
Western Avenue from his new squat in Putney; he has scars
on his knees because he often cycles home drunk at night.

– – –

A kind of insurrection took place across London in the early seventies. A coalition of community groups, tenants associations and impromptu political parties led the protests against the motorway box, and in 1973 the GLC abandoned its controversial scheme. The urban renewal project in both Britain and the United States had run its course.

In the seventies, the population of inner London fell by more than 700,000 people, while its satellite towns continued to expand. On the east coast of America an immense urban region had begun to take shape: stretching from Boston to Washington, the conglomeration was dubbed 'megalopolis', and there were fears that cities like New York would be lost amidst its enveloping anonymity.

- - -

The manager of the pizza parlour at Western Circus is a Kurdish refugee called Hiwa. In 1991, he fought against Saddam Hussein's government troops in the short-lived uprising that marked the end of the Gulf War, and he now lives in a tower block overlooking the M41 – the truncated stretch of the 'West Cross route' which connects Shepherd's Bush to the Westway. When the uprising failed, he escaped across the mountains to Iran. Hiwa has never forgiven the Western powers for not supporting the uprisings in Iraq, as they had said they would. The plate-glass windows of his shop overlook the tangled junction at Western Circus, and his flat on the ninth floor overlooks one of the few completed sections of the motorway box. He says he would rather be living in Iraq.

- - -

Once again, I have underestimated Robin Green. I thought he would be dismayed by the decision to abandon the work

on Western Avenue, but I was wrong. Eight years after
Robin's presentation at the public inquiry was dismissed,
the government has conceded that he was right after all –
his work has been vindicated, and he is jubilant. 'It's
flattering that my opinion has been subsequently upheld.'
He smiles, his still features alight with pleasure.

We are sitting at the dining-room table in the Greens'
house in Hayes. Robin looks more relaxed than I have ever
seen him; his hair has grown long, and he is casually dressed
in jeans and trainers. But it soon becomes apparent that he
has lost none of his terrifying thoroughness. 'To abbrevi-
ate,' he begins, 'the benefits of completing the scheme which
necessitated the demolition, I think, of 182 homes and 28
commercial properties, were outweighed by the environmental damage the scheme has and would cause, and the
scheme was rejected . . . That was my impression. In which
case – you're not correcting me? No. No . . .' I would not
dare to correct him.

Robin dismisses the lazy assumption propagated by the
media that the scheme was abandoned purely to save
money. He insists it was cancelled because it was 'flawed
both in principle and in detail'.

He selects a document from a bookshelf behind him,
and flattens it on the dining-room table. It is a White Paper
published in 1989 – a document that attempted to define
an integrated transport policy for London. He shows me an
aerial photograph of London: the city is a purple mass – a
blue-black bruise bisected by the river's thin trail, its bor-
ders tinged a livid green. He flicks through the pages until
he finds the relevant section: in areas like Gipsy Corner, it
argues, money should be invested in railways rather than
roads. At the public inquiry, Robin pointed out that the
proposed reconstruction of the A40 contradicted govern-

ment policy, and last month, the Department of Transport finally conceded that he was right.

He shows me the transcript of the transport minister's statement in the House of Commons on 28 July 1997, which states simply that '. . . the A40 scheme in the west of London would have the effect of encouraging car commuting where public transport alternatives exist. This would not be justified and the scheme will therefore be cancelled. Alternative solutions to local problems will be sought.' Nothing more. I find it difficult to believe that such a lengthy, disruptive and expensive process could be brought to a halt with such a brief statement. But Robin has already moved on to the next document – his Proof of Evidence.

Recognizing the need to improve the A40, but dismissing the Department of Transport's scheme as 'inordinately damaging to the urban environment', Robin's Proof of Evidence argued that the government should abandon its clumsy proposals for the reconstruction of Western Avenue and initiate a new approach towards transport planning. He believed that public opinion had begun to turn against road-building, and suggested implementing small measures such as improved traffic junctions and pedestrian crossings as a means of buying time while a new consensus emerged. He reads out a sentence from his Proof of Evidence: 'There may well be a different planning and transportation scenario in the mid-1990s for Greater London, a situation more "green" in nature, where policies of traffic restraint and management and the assignment of priority to public transport predominate.'

Had the government been brave enough to accept his arguments, Western Avenue would still be intact. 'I thought it would take five or six years for the government to catch up with my thinking. Obviously, it took eight or nine – I

was a little ahead of myself there,' he concedes magnani-
mously. 'I'm glad they got there in the end, though I'm a
bit sad that it should have taken so long and extorted such
a cost.' He puts his notes aside contentedly.

There is silence for a moment. The window-sill beside
us is crowded with family photographs, and through the
net curtains beside me, I can see the house on the far side
of the crescent where Robin's sister lives. I have to say he
does not seem sad – in fact, he seems happier than I have
ever seen him. The significance of his performance at the
public inquiry is finally becoming apparent, and he is
relishing the scale of his victory. The fact that his judgement
has been vindicated gives him enormous satisfaction – and
so it should – yet it does not seem enough to explain his
reaction to the news; it seems to me that there is more
involved.

From almost every perspective, it made no sense to
abandon the work, but when the objective criteria of town
planning were applied to assess the merits of the scheme, it
was found to be lacking, and so it was cancelled. The
decision accords with Robin's perception of the natural
order of things. The rituals and procedures of town planning have been validated, and order reigns once more. It
hardly matters that he has been forced from his home.

Still, it must be frustrating, I suggest, to consider the
amount of time and money wasted. Robin rebuts the idea:
'It's not frustrating for me, because I can divorce it from a
personal level. I can view it objectively as a professional.'
But from a professional point of view, I suggest, the scheme
has been a disaster. Robin smiles broadly. 'So which hat do
I wear when I reply? As a professional, you can't knock
other professionals – dog don't eat dog!' He laughs, which
is rather disconcerting. He tries to explain: 'White-collar
middle-class professions – or people with pretensions to

belong to white-collar middle-class professions – don't attack one other.' He knows he was right, and the highly paid consultants who devised the scheme were wrong; he does not want to gloat, yet he cannot help but laugh at their professional embarrassment.

He enjoys his new life in Hayes – 'there are many more community events, and the local council seems to be involved in consulting the local populace more' – but he acknowledges that many of their neighbours did not want to leave Western Avenue; nor did his parents. He does not know how they will react to the news of the scheme's cancellation – they left for Ireland before the decision was announced – but he knows that they miss the road. 'Or at least,' he adds, strangely, 'they say that they do. It's hard for me to judge.'

Plainly, he is dissatisfied by their emotional reaction to the move, and he begins to consider the reasons why they might miss Western Avenue. In the first place, he begins, the new house has many 'technical deficiencies'. He gives me an example: the bedroom that contains the hot-water cylinder, and is already overheated, faces directly south, so it attracts 'solar gain' and becomes unbearably hot during the day. Unfortunately, the room also overlooks the M4 and Heathrow Airport, and if you open the window, then the 'consistent noise' of planes and cars becomes an irritation. In other words, the room is either too hot or too noisy. 'On Western Avenue, on the other hand,' says Robin, 'the windows were east–west oriented – rather than north–south, as they are here – and you'd get more diffused solar gain in the evenings and mornings.'

I had forgotten how extraordinary Robin's perception of the world can be. The image of him methodically opening and closing the window in an attempt to gauge the comparative disadvantages of heat and noise makes me laugh; I try and concentrate on what he is saying. Secondly, he points out that ten per cent compensation to counteract the stress of moving is hardly adequate. He once saw a programme in which a group of old-age pensioners were moved from one home to another: a third died subsequently from natural causes – or rather, from the stress of reloca-tion. 'So,' he concludes, 'they may prefer to go back and live on Western Avenue, and I think there's a great deal of rational basis for doing so.' I had never suggested that their desire to return to the road was irrational – or that it would be less valid if it were – but Robin is reassured.

In the future, he believes that they will build new flats and houses on the empty land. The new buildings will face away from the road, and will serve to screen the surround-ing houses from it. He estimates the scheme has cost around £20 million so far, yet the true costs are hard to estimate, for over the years, money has been spent on preparing one scheme after another. 'The benefits to those with preten-sions to being white-collar middle-class professionals, you know, have been immense.' Again, he chuckles. 'So the consultants didn't mind if there were umpteen revisions made; nor did the legal people while they were processing the inquiry. It's like some super-large taxi meter, and you know the way they go – when the flag's down . . . And perhaps that accounts for the reason why the top ten per cent of the country have dramatically increased their income – those people who are involved in legal affairs and accountancy and other such highly paid professions – and the majority of the population have not.'

Does he genuinely believe that the episode was intended to provide employment for consultants? Perhaps it is not such a far-fetched idea – it might appeal to Reverend Arnott, eager to establish who is responsible for the devas-tation of his neighbourhood, and it certainly appeals to

Robin. One day, on Western Avenue, he closed the door of the room where his parents were sitting, and told me, in a confidential whisper – as though it were a revelation their frailty would not bear – that he often suspected that sinister conspiracies lay behind seemingly random events. Today, he takes a different approach: 'Having been in local government, I think a lot of things happen by accident – they just arise.' He laughs. 'I'm literal-minded – I can't necessarily relate to such manoeuvrings, because I can't think of them myself, but mandarins are very intelligent: they may well have been capable of such an approach . . .' He laughs again. 'But I'm not really into conspiratorial theories – especially if I put my name to what I'm saying.'

There is silence for a moment. I am confused. Then, as though he is revealing something of great significance, Robin says, 'I just want to point out that I haven't concluded the compensation negotiations – so anything I say is with that in mind.' He cannot say anything which might prejudice his case; the bureaucrats at the Department of Transport might hear of his accusations. So attentive is he to the mechanism of government that he cannot imagine that the government is deaf to him. And maybe he is right to be concerned: he understands better than I do how the government operates. He has always conducted our conversations like official press briefings – in which case, perhaps he is merely using me to present his arguments to the world. I might have misunderstood him from the start.

— — —

By the beginning of the seventies, our perception of the demands of traffic had begun to change: roads are like sponges, claimed *The Times*, they will always fill to capacity. Deriding the engineers responsible for the motorway box, *The Times* noted scornfully they had been led by 'a visceral feeling that it was "necessary to come to terms with the motorway age"' – as though they alone had been seduced by the allure of what Moses called 'city modernisation'. The machine that had driven the spectacular boom of the post-war years was increasingly seen as an agent of doom. In 1977, John Tyme, a former lecturer in environmental studies, declared himself the world's first full-time roads protester: man '. . . is a flawed species,' he declared, 'and the car is our executioner.' If so, then our demise was imminent: between 1950 and 1980, the number of cars in the world increased from 50 million to 350 million.

11. The Patron Saint of Travellers

It is January, 1998: three years after the evictions began – and more than three decades since the first plans to widen the road were considered – the Highways Agency has just announced its latest scheme for Western Avenue. The bridges between Western Circus and Gipsy Corner will be replaced, increasing the road's capacity by fifty per cent, and creating an extra lane which will be dedicated to 'non-car traffic' – commercial traffic and public transport.

I am in room 5033 of St Christopher House, a dusty slab of glass in Southwark, south-east London. Opposite me sits Alan Mellors, the Highways Agency Area Manager for West London and the man responsible for the mainten-ance of Western Avenue. Does he expect a hostile reception at the public meetings scheduled to discuss the new proposals?

'I expect some people will be critical of us – and I think they've got reason to be critical.' He sits back in his chair and locks his hands behind his head; he looks relaxed and composed – at ease in his surroundings and his role. 'People will be quite upset that over the last few years lots of things have been going to happen and haven't happened. Proper-ties have been demolished in the expectation that things were going to happen, and they haven't happened, and I think if I was in their position, I would feel pretty upset at the way things have gone on. But I mean, hindsight is a wonderful thing, isn't it?' Now Mr Mellors flattens his palms on the lacquered surface of the conference table. 'What I want to say is this: the past is the past – what we

must do now is look to the future, and make sure we move
ahead as quickly as we can to improve things *temporarily*
and to improve things *permanently* in that area.'

It is a rather disconcerting speech: I did not expect Mr
Mellors to be proud of the fact that the project had been
abandoned half-finished, but nor did I expect him to dismiss
the subject with vapid exhortations to 'look to the future'.
For a moment, Mr Mellors sounded like a second-rate
politician. His reply was not quite an apology, nor a
statement of regret – nor, even, an admission of responsibility. Somehow, he managed to suggest that the 'things
that were going to happen' were disrupted by mysterious
forces beyond anyone's control.

'You see, a lot of the decisions were taken by ministers
taking into account the policies of the day and the situations
of the day,' resumes Mr Mellors. 'And you could say none
of those decisions were ever wrong – it's just that the way
it's all worked out, we've ended up in a situation which
I don't think anybody could ever foresee. And it's an
unfortunate situation.'

Mr Mellors has a strange habit of presenting everything
in the passive voice: it is almost as if he believes the
'unfortunate situation' had evolved without his active par-
ticipation. When I first met him, there was nothing in his
manner to suggest he would prove so evasive. He seemed a
confident and approachable character; a compact, apparently vigorous man in his early fifties, dressed in a blue shirt
and a yellow tie, whose brisk and purposeful air might have
been designed to advertise what I'd been told repeatedly in
the months it took to organize our meeting – Mr Mellors is
a busy man and an important member of the Highways
Agency hierarchy.

Feeling formal and constrained in a suit – worn not out
of courtesy to the Highways Agency, but because I am

going to a funeral later in the day – I took a seat at the table. Opposite me sat Mr Mellors and his deputy, Hugh Richards, the Route Manager of the A40, while to my left was my escort for the day: Howard Cohen is a representative of the Central Office of Information – the government's press office – and the man who had brokered the meeting.

Mr Mellors is right to insist that if we view each decision within the context of the circumstances that prevailed at the time it was taken, then its justification will become apparent. It is a perfectly logical argument, and yet it is also patently absurd: everything has gone according to plan; unfortunately, the plan kept changing.

'It's just a shame that elections come when they do,' says Hugh Richards mildly. His pale hands are folded around a mug of tea ('Yipes!' says Wile E. Coyote through his intermeshed fingers). 'Had it all happened a year earlier, then we might not have demolished the houses by that time, but it's very easy to use hindsight. Unfortunately, at the time, it was considered the best thing to press on – to implement the policies as soon as possible.'

I want to establish how Mr Mellors and Mr Richards felt when they were told to abandon the scheme to rebuild the road: was it not disappointing to be forced to give up a project that had been planned for more than thirty years – a project in which they had both invested considerable time and effort, and one that had already exacted significant costs?

Mr Mellors and Mr Richards look at me quizzically. They do not seem to understand the question, so I rephrase it: is it not frustrating to be forced to work within constantly changing guidelines? It is Hugh Richards who speaks first, and when he does, it is with a studiously sympathetic air – as though he were attempting to rescue me from a socially embarrassing situation.

'No, it's quite interesting, really, isn't it?' he says, airily. His slender shoulders are still, but his head pivots sideways, turning above his splayed elbows, as he appeals to his boss.

'Not at all,' says Alan Mellors, decisively. 'I think it's quite challenging. I mean, if your car is rusting away, do you keep sending it to the garage to have the rust removed? No – you say, enough's enough. Do I throw £75 million of scarce taxpayers' money at these schemes if in actual fact they're not delivering what I want? It was a brave decision to say stop, but I think ministers feel – and I understand totally why – that it was the right decision. The idea of being absolutely attached to something, of wanting to see it through come hell or high water, even if it's the wrong thing . . . none of us have that.'

It is another perfectly logical argument, and again it is absurd: of course it's 'right' to abandon something that is 'wrong' – but if it's 'wrong' now, then how can it have been 'right' before? And if it was 'wrong' in the first place, then why was it ever begun? I know what Mr Mellors' answer will be: he is a civil servant, and it is not up to him to judge the merits of a policy. I accept that it is his job to implement policies devised by his political masters, but I still feel as though something is eluding me: it was Mr Mellors who managed the demolition of the houses, and yet Mr Mellors now denies all responsibility for his actions, for he was merely obeying instructions. I would be much happier if he were to concede that he would have liked to have completed the work he had begun, or that he was glad to abandon it – or if he were to admit to having any opinion on the subject at all. Accommodating the conflicting policies of successive governments requires either remarkable mental agility or remarkable stupidity, but one thing is clear: it has become almost second nature to Mr Mellors. Or perhaps his apparent reluctance to acknowledge responsibility for Western Avenue is not evasiveness at all: perhaps it is merely a reflection of the fact that responsibility for it is spread so widely between successive generations of politicians and civil servants that no one actually knows where it resides anymore.

Just as I have begun to establish the way in which he views his role, Mr Mellors suddenly shifts his position: 'What is fortunate is that we're not yes-men, in the sense that politicians say, "That's our policy – get on with it, I don't want to hear anything." We have the opportunity to shape changes in policy, so that if we see things need to be changed, then we have that opportunity . . . Ministers are looking ahead to the future, we're looking at what we're trying to do today, and often we get a meeting of minds.'

Mr Mellors – who talks about ministers with the same exaggerated reverence as Robin Green – is now claiming to play a part in shaping the policies that he initially said he was charged with implementing. It is another instance of his infuriating elusiveness – Mr Mellors can blame the politicians when it suits him, but he does not want to be regarded as a mere functionary.

Sensing my confusion and frustration, Mr Cohen interrupts to suggest that Mr Mellors explain the context within which the Highways Agency operates – at least, that is the gist of what he says, though it takes him the best part of a minute to say it. Mr Mellors listens patiently, and then agrees; since the sixties, he begins, mobility has been regarded as all-important. 'So, I mean, looking at things like the A40, we will have been developing improvements and maintaining that road in the light of ever-increasing traffic volumes, because it's government policy to enable people to be able to move around, to stimulate the economy and that sort of thing . . .'

I try to listen to what Mr Mellors is saying, but it is

hard to concentrate because I do not feel as though he is
really talking to me at all. He seems to think he is address-
ing a press conference: his speech is stuffed with words and
phrases lifted from policy documents and ministerial briefings, and his delivery is lifeless and impersonal. I do not
know how I am supposed to respond to this rambling,
jargon-freighted monologue.

Perhaps this is what Mr Cohen had in mind when he
said he had arranged an 'official briefing' for me. Perhaps I
ought to have drafted an official press release outlining my
own position on the subject of Western Avenue, which I
could have passed to Mr Cohen of the Central Office of
Information, who would then have passed it to Mr Mellors
of the Highways Agency. While Mr Mellors considered his
response, Mr Platt and Mr Richards could have avoided
each other's gaze.

Mr Mellors' argument is easily summarized: in the early
seventies, public opinion turned against road-building, particularly within urban areas, and expenditure on new roads
fell dramatically. Of the GLC's plans for three concentric
motorway rings encircling London, the outer ring was the
only one to be built. The volume of traffic on the M25
exceeded the road's capacity almost as soon as it was
completed, though as Mr Mellors points out, that was
partly because it had 'stimulated the economy'.

The road lobby was in retreat, but it had not been
defeated, and in the eighties, Mrs Thatcher's government
launched what was billed as the greatest programme of
road-building since the Romans – a project that culminated
in protests at Twyford Down, Leytonstone and Newbury.
Last year, the new government assessed the scheme to
rebuild Western Avenue. 'They concluded that what was
going to be achieved were not the objectives they were now
seeking. And I think, increasingly, the previous adminis-

tration, towards the end . . .' For the first time since he started talking five minutes ago, Mr Mellors pauses momentarily – long enough for Mr Richards to interrupt: 'There were doubts,' he says, helpfully.

'There were doubts. But they were such a long way along the route: property had been purchased, property had been demolished – "We've got so far, we'll finish off." And I think perhaps the new administration had the opportunity to be able to say, "Let's abandon it." '

The decision to cancel the long-delayed reconstruction of Western Avenue signals the end of the 'Motorway Age' of the post-war years. The government has declared that it intends to implement an 'integrated transport policy' – a sound principle, though Mr Mellors is well aware of the difficulty of putting it into practice. 'Is the public transport good enough at the moment for the commuters to transfer to?' he asks. Yet, loyal as ever to the official message, he adds that there are many initiatives under way to improve it.

Had they built the flyover and underpass on Western Avenue, it would have sent the 'wrong signal' to commuters: ' "Oh look, this is a nice road – we'll come in this way." ' I ask Mr Mellors when it was that the Highways Agency acknowledged that building new roads generates more traffic, and he replies, calmly, that it has known all along: 'I think it's probably something that people have been saying for twenty years – most people agree that it happens, but I think also most people agree that it doesn't happen as much as some people might have suggested it happens.'

Mr Mellors' response only serves to obscure the issue, but his perplexing rhetoric conceals a deeper evasion: despite the fact that he has been building roads for years, Mr Mellors now professes to have always known it to be a self-defeating exercise. He seems to be disclaiming responsibility for his actions, while simultaneously laying claim to a kind of omniscience – Mr Mellors is aware of everything and responsible for nothing.

On the desk between us, Hugh Richards unrolls the latest set of plans for the road. Coloured shading infuses the chequered map of the suburb of East Acton; yellow marks the 'surplus land area', while the lane for 'non-car traffic' is shaded purple. At the moment, the development does not encroach upon the land where the houses once stood, but the public consultation process has only just begun, and if the experience of the last thirty years is any guide, then it seems likely that their plans will be revised many times before they are finally implemented. But Mr Mellors and Mr Richards do not agree. When I ask why the stretch of road between Western Circus and Gipsy Corner has remained untouched for so long, the response takes me by surprise: 'You do the worst bits first,' says Hugh Richards, patiently, as though he were explaining something to a child. 'It was never intended that it wasn't going to be done – it's been on the list for a long time, but there were always schemes of more urgency.'

'It was done on a priority basis,' confirms Mr Mellors.

I had assumed that any number of factors – political indecision or bureaucratic incompetence or public antipathy – had played a part in delaying the scheme to rebuild Western Avenue, but I was wrong. From the perspective of Mr Mellors' airless office, there has been no delay at all: the bureaucrats of the Highways Agency have simply been working through an ordered list of projects until the time came to begin work on Western Avenue. Their insistence that everything has been proceeding according to plan is so ridiculous that I find it hard to believe they are serious – but Mr Mellors and Mr Richards are not the kind of people to joke about their work.

The bureaucrats of the Highways Agency are charged with a more or less impossible task, but I am beginning to understand why people like Mr Mellors arouse such resentment among the residents of Western Avenue. His strange evasiveness, his peculiar language, his apparent complacency, and, above all, his bizarre optimism combine to create a sense that he operates in a realm governed by obscure and meaningless rules. Despite his protestations that the Highways Agency has a 'customer focus', Mr Mellors seems blind to every concern, except for one – the mechanism of government. Inevitably, perhaps, he is turned inwards, more attuned to the functioning of the civil service than he is to the consequences of his actions.

There is a knock on the door: it is the Divisional Director, Mr Mellors' superior. My briefing is coming to an end, but as Mr Mellors leaves the room, Mr Richards returns to the map, and his long fingers trace the road's route, pointing out the various features they have devised to adapt Western Avenue to meet the demands of the next century. 'We could go on for hours,' he says, happily. In contrast to Mr Mellors' studied indifference, Mr Richards is boyishly enthusiastic about his work; he has worked on the A40 for fourteen years now, and since he became Route Manager a year ago he has been 'thoroughly enjoying himself'. I find his attitude infinitely preferable to Mr Mellors' shifty charm.

Mr Richards folds up the map reluctantly. The public consultation process has only just begun, but he is confident that the work will proceed according to plan. It is tempting to believe that it will all work out exactly as he has envisaged.

— — —

My broken speedometer flickers aimlessly as a car drifts past in the outside lane. To the left, railway lines converge

on the translucent hangers of Paddington Station, while the
gantries that pass overhead signal distances to Guildford
and Oxford – towns drawn within London's compass by
the road which spins beneath the wheels of my car. Even
my car loves the Westway – and on the Westway, even I
love my car. The car's potential is rarely exploited in
London's congested streets, but it finds fulfilment on the
Westway, for the city has been prised apart to make way
for its broad carriageways.

My journey began a moment ago on Marylebone Road.
The mass of traffic which congealed at the lights dissolved
into its constituent parts as the cars began to gather speed.
There is a glass tower planted beside the flyover: my car
ascended its gridded, graph-paper façade, and then fell into
a valley formed by the slip-roads which feed and drain the
Westway's carriageways. To the right, the clocktower of a
church showed through a thick canopy of trees – a relic of
the older city preserved amongst the tower blocks and
carriageways of modern London, much as Le Corbusier
had planned to preserve the churches of the Marais
amongst the immense cruciform towers of the Contemporary City ('They would stand surrounded by verdure; what
could be more charming!') The city fell away beneath me.

With the irresistible grace of a bubble sliding down a
tilted bottle, another car drifts past me. My broken speedometer hardly matters, for the only true measure of speed on
the Westway is the relative motion of the other cars on the
road. The tower blocks that flank the road are dark, except
for the sea-green spine of their illuminated stairwells: it
looks as though the buildings are structured around a series
of water-tanks stacked one upon the other. They are visual
markers which measure my momentum across the city; they
are monuments to the power and speed of the car, built to
the scale it demands.

Signs flag the exit to Shepherd's Bush: I leave the road and descend to the flat carriageways of the M41. Overhead, a twin row of lights flower like metallic daffodils. It is 10.00 pm, and the road is clear. 'Motorway Ends' reads the blue sign at the roundabout, five hundred yards from my house.

— — —

Several years ago, Tony visited the north Norfolk coast and was overwhelmed by the vastness of the Norfolk sky. Sometimes, the city makes him claustrophobic, and when he leaves London, he would like to live in Norfolk, beneath its 'big sky'.

— — —

The shuttered room is freighted with the scent of the melon that rests in the bowl on the wooden table. Mr Johnson gestures to a chair beside him, and places his hands squarely on the table. 'My personal feeling is that the project was necessary. I've lived here and I can see the congestion, and I can see that it was increasing between the two points – Gipsy Corner and Western Circus.' He raises his hands, and gestures to the left and the right, with the studied deliberation of an air-hostess indicating the location of the emergency exits. 'It should have gone ahead – in my opinion, a project of £110 million could have been found by the government. It would have saved a lot of aggravation. Having demolished 200 houses and caused a lot of hardship to the families, it's sad that it should have been discontinued. So what do they want to do with the land – turn it into a garden? It will be the garbage of the city.'

He lifts both hands from the table, and then lowers them again. His grey hair is curling, cropped short, and lightly greased, and he wears a crisp blue shirt with a designer monogram on the pocket; the cuffs are tucked back to reveal tanned forearms. He has not shaved, and his chin and cheeks are stubbled. Mrs Johnson, who has been standing in the kitchen doorway, crosses the room silently, and sits on an armchair in the sitting-room. She does not look at us: she folds her hands neatly on her lap, and stares towards the far wall, her face in profile. When Mr Johnson is not talking, the room is very quiet, and the artificial light inside the wood-panelled hall makes the house seem older than its sixty-odd years.

Mr Johnson's case is still in court, and he does not know when it will be resolved. He is waiting for the council to provide alternative accommodation – and once it does, he will happily leave the road. There is little incentive to stay: their neighbours have gone, the shops are closing and the traffic is getting worse. The rush-hour used to be over by nine-thirty in the morning, but it now lasts until midday, and then begins again mid-afternoon. 'We'd like to leave this behind. I don't want to be an obstacle in the project. How could I be? For what reason? It's stupid not to want to go. The tractors will cut in a straight line whether you want to go or not. You don't want to go? Fine. Then the tractors will cut straight over your head.' His hand, stiff-palmed, flashes over the crown of his head.

Life on Western Avenue is not as strange as I once liked to imagine: as Robin Green told the public inquiry in 1989, the road is an 'integral multi-functioning element of the suburban landscape'. It is cramped and constricted by the car, yet the same is true of much of London. The street in Shepherd's Bush on which I live is lined with terraced Victorian housing and thinly sown with trees: it contains a church and old people's home, but it is not a quiet road, for it serves as a through-route between the backstreets of Olympia and Shepherd's Bush Green. The area is thick with 'traffic-calming measures' – mini-roundabouts, traffic lights, one-way streets, chicanes and speed bumps – but the most effective restraint on the traffic is the double-parked cars. The street does not belong to me or my neighbours, few of whom I have ever met: it belongs to the car.

Two years ago, the Johnsons were woken in the middle of the night when the neighbouring house was set on fire. The next night, it was set on fire again. The arsonist – who was drunk when the police caught him – is now serving a four-year sentence. 'In my case, it's not a question of not wanting to go, but of wanting to go to the right place,' concludes Mr Johnson.

Mr Johnson has explained his 'situation' in a precise, faintly weary manner; he is polite, but hardly effusive. It is plain that he has nothing more to say.

'I'm in court, and I intend to pursue the matter in court,' he says, as he follows me to the door. 'Not for my sake, but for the sake of the supposedly responsible functionaries of local government. It's time someone gave them a kick up the arse.' He gestures towards the charred Tudorbethan façade of the house next door: 'You can see the fire damage.' He nods briefly, and goes back inside the house. Having survived here for so long, it now seems unthinkable that the Johnsons will ever leave.

Outside, the air is cold and dry, thickened by a dust that catches at my throat. It is March 1998: a fortnight has passed since I visited the Highways Agency, and resurfacing work has begun at Western Circus. A spray of blood-red roses stains the luminous orange jacket of the flower-seller stationed on the Westway.

– – –

Le Corbusier hoped the invention of the car would inspire the construction of a machine-age city – a 'vertical city' of towers and elevated motorways. His vision was partially realized in the construction of the Westway and the towers that flank its carriageways, but in the end, the car served to fulfil a different prophecy: H.G. Wells' vision of a city described by a radius of a hundred miles came true, twenty years sooner than he had anticipated.

Today, what is defined as 'the functional London region' stretches from Bournemouth to Brighton and from North-ampton to Chelmsford. Seventeen million people live within a fifty-mile radius of Oxford Circus.

— — —

Headlights spill across the unlit windows and illuminate the porches and gables of the houses lining Western Avenue's northern boundary. I am standing beside Western Circus: the top layer of the junction has been broken up; its rough surface lies several inches below the surrounding roads, and temporary traffic lights marshal the cars traversing its unmarked expanse of tarmac.

It is 11.00 pm. A moment ago, I parked in a side-road above Western Circus and walked on to the road. The dimly lit interior of a passing car reveals a face as pale and indistinct as a painted balloon. I know that the occupants of each car will be staring at the neon-lit mock-Georgian buildings which clutter the junction and the houses which crowd the hillside.

To descend from the high ground of the Westway's elevated carriageways to the plains of East Acton is a frustrating experience, for the houses that remain beside the road – and the traffic lights and crossings which their inhabitants require – interrupt the smooth passage from central London. The car has not only dispersed the city across a wider area – it has also changed our perception of the city: as Richard Sennett puts it, 'we now measure urban space in terms of how easy it is to drive through them, to get out of them'. The Westway has aged better than Western Avenue: while Western Avenue's decline has continued, the Westway has become an iconic feature of London's landscape, and the city has reknitted around its concrete carriageways. Ladbroke Grove is as fashionable now as the King's Road was in the sixties, when the demolition of North Kensington began.

Ten minutes pass before Hugh Richards arrives to meet me. For a moment, we watch as the westbound cars approach the junction and draw up behind one another. 'It's actually a very interesting process trying to carry out works – how on earth do you resurface a junction and still keep traffic flowing through it in all directions?' he says, almost to himself. 'It's an incredibly difficult problem and takes an awful lot of planning.'

A lane has been closed for resurfacing on the eastbound carriageway of the Westway, and Mr Richards is pleased to see that the traffic is flowing smoothly through the chicane the workmen have set up. Tony Jacklin, the works foreman, has been arranging the work details for the night. A hundred and forty tons of asphalt ordered for Western Circus will be laid on the Westway instead, where the council are doing maintenance work on the hill above the junction. Tony Jacklin – a stocky man in boots and fluorescent jacket, with mobile phone and clipboard – is composed and confident, and in contrast, Mr Richards seems willowy and endearingly ineffectual, ill at ease in his casual clothes. A balding workman ambles across the junction to talk to his foreman; his stomach, barely contained within a flimsy fluorescent vest, barrels ahead of him – it is a cold night, but his arms are bare.

Resurfacing has been under way for eight weeks, and the work is almost complete. 'If I have my way, I'll have you digging all this up in a few months anyway,' says Hugh Richards, bullishly – almost as if he were trying to assert his status as the Route Manager of the A40. He plans to reconfigure the junction by moving the central reservation a few yards to the south – a move which he believes will improve the traffic flow through Gipsy Corner.

We cross the junction and follow Tony Jacklin as he walks along the Westway. Beside the vans scattered along the fenced-off carriageways, there are men gathered in small groups, drinking tea and smoking. They are allowed to work only between 11.30 at night and 4.00 in the morning when the commuter traffic picks up again. Even so, there are often traffic jams on Western Avenue in the middle of the night while the works are under way.

Mr Richards points out the work that the Highways Agency has recently completed. He is proud of the relaid central reservation, and the newly built lay-bys, but he knows there is more to be done: 'Because of the never-ending scheme, everything has been put off and put off – but we're going in big-time to rectify years of neglect.' It is almost midnight: we cross the road by the subway, and as we walk back towards Western Circus, I ask him yet again whether he regrets the fact that the plan to rebuild the road has been abandoned. 'I did a lot of the design work on the tunnels, so I'm sorry that it's not going to happen, but I think what we're doing is right for a sustainable transport policy for the future . . .' So far, it might have been Mr Mellors speaking, but Mr Richards is a less accomplished civil servant than his colleague and he cannot sustain the official line indefinitely: 'I have doubts about the traffic capacity . . .' he adds uneasily. 'But then you'll never get a perfect solution.' He is right, of course, and it is reassuring that he should admit as much – Mr Mellors would never be as honest and straightforward.

Suddenly, Mr Richards begins to quicken his stride: there has been an accident at Western Circus. I reach the junction a yard behind him: 'Well there's no excuse for that – the traffic management ended before that point,' he says, quietly, with a combination of relief and disdain.

Bonnet to bumper, two cars are interlocked on the unmarked expanse of tarmac. An Indian woman in a white sari stands beside the cracked shell of her car, with a child cradled in her arms. The impact seems to have sealed shut the rear doors, for another woman sits on the back seat, her face pressed to the glass. Three solidly built men stand beside the other car: they are identically dressed, with shaven heads, black jackets and sharply creased trousers. I cannot read the logo embossed on the back of their jackets, but it seems as though the Indian family's white Mercedes has collided with a car containing a crew of bouncers. Lit by the glare of the traffic lights, the men guard the site of the accident as the London-bound cars attempt to negotiate the blocked junction. Already, the queue stretches as far as the first of the houses which flank the road's northern boundary.

A policeman on a motorbike arrives – his limbs seem heavy and cumbersome in their leather cladding as he walks across the junction – and an ambulance draws up behind him, spilling amber light across the sunken puddle of unmarked tarmac.

– – –

My car has played another trick on me: the driver's door is jammed. I have to shuffle across the passenger seat when I

want to get in or out. Fortunately, it now goes backwards
as well as forwards, but when the brakes lock and the car
turns over on the motorway, it will be difficult to release
me from the wreckage.

– – –

'Stop the motorways now,' said the *Sunday Times* in 1973,
'before motorway begets motorway, and the ordinary English landscape goes under.' The motorways were stopped,
but to no avail, or so the *Sunday Times* believes. In April
1998, in an article claiming that 1,700 people were leaving
Britain's cities every week, the paper listed the factors that
would finally ensure the long-anticipated demise of the
English countryside: the roads and roundabouts; the incur-
sions of the retail and leisure industries; the skyline littered
with pylons and masts; the erosion of local identity and
distinctiveness; the suburban housing estates.

The process of mass-suburbanization which Wells had
anticipated in 1901 is not yet complete: in 1995, the
Department of Environment declared that four million new
houses must be built in Britain by the year 2016 – the same
number built in the great housing boom of the twenties and
thirties.

– – –

It is three years since she last visited Western Avenue, but
Sinitta – the Housing Association official – has not forgotten the strange atmosphere on the road during the summer
of 1995. 'It was very eerie up there,' she says. 'As they
boarded up the houses, it looked very strange – you could
have used it as a film set: you'd be sitting in a traffic jam
with all these people in their cars, just looking around
them, staring at the empty houses.'

We are sitting in an empty attic room with sloping roof

– a bland meeting room in the Housing Association's offices in Kilburn. Sinitta's life and her career have moved on since 1995 – she has been promoted and has just returned from maternity leave – but she recalls the tenants' meeting clearly, and she does not blame them for being angry. She avoids the A40 now, if she can, for the empty sites beside the road remind her of the summer when so many houses were needlessly demolished.

– – –

The tailback begins half a mile before Western Circus: the serried ranks of cars on the Westway stretch as far as White City, where the carriageways rise to form the flyover which carries traffic above the inner suburbs of west London. Beside me, the driver of a sapphire-blue car lights a cigarette and rests his head against the window. It is three o'clock on a mid-week afternoon in April, and the traffic is mired in the unseasonal heat-haze which shimmers above the road.

There is a story by Dr Seuss about two animals called the Zax – a South-Going Zax, and a North-Going Zax. One day, as they are crossing a place called the Prairie of Prax, the Zax bump into one another: 'There they stood. Foot to foot. Face to face.' The North-Going Zax always goes north, yet his path is blocked by the South-Going Zax. He asks him to step aside, but the other Zax refuses, for he lives by a rule he had 'learnt as a boy back in South-Going School': 'Never budge! That's my rule. Never budge in the least! / Not an inch to the West! Not an inch to the East! / I'll stay here, not budging! I can and I will / If it makes you and me and the whole world stand still!' Years pass, and a new highway is driven through the Prairie of Prax. A flyover – a Zax Bypass – is built above the 'two stubborn creatures', who have not moved from the spot where they so disastrously collided: they are left standing 'unbudged in their tracks'.

On the hoardings sealing Mrs Buchan's site, there is a poster advertising a game called Carmaggedon: 'So many Pedestrians, so little time'. A red-eyed, leather-headed ghoul grips the steering-wheel of a powerful machine and surveys the queues of cars stalled at Western Circus. The image is hardly appropriate – for the moment, at least, the pedestrians on Western Avenue are in no danger from the traffic.

At first, the car was expected to provide a cure for most of the problems it is now charged with creating: pollution, congestion and death on the roads. In 1901, H.G. Wells lamented the 'unprecedented state of congestion' in London's streets – 'the omnipresence of mud, filthy mud, churned up by hoofs and wheels under the inclement skies, and perpetually defiled and added to by innumerable horses . . .' He described a young woman attempting to cross the road at Marble Arch, 'breathless, foul-footed, splashed by a passing hansom from head to feet, happy that she has reached the further pavement alive . . .' Wells was excited by the prospect of a city freed from 'battering horse-shoes, the perpetual filth of horse traffic and the clumsy wheels of London carts'. But today the car's conquest of London is more or less complete: it has begun to destroy the city, as Le Corbusier said it would – though the city exacts its revenge by smothering the car and frustrating its drivers.

J.G. Ballard believed that as 'a basically old-fashioned machine', the car '. . . enshrines a basically old-fashioned idea – freedom: in terms of pollution, noise and human life, the price of that freedom may be high, but perhaps the car, by the very muddle and congestion it causes, may be holding back the remorseless spread of the regimented, electronic society.' But there seems no reason why an electronic society should be any more 'regimented' than a society governed by primitive technology – and as Ballard acknowledges, the car is a primitive machine. What's more, as the number of cars increases, the terms of Ballard's equation shift: the freedom which the car undoubtedly bestows is restricted by the congestion on the streets, and the price we pay – 'in pollution, noise and human life' – becomes steadily higher.

The east-going Zax in his sapphire machine finishes his cigarette: he has progressed fifty yards. All being well, he will pass the site where the Greens used to live, half a mile to the west, in about twenty minutes.

＿   ＿   ＿

Trevor still lives within sight of the A40, though he has moved a mile to the east. When he left Western Avenue, he went to live on a canal boat, and the noise of the traffic on the Westway echoes across the rubble-strewn basin where it is moored. He is not at home on the day I visit him, and I never see him again.

＿   ＿   ＿

The arm of the digger which is destroying the Johnsons' house is as delicate as a bird's beak – it can pick a worm-thin piece of piping from the house's guts – and yet as blunt and strong as a wrecking ball. Wood splinters as it crashes through the panelling in the hall. The man operating the machine stops work for a moment, and I venture into the site to talk to him. Deep indentations criss-cross his face; the protective mask he wears while he manipulates the giant metal beak of his wrecking-machine has etched lines into his skin, like duelling scars or tribal scarifications. His name is Charlie Angell, and he tells me he has been using diggers since he was ten years old and he started working with his father on land owned by the Ministry of Defence.

Preceded by two police outriders, a horse-drawn funeral cortège crosses the first of the railway bridges, and passes beneath the Bridge of Fools. It was the railway bridges – hailed as gateways to a new age of concrete and steel – which were the first part of the road to become outdated. They will soon be replaced.

– – –

On Western Avenue, the general manager of the Renault showroom commutes from Solihull, near Birmingham. The manager of the Warner Bros multiplex commutes from Northampton (though his casual staff live nearby). Tony commutes from the far side of London. On Western Avenue, a simple rule prevails: the further you travel to work, the more important you are.

– – –

Irene says she would like to retire to an island – like the island on the west coast of Scotland where Norm grew up. Norm is happy to leave the city, too: 'When you're younger, you want the wild life, but when you get a bit older, you start to realize what you've missed ... Do you know anyone my age who wants to live in London?'

– – –

'It's zero-rated.' The estate agent is abrupt to the point of rudeness. The posters in the window of the shop at Western Circus advertise the firm's successes – in the last few months, they have sold several of the houses that the Highways Agency owned on Western Avenue – but he will not condescend to talk to me about any aspect of life on Western Avenue. 'Much of our business is confidential government business. We couldn't possibly discuss it.' He folds his hands on his desk, and stares at me blankly until I leave the shop.

Outside, a fence encloses the triangular paddock of virulent grass where the bingo hall once stood. It is May, and the Highways Agency has completed the first of the tasks scheduled for the coming months: it has 'landscaped' the derelict sites beside the road. On the hill above Western Circus, where Mrs Buchan used to live, trees and shrubs have been planted in freshly dug flowerbeds, and a chain-link barrier protects the green wooden fences from fly-posters and graffiti. The southern edge of Western Avenue looks almost as it might have done in the twenties, before houses and factories were built beside the road: it has begun to resemble the wide, tree-lined road Mrs Buchan remembers from her childhood.

\- \- \-

There are now an estimated 500 million cars in the world, and the number is expected to double by 2030.

\- \- \-

'Why don't you tell this young man what you think?'

Mr Green draws out the wire of his hearing-aid to its full extent, and then watches carefully as it recoils upon itself. He lifts it rather hopefully towards his ear. He seems transfixed by the apparatus. No one speaks. 'Can you hear now?' says Mrs Green, after a moment. 'Well, why don't you give your opinion and talk?' Mr Green is sitting in a chair inside the window. His features are beaked with age and his skin is thickly wrinkled: his head falls forwards

under the pressure of its own weight, and he watches me
with heavy-lidded, red-threaded eyes, his gaze patient,
steady and, as far as I can tell, uncomprehending.

'We're saddened. We feel buried alive out here. I feel as
if my life has finished.' It is Mrs Green who finally answers
my question. I do not know what to say. The room is silent.
Mr Green looks at his wife expectantly, yet still he says
nothing. 'Can you hear, Freddie? Well, why don't you tell
him?' Like a shy child asked to perform in front of adults,
Mr Green says nothing, guiltily relishing his refusal to
speak.

Then, suddenly, for no apparent reason, he begins to
talk. 'You see, when we lived on Western Avenue, I could
walk out of the door, and get a bus to Greenford! If I
wanted to get into town, I'd only got a short walk, and I'd
be on the Underground.' Each word is an isolated foot-fall
– a tentative step forward – yet, gradually, his words form
sentences, and his sentences form thoughts, and it is a relief
to realize he has not lost his mind.

The last time he went to London, he says scornfully, he
left home at ten past five, and he did not reach Victoria
until twenty past seven. 'And that's no exaggeration. Well!
It's out of this world – you would think you could have
walked it by then!' I ask them about Western Avenue.
Unlike their son, Mr and Mrs Green believe that the scheme
was abandoned on grounds of cost. 'We weren't surprised
by the news – we were annoyed, mostly,' says Mr Green.
'To think they'd got us out, and then done a thing like
that!'

Mrs Green has, as always, placed herself discreetly inside
the door to the sitting-room. Eager to push her husband
forward – and relieved that he is, at last, co-operating –
she explains that he thinks the work will still proceed.
'He thinks private enterprise will get involved. Don't you,

Freddie? That's his idea.' Mr Green thinks Western Avenue will become the first of many toll roads leading into London. He might be right, though the road's future is far from settled: a Park Royal firm has begun to petition motorists stalled in the rush-hour queues on Western Avenue – it wants to see the scheme to rebuild the road reinstated. Mr Green soon tires of the subject: the future is of little interest to him.

'There's one thing I remember. It was after the war . . . The Germans – no, the Russians captured an Englishman . . .' It is the story he told me the first time we met, and I probably know it better than he does – I could tell the story in half the time it is taking him to recall it.

'He had a very interesting life in the police,' says Mrs Green, loyally, when her husband falters. 'He should write his memoirs . . . Except he's forgotten half of it now.' She looks at her husband affectionately. Mr Green's control of the past is fading, yet though his wife knows the territory better than he does, she lacks his ceaseless determination to map its fading contours.

'It's rather strange, you know, that I should have ended up living here,' he says, abruptly. In 1930, a year after he joined the police, Mr Green was transferred to a station in Norwood Green – the village next to Hayes. It was surrounded by farmland and market gardens: in the morning, he would see teams of women in the fields, and in the evening, he would watch them load a truck with produce for the market at Covent Garden.

'It's strange that I should have come back to Norwood Green,' he says, wonderingly. To return to the place where he began his career lends his life a certain symmetry, but there is no comfort to be derived from it: Mr Green would rather be living on Western Avenue.